1 CORIN

fo

EVERY

20TH ANNIVERSARY EDITION WITH STUDY GUIDE

NEW TESTAMENT FOR EVERYONE

20TH ANNIVERSARY EDITION WITH STUDY GUIDE

N. T. Wright

Matthew for Everyone, Part 1

Matthew for Everyone, Part 2

Mark for Everyone

Luke for Everyone

John for Everyone, Part 1

John for Everyone, Part 2

Acts for Everyone, Part 1

Acts for Everyone, Part 2

Romans for Everyone, Part 1

Romans for Everyone, Part 2

1 Corinthians for Everyone

2 Corinthians for Everyone

Galatians and Thessalonians for Everyone

Ephesians, Philippians, Colossians and Philemon for Everyone

1 and 2 Timothy and Titus for Everyone

Hebrews for Everyone

James, Peter, John and Judah for Everyone

Revelation for Everyone

1 CORINTHIANS
for
EVERYONE

20TH ANNIVERSARY EDITION WITH STUDY GUIDE

N. T.
WRIGHT

STUDY GUIDE BY SALLY D. SHARPE

First published in Great Britain in 2003 by the
Society for Promoting Christian Knowledge
36 Causton Street
London SW1P 4ST
www.spckpublishing.co.uk

Copublished in 2004 by the Society for Promoting
Christian Knowledge, London, and Westminster John Knox Press,
100 Witherspoon Street, Louisville, KY 40202.

20th Anniversary Edition with Study Guide
Published in 2023
by Westminster John Knox Press
Louisville, Kentucky

23 24 25 26 27 28 29 30 31 32—10 9 8 7 6 5 4 3 2 1

Cover design by Allison Taylor

Library of Congress Cataloging-in-Publication Data

Names: Wright, N. T. (Nicholas Thomas) author. | Sharpe, Sally D., 1964- writer of supplementary textual content.
Title: 1 Corinthians for everyone / N. T. Wright ; study guide by Sally D. Sharpe.
Other titles: First Corinthians for everyone | Bible. Corinthians, 1st. English. Wright.
Description: 20th anniversary edition with study guide. | Louisville, Kentucky : Westminster John Knox Press, 2023. | Series: New Testament for everyone | Summary: "This translation shows the liveliness of cosmopolitan Corinth and reveals the wisdom and challenge of Paul's writing, bringing out the pastoral sensitivity and deep insight that make this letter one of Paul's crowning achievements. This anniversary edition contains a glossary and a study guide that is suitable for group study, personal study, or daily devotions"-- Provided by publisher.
Identifiers: LCCN 2023008472 (print) | LCCN 2023008473 (ebook) | ISBN 9780664266462 (paperback) | ISBN 9781646983087 (ebook)
Subjects: LCSH: Bible. Corinthians, 1st--Commentaries. | Bible. Corinthians, 1st--Textbooks.
Classification: LCC BS2675.53 .W746 2023 (print) | LCC BS2675.53 (ebook) | DDC 227/.207--dc23/eng/20230516
LC record available at https://lccn.loc.gov/2023008472
LC ebook record available at https://lccn.loc.gov/2023008473

Most Westminster John Knox Press books are available at special quantity discounts when purchased in bulk by corporations, organizations, and special-interest groups. For more information, please e-mail SpecialSales@wjkbooks.com.

For
Monsignor Liam Bergin
Rector of the Pontifical Irish College in Rome
and his colleagues and students
in the grounds of whose College
this book was written

CONTENTS

INTRODUCTION TO THE ANNIVERSARY EDITION

It took me ten years, but I'm glad I did it. Writing a guide to the books of the New Testament felt at times like trying to climb all the Scottish mountains in quick succession. But the views from the tops were amazing, and discovering new pathways up and down was very rewarding as well. The real reward, though, has come in the messages I've received from around the world, telling me that the books have been helpful and encouraging, opening up new and unexpected vistas.

Perhaps I should say that this series wasn't designed to help with sermon preparation, though many preachers have confessed to me that they've used it that way. The books were meant, as their title suggests, for everyone, particularly for people who would never dream of picking up an academic commentary but who nevertheless want to dig a little deeper.

The New Testament seems intended to provoke all readers, at whatever stage, to fresh thought, understanding and practice. For that, we all need explanation, advice and encouragement. I'm glad these books seem to have had that effect, and I'm delighted that they are now available with study guides in these new editions.

N. T. Wright
2022

INTRODUCTION

On the very first occasion when someone stood up in public to tell people about Jesus, he made it very clear: this message is for *everyone*.

It was a great day – sometimes called the birthday of the church. The great wind of God's spirit had swept through Jesus' followers and filled them with a new joy and a sense of God's presence and power. Their leader, Peter, who only a few weeks before had been crying like a baby because he'd lied and cursed and denied even knowing Jesus, found himself on his feet explaining to a huge crowd that something had happened which had changed the world for ever. What God had done for him, Peter, he was beginning to do for the whole world: new life, forgiveness, new hope and power were opening up like spring flowers after a long winter. A new age had begun in which the living God was going to do new things in the world – beginning then and there with the individuals who were listening to him. 'This promise is for *you*,' he said, 'and for your children, and for everyone who is far away' (Acts 2.39). It wasn't just for the person standing next to you. It was for everyone.

Within a remarkably short time this came true to such an extent that the young movement spread throughout much of the known world. And one way in which the *everyone* promise worked out was through the writings of the early Christian leaders. These short works – mostly letters and stories about Jesus – were widely circulated and eagerly read. They were never intended for either a religious or intellectual elite. From the very beginning they were meant for everyone.

That is as true today as it was then. Of course, it matters that some people give time and care to the historical evidence, the meaning of the original words (the early Christians wrote in Greek), and the exact and particular force of what different writers were saying about God, Jesus, the world and themselves. This series is based quite closely on that sort of work. But the point of it all is that the message can get out to everyone, especially to people who wouldn't normally read a book with footnotes and Greek words in it. That's the sort of person for whom these books are written. And that's why there's a glossary, in the back, of the key words that you can't really get along without, with a simple description of what they mean. Whenever you see a word in **bold type** in the text, you can go to the back and remind yourself what's going on.

There are, of course, many translations of the New Testament available today. The one I offer here is designed for the same kind of reader: one who mightn't necessarily understand the more formal, sometimes even ponderous, tones of some of the standard ones. I have tried, naturally, to keep as close to the original as I can. But my main aim has been to be sure that the words can speak not just to some people, but to everyone.

Let me add a note about the translation the reader will find here of the Greek word *Christos*. Most translations simply say 'Christ', but most modern English speakers assume that that word is simply a proper name (as though 'Jesus' were Jesus 'Christian' name and 'Christ' were his 'surname'). For all sorts of reasons, I disagree; so I have experimented not only with 'Messiah' (which is what the word literally means) but sometimes, too, with 'King'.

Paul's first letter to Corinth – a lively seaport where people and cultures of every sort jostled together, just like so many places in today's world – is full of wisdom and challenge. The young church there was as lively as the place itself, with as many questions and problems – and as much joy and excitement – as any growing church today. Paul's pastoral sensitivity and deep insight come together to make this letter one of his crowning achievements, full of good things for us to ponder and enjoy today. So here it is: Paul for everyone – 1 Corinthians!

Tom Wright

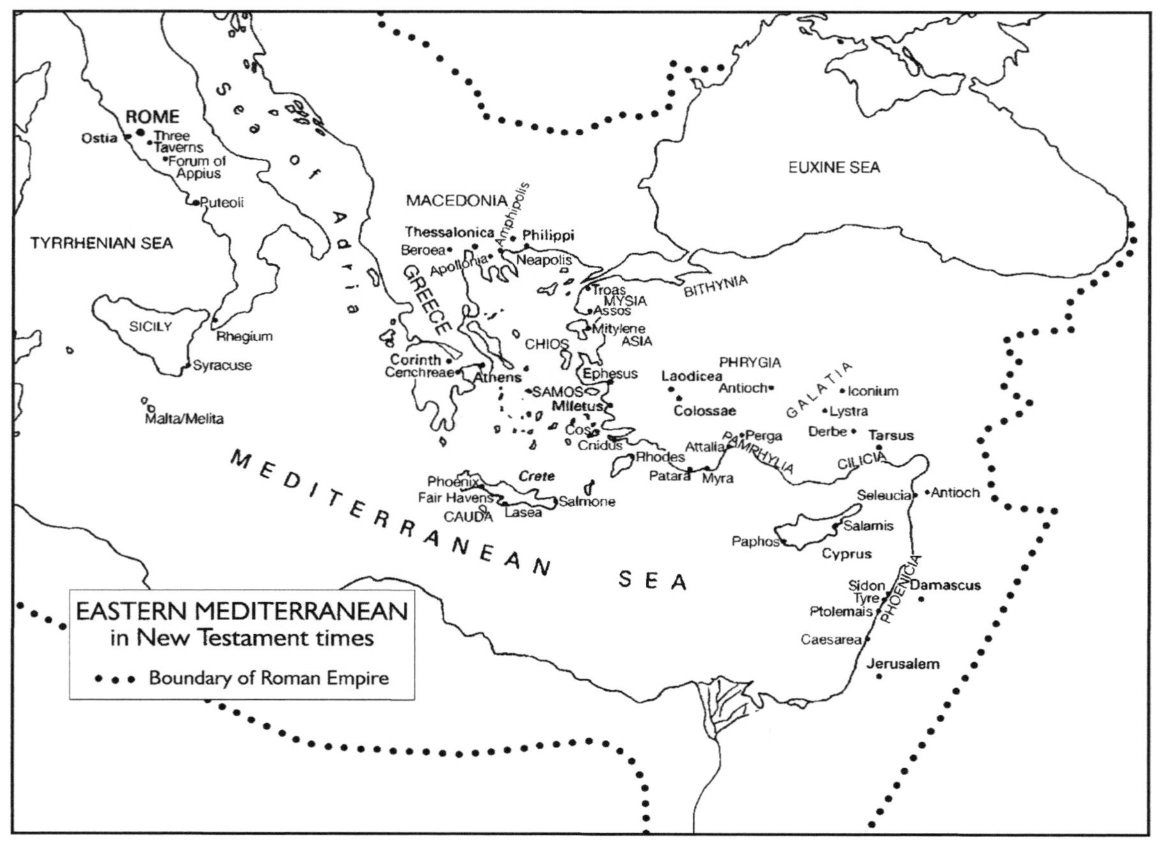
EASTERN MEDITERRANEAN
in New Testament times
Boundary of Roman Empire
ROME
Ostia
Three Taverns
Forum of Appius
Puteoli
TYRRHENIAN SEA
Sea of Adria
SICILY
Rhegium
Syracuse
Malta/Melita
MACEDONIA
Amphipolis
Thessalonica
Philippi
Beroea
Apollonia
Neapolis
GREECE
Corinth
Cenchreae
Athens
CHIOS
SAMOS
Miletus
Cos
Cnidus
Troas
MYSIA
Assos
Mitylene
ASIA
Ephesus
BITHYNIA
EUXINE SEA
PHRYGIA
Laodicea
Antioch
Colossae
GALATIA
Iconium
Lystra
Derbe
Tarsus
Perga
Attalia
PAMPHYLIA
Rhodes
Patara
Myra
CILICIA
Crete
Phoenix
Fair Havens
Salmone
CAUDA
Lasea
Seleucia
Antioch
Salamis
Paphos
Cyprus
MEDITERRANEAN SEA
Sidon
Tyre
Ptolemais
PHOENICIA
Damascus
Caesarea
Jerusalem

1 CORINTHIANS 1.1–9

Thankful for God's Grace

[1]Paul, called by God's will to be an apostle of Messiah Jesus, and Sos-
thenes our brother; [2]to God's assembly at Corinth, made holy in Mes-
siah Jesus, called to be holy, with everyone who calls on the name of
our Lord, Messiah Jesus, in every place – their Lord, indeed, as well as
ours! [3]Grace to you and peace from God our father and Messiah Jesus
the Lord.

[4]I always thank my God for you, for the grace of God that was given
to you in Messiah Jesus. [5]You were enriched in him in everything, in
every kind of speech and knowledge, [6]just as the messianic message
was established among you, [7]so that you aren't missing out on any
spiritual gift as you wait eagerly for our Lord, Messiah Jesus, to be
revealed. [8]He will establish you right through to the end, so that you
are blameless on the day of our Lord, Messiah Jesus. [9]God is faithful!
And it is through God that you have been called into the fellowship of
his son, Messiah Jesus, our Lord.

It wasn't long into the phone call before I noticed something different. It was the first time I'd spoken to this friend for some weeks, and whichever way the conversation turned, one name kept coming back. She and James had been talking over dinner last night . . . James was hoping to get promotion soon and would be working much closer to where she lived . . . perhaps I knew so-and-so who'd been at school with James? . . . and so on, and so on. There was a warmth, an excitement, and the conclusion was obvious; any minute now, she hoped, James would ask the key question, to which her answer was ready and waiting.

Well, it happened of course, and they are now married. But my point is to notice how people give themselves away by what they go on talking about, almost (it sometimes appears) to the point of obsession. It doesn't take long in someone's company, or even in a phone call, before you discover what's really exciting them, what is at the centre of their waking thoughts.

If we had any doubts about what Paul was excited about, what was at the centre of his thoughts and intentions, this first paragraph of one of his most varied and lengthy letters would soon put us straight. One name keeps coming up, over and over again, like a motif in an opera. It's good to remind ourselves where Paul's heart lay, because we can easily read the whole letter merely as an argumentative tract, almost bossy sometimes, setting the Corinthians right about this and that, as though his only concern was to lick them into shape.

It wasn't. His central concern, here and throughout his life and work, was quite simply Jesus. The name occurs eight times in these nine verses. Paul couldn't stop talking about Jesus, because without Jesus nothing else he said or did made any sense. And what he wants the Corinthians to get hold of most of all is what it means to have Jesus at the middle of your story, your life, your thoughts, your imagination. If they can do that, all the other issues that rush to and fro through the letter will sort themselves out.

In particular, he wants them to have Jesus at the centre of their understanding of the world and of history. Most of the Christians in Corinth had not been Jews, but ordinary 'pagans'. They had been **Gentiles**, believing in various gods and goddesses, but without any idea that history, the story of the world, was *going* anywhere, or that their own lives might be part of that forward movement. Again and again Paul wants them to learn this lesson: that they have been caught up into a great movement of the love and power of the one true God, the God of Israel, whose work for the whole world had now been unveiled through the events concerning his son. That's why Jesus is at the centre of the picture.

Look how, with a few deft strokes of the pen, he sketches a picture of the Christians in Corinth so that at every point their story is intertwined with Jesus' story. To begin with, God has set them aside for his own special purposes in King Jesus; that's what 'made holy' means (verse 2). I don't possess very many suits of clothes, but there is one which I keep for best, which only comes out on the most special of occasions. That's what being 'holy' means, from God's point of view; it means that he has set people aside for special purposes; and the people in question are expected to co-operate with this. That, indeed, is what quite a lot of the letter will be about.

But once they've been set aside as special, they discover that they are part of a large and growing worldwide family, brothers and sisters of everyone who 'calls on the name of our Lord King Jesus'. In fact, 'calling on' this name is the one and only sign of membership in this family, though people in Paul's day and ever since have tried to introduce other signs of membership as well. And the idea of 'calling on his name' links this worldwide family back to the earlier story of Israel, the people who 'called on the name of the Lord' in the sense of the Lord **YHWH**, Israel's God. Right from the start, Paul shows what's going on: in Jesus, Israel's true king, the world's true Lord, Israel's one God has become personally present in the world, summoning all people into his family. This is so central to his thinking, and to the life of the communities founded by his royal announcement of Jesus, that he has developed ways of talking about it that almost become formulae. Verse 3 is one such, praying that grace and peace will come to them 'from God our father and King Jesus the Lord'.

As in most of his letters, Paul follows the opening greeting by telling them what he thanks God for when he thinks of them – using the opportunity, in the process, to hint at some of the things he's going to be talking about later on. Notice how he moves from what happened to them in the past, through the sort of people they are in the present, to the hope they have for the future, with Jesus at the centre at every stage. God gave them his 'grace' in King Jesus (verse 4). 'Grace' is one of those little words that contains a whole universe of meaning, summing up the fact that God loved them and acted decisively on their behalf even though they had done nothing whatever to deserve it, but rather the opposite.

The result of this 'grace' was that God's riches had enriched them (verses 5, 6). They had become a community of learners, growing eagerly in knowledge about God and his new **life**, able to teach one another, and so strengthening and confirming the original royal proclamation, 'the **messianic message**', that had been made to them. In fact, when it comes to 'spiritual gifts' (the special things God gives to people by the **holy spirit** to enable them to serve him and one another in ways they couldn't otherwise have done), the Christians in Corinth are as well equipped as anybody could wish. So much so that it has become something of a problem.

But Paul isn't talking about problems at the moment. God called them in the past, God equips them in the present, and God will complete the whole process in the future. World history, and the story of the Christian life, has a shape, and Jesus is its shaper at every point. Just as a runner sprinting along the track leans forward to go faster and to get to the finishing line quicker, so the Christian must always be leaning forwards towards God's finishing line, 'eagerly waiting for our Lord, King Jesus to be revealed'. There is coming a day – like 'the day of the Lord' in the Old Testament, only more so – when the hidden truth about the world will be unveiled; this truth will turn out to be a person, and the person will turn out to be Jesus. That's why it's the central Christian badge or sign to 'call on him', to pray to the father through him, to learn to love him, to know his friendship and love throughout our lives, to have his name always in our hearts and often on our lips.

When two or three people like that (or more!) get together, they have much to share, much in common. The early Christian word for that was 'fellowship' or 'partnership', and that's what Paul says they now enjoy: membership in the family that has God for its faithful father and Jesus, his unique son, as its older brother. This opening holds together a view of the whole world (God's world, with Jesus as its true Lord) and of the individual (called to faithful holiness, equipped for God's service). It also brings together Paul's task (being responsible to God for the Christian fellowships that have come about through his work), and his gratitude to God for what he has already done and for what he will continue until all is completed. Writing this letter, in other words, is part of the process by which God intends to take these Christians from the one to the other, from God's past achievement to God's future finishing of the job. May God grant that it will have that effect on us, too.

1 CORINTHIANS 1.10–17

Beware of Divisions!

[10]Now I must appeal to you, my brothers and sisters, through the
name of Messiah Jesus our Lord, that you should all be in agreement,
and that there should be no divisions among you. Instead, you should
be fully equipped with the same mind and the same opinion.

[11]You see, my dear family, Chloe's people have put me in the picture
about you – about the fact that you are having quarrels. [12]What I'm
talking about is this. Each one of you is saying, 'I'm with Paul!', 'I'm
with Apollos!', 'I'm with Cephas!', 'I'm with the Messiah!'

[13]Well! Has the Messiah been cut up into pieces? Was Paul crucified
for you? Or were you baptized into Paul's name?! [14]I'm grateful to God
that I didn't baptize any of you except Crispus and Gaius, [15]so that
none of you could say that you were baptized into *my* name. ([16]All
right, I did baptize Stephanas and his household as well. Apart from
that, I don't know if I baptized anybody else.) [17]This is the point, you
see: the Messiah didn't send me to baptize; he sent me to announce
the gospel! Not with words of wisdom, either, otherwise the Messiah's
cross would lose its power.

I was woken up early this morning by beautiful birdsong. Right outside my window some little fellow was chirruping, squeaking and whistling like a virtuoso musician showing off before an admiring crowd. Then others joined in. The trees around the garden seemed to be full of them. I hadn't intended to wake up quite that early, but I couldn't help admiring them and enjoying the morning symphony.

But as I put the coffee on, I reminded myself why they do it. The sound may be beautiful in its way, but what it means is: this is *my* bit of the garden, or the tree, and *you* don't belong here! It's a territorial claim, staking out a precarious identity in a potentially dangerous world. And as I thought of that, my mind went naturally to the problem Paul faced as messengers came from Corinth to tell him how things were getting on in the young Christian community. There was plenty of noise, plenty of birdsong, plenty of squeaking and whistling, and it all meant the same thing: this is *my* vision of what Christianity is, and *you* don't belong here!

The way they were marking out different styles was in terms of different teachers. 'I'm Paul's man!' one would say, trumpeting his loyalty to the **apostle** himself, who had first told them the news about Jesus as king and Lord. But Paul hadn't been the only teacher they'd had in Corinth.

Not long after he'd gone, a wonderful speaker, greatly learned in scripture and able to explain it powerfully, had arrived. His name was Apollos, and we shall meet him quite a bit in the next few chapters. Apollos came from Alexandria in Egypt, where there was a strong Jewish community which included a great Jewish philosopher by the name of Philo. Apollos had been in Ephesus, where he had met some of Paul's colleagues (the story is told in Acts 18.24–28). They had helped him into a full understanding of the Christian **message**. He had then himself gone to Corinth (Acts 18.27—19.1), and was there when Paul came back to Ephesus (that's where Paul was while writing this letter). By this stage it seems that Apollos, too, had returned to Ephesus once more. In 16.12 Paul declares that he had urged him to visit Corinth again, but that it wasn't possible at the moment.

Anyway, we should not be surprised that there were some in Corinth who had decided that they preferred Apollos's teaching, style, methods and perhaps content, to Paul's. Go to any church where two preachers have worked side by side, or in quick succession, and you will find people comparing them. That's natural; but how easily it can pass into factions and rivalry. 'I'm with Apollos!'

But that wasn't all. Some in Corinth were saying they belonged to Peter. ('Peter' is the Greek word meaning 'rock'; the Aramaic equivalent was 'Cephas', and that's what the early church often called him.) We don't know whether Peter had visited Corinth himself, or whether some other travelling Christians had been to Corinth claiming to teach what Peter himself taught. But someone had made sufficient impact for another group in the church to say they belonged to Peter. 'I'm with Cephas!' (People have sometimes speculated about whether Peter and his followers represented a more Jewish type of Christianity, and Paul and his followers a version which had cast off Jewish restraints. This is almost certainly misleading.)

Meanwhile, there seems to have been a fourth 'party' – claiming that *they* were the real **Messiah**-people! Everyone else was following this leader or that leader, but they were simply following King Jesus! This, too, alas, is a well-known power-play in the church ('We've heard your opinions; now let me tell you what Our Lord thinks about it all!'). 'I'm with the Messiah!'

It's a sobering thought that the church faced such division in its very earliest years. People sometimes talk as if first-generation Christianity enjoyed a pure, untroubled honeymoon period, after which things became more difficult; but there's no evidence for this in the New Testament. Right from the start, Paul found himself not only announcing the **gospel** of Jesus but struggling to hold together in a single family those who had obeyed its summons.

But he doesn't just get stuck in and knock their heads together. There is a bit of that in verse 13, where he basically tells them not to be so silly: they are implying that the Messiah himself has been carved up into little pieces, or they are suggesting that Paul (and Apollos and Cephas, though he wisely doesn't say that here) is somehow on a level with the Messiah himself. But even these rhetorical questions ('Is the Messiah split up? Was Paul crucified for you?') make the main point, the point which from one angle is what the whole letter is about. The Messiah is the one who matters; and all others, from the most senior apostle to the youngest convert, are simply members in his body (see chapter 12).

In particular, Paul digs down underneath any suggestion that special significance was to be attached to the person who baptized a new Christian. He assumes that they have all been baptized, and he will from time to time return to this to make particular points. Paul took **baptism** extremely seriously. It was the formal, outward sign, before God, one's family, the wider community, and the whole church, that you were leaving your old identity behind and entering the new life of God's people in the Messiah. Baptism to the Christian was like crossing the Red Sea for Israel, at the time of the **Exodus**: it meant coming out of slavery into freedom – and responsibility (10.1–13). But the only name to be baptized into was the name of the Messiah. The person who did the baptizing was quite irrelevant.

The relevant fact – and here we get to the heart of it, as we shall see from now on – was the clash between the **good news**, the gospel, of Jesus, and the apparent power of human wisdom. Here we need to know something about Corinth and its public life, which will be important as we proceed. Corinth had been destroyed by the Romans in 146 BC, and rebuilt by Julius Caesar in 44 BC as a Roman colony. Since that time, about a hundred years before this letter was written, Corinth had prided itself on being a Roman city on Greek soil. It celebrated its Roman style of buildings, its Roman culture, its special links to the capital of a worldwide empire.

And it prided itself on its intellectual life. In our day, if a famous symphony orchestra visits a city, we might say that 'the whole town turned out to hear it' – not that every single person would go, but that many would make it their business to hear the concert, and everybody would be talking about it and comparing it with other orchestras they'd heard. In Paul's day, a city like Corinth would do that with visiting intellectual teachers, men with a reputation as philosophers, instructors in the theory and practice of wisdom. 'The whole town', or a good many of them, would turn out to listen to them speak, and everyone would discuss what they had to say.

One of the words for such people was 'sophists'. That word has a bad sound to us, indicating someone who gives themselves airs, who is a bit puffed up with their own self-importance. And one of the reasons we think of sophists like that is because of this very letter. Paul is about to launch an attack on such 'wisdom', and to show that you have to make a choice between the world's wisdom and the power of the Messiah's cross.

But the key point here is this: the 'sophists' who travelled around the ancient world were keen on making **disciples** for themselves, and their followers often quarrelled and scrapped among themselves as to which teacher was the greatest. Paul has realized, with the report from the family of Chloe, visiting him in Ephesus, that the Christians in Corinth have begun to treat him, Apollos, Peter and even King Jesus himself, as a bunch of teachers to be played off against one another. And that is to miss the whole point. The church still (God help us!) sometimes makes the same mistake today.

1 CORINTHIANS 1.18–25

God's Folly

18 The word of the cross, you see, is madness to people who are being
destroyed. But to us – those who are being saved – it is God's power.
19 This is what the Bible says, after all:

> I will destroy the wisdom of the wise;
> the shrewdness of the clever I'll abolish.

20 Where is the wise person? Where is the educated person? Where
is the debater of this present age? Don't you see that God has turned
the world's wisdom into folly? 21 This is how it's happened: in God's
wisdom, the world didn't know God through wisdom, so it gave God
pleasure, through the folly of our proclamation, to save those who
believe. 22 Jews look for signs, you see, and Greeks search for wisdom;
23 but we announce the crucified Messiah, a scandal to Jews and folly
to Gentiles, 24 but to those who are called, Jews and Greeks alike, the
Messiah – God's power and God's wisdom. 25 God's folly is wiser than
humans, you see, and God's weakness is stronger than humans.

On 15 March 44 BC, Julius Caesar was assassinated in Rome, a mile or so away from where I am writing these words. His killers were a group of conservative Republicans who thought, with good reason, that Caesar was planning to make himself king of Rome – something the city had set its face against for hundreds of years.

Thousands of people who know little ancient history know about this incident because of Shakespeare's play *Julius Caesar*. One of the most famous scenes in that play is when, after the murder, the leading conspirator, Marcus Brutus, steps forward to explain to the anxious crowd why it was necessary, for the good of the state, that Caesar should have been killed. He speaks in flat, straightforward, simple prose. His sentences plod along, clear enough in their way, but without life, energy or passion. The crowd are more or less convinced, but not excited.

Then there steps forward a very different man. Mark Antony was a friend of Caesar, and begins by saying he's come to bury Caesar, not to praise him; he isn't trying, he says, to argue against Brutus and what he and the others have done, just to do the decent thing by his friend. But already, in Shakespeare's magic lines, Antony's speech begins to move us. It is poetry. It dances, casts a spell, entrances the crowd. Antony, well aware of what he is doing, disclaims all such artistry: 'I am no orator, as Brutus is', he protests, even while charming the birds out of the trees in a way that poor, pedestrian Brutus could not have imagined. By the end of the speech the crowd has been pulled right round, ready to do whatever Antony suggests. It is the turning-point in the play, and, in a measure, in the actual history of Rome.

There are two moments in Paul's writings where (though with very different intent) he plays the same trick as Mark Antony. One is 2 Corinthians 11, where he constructs an upside-down list of his 'achievements', which only mentions his failures. The other is the section of the present letter which opens with the passage now before us.

He is contrasting 'the wisdom of the world' with 'the wisdom of God'. His basic claim is that the **message** about the **Messiah** and his cross carries a power of quite a different sort to the power of human rhetoric, with its showy style designed to entertain the ear and so gain an undeserved hearing for a merely human message. But, in making this point, he himself writes a paragraph of such wonderfully flowing and balanced rhetoric that one can only assume he was deliberately teasing them, perhaps hoping to make, by humour and irony, the deadly serious point underneath.

The point is that when Paul came into a pagan city that prided itself on its intellectual and cultural life, and stood up to speak about Jesus of Nazareth, who had been crucified by the Romans but raised from the dead by God, and who was now the Lord of the world, summoning people to faithful obedience, he knew what people would think. This was, and is, the craziest message anybody could imagine. This wasn't a smart new philosophy; it was madness. It wasn't an appeal to high culture. It was news of an executed criminal from a despised race.

Nor would the Jewish people themselves enjoy it. As Paul knew, it was a 'scandal' to them. (The word 'scandal', in his world, meant 'something that trips someone up'. No Jew of the time was expecting a Messiah who would be executed by Rome; a Messiah ought to be defeating the pagans, not being killed by them!) Paul had no illusions, then, about the **gospel** message, the royal announcement of King Jesus. Simply to make the announcement, to tell the story of Jesus and his cross, was to invite people to mock.

So when he announced it, when he stood up in the synagogue or the marketplace or the debating-chamber, he didn't use clever words to trick people into thinking they believed it because they enjoyed his speaking style. Now, writing this letter, looking back on his initial announcement, he can for a moment spin some good sentences together, to tease them into seeing the point. But he didn't do that when making the original proclamation. The cross had to do its own work. Simply telling the story released a power of quite a different sort from any power that human speech could have: God's power, beside which all human power looks weak; God's wisdom, beside which all human learning looks like folly.

Paul says it the other way round, to make the point with stunning rhetorical effect: God's folly is wiser than humans, and God's weakness is stronger than humans! Of course, it's very easy for humans, when they believe the gospel, to turn it into a way of inflating their own personal or political power, or showing off how clever they are. But to do so is to undermine the very point of the message. The Christian **good news** is all about God dying on a rubbish-heap at the wrong end of the Empire. It's all about God babbling nonsense to a room full of philosophers. It's all about the true God confronting the world of posturing, power and prestige, and overthrowing it in order to set up his own **kingdom**, a kingdom in which the weak and the foolish find themselves just as welcome as the strong and the wise, if not more so. Think back to Jesus himself, and the people he befriended, and ask yourself whether Paul is not being utterly loyal to his master.

In other words, as he says in Romans 1.16, the gospel, the royal announcement that Jesus is Lord, because God has raised him from the dead, is 'God's power for salvation to those who believe'. When this announcement is made, people discover to their astonishment that things change. Lives change. Human hearts change. Situations change. New communities come into being, consisting of people grasped by the message, believing it's true despite everything, falling in love with the God they find to be alive in this Jesus, giving Jesus their supreme loyalty. That is the evidence Paul has in mind. 'To us who are being saved, it is God's power.' That is as true in the twenty-first century as it was in the first – however much people today, exactly as in Paul's day, defend their own power and prestige by declaring that it's all folly.

1 CORINTHIANS 1.26–31

Boasting in the Lord

> 26Think back to your own call, my brothers and sisters. Not many of
> you were wise in human terms. Not many of you were powerful. Not
> many were nobly born. 27But God chose the foolish things of the
> world to shame the wise; God chose the weak things of the world to
> shame the strong; 28God chose the insignificant and despised things
> of the world – yes, even things that don't exist! – to abolish the power
> of the things that do exist, 29so that no creature could boast in God's
> presence. 30Who and what you now are is a gift from God in Messiah
> Jesus, who has become for us God's wisdom – and righteousness,
> sanctification and redemption as well; 31so that, as the Bible puts it,
> 'Anyone who boasts should boast in the Lord.'

There is a true but sad story about Cosmo Gordon Lang, who was Archbishop of Canterbury from 1928 to 1942. In his day there was no compulsory retirement age for archbishops; but, when he reached his late seventies, realizing that he was becoming physically frail, he decided to leave office. But, in a revealing remark to a colleague, he showed his real fear, a fear which one might have hoped an archbishop would long since have outgrown: 'Having been Somebody,' he remarked, 'I shall now be Nobody.'

The world is full of 'somebodies' and 'nobodies', and it does neither of them any good. That's not the way God intended it to be. Every human being, man, woman, child and even unborn child, bears the image and likeness of God, and has neither more nor less dignity because some other people have heard of them, look up to them or think they're special. But in most parts of the world, at most periods of history – and, as the story shows, often enough in the church itself – people feel that it's better to be 'somebody'. The cult of fame has reached monstrous proportions in recent days, to the absurd point where many people are now famous for being famous. We know their names, we recognize their faces, but can't remember whether they are footballers, film stars or fashion models. Or perhaps even archbishops.

Corinth, as a proud Roman city, was exactly the sort of place where people would look up to the 'somebodies', and do their best to join them. Then, as now, there were the obvious routes to fame: political power, and royal or noble birth. And, as we've seen (though this doesn't hold for all cultures), Corinth paid special attention to people who could speak well, public rhetoricians, lawyers and the like. The wise, the powerful, the noble: these were the 'somebodies' in Corinth.

And Paul reminds his readers that most of them were, on the same scale, 'nobodies'. When he first came to town and announced the **gospel** of King Jesus as Lord, and they believed it, most of them weren't among the 'wise' whom society looked up to. Most of them didn't have any social power (though Erastus, the city treasurer, is mentioned as a Corinthian Christian in Romans 16.23). Most of them didn't come from well-known, 'noble' families.

'But God . . .' Those are some of Paul's favourite words. He often describes a human situation or problem and then takes delight in showing that God has stepped in and done something to change it drastically. They were 'nobodies', but God has made them 'somebodies'. Not the sort of 'somebodies' the world would recognize as such, but the only sort that mattered. And what is important in this paragraph is the fact that God has taken the initiative in it all. The Christian gospel is a matter of grace from start to finish. God chose these Corinthian 'nobodies' (verses 27, 28); God 'called' them through Paul's announcement of the crucified Jesus as Lord (verse 26; the word 'call' is Paul's regular word for what we sometimes call 'conversion'); God gave them the status in his eyes that the **Messiah** himself has (verse 30). They are who they are, as he says in a rather shorthand way, 'from God in the Messiah' (verse 30). This is the same sequence (chosen, called, justified) as Paul sketches in the famous summary in Romans 8.29–30, though there he extends the sequence backwards to God's original plan and forwards to ultimate glorification as well.

The result of it all, of course, is that they have nothing to boast of. As he says later in the letter (4.7), they have nothing that they haven't received as a gift; and if someone gives you a present you didn't deserve, you haven't got anything to boast about. This is essentially the same point that Paul makes in several other places, where he speaks of 'boasting' as being ruled out by the gospel, both the actual message (the foolish announcement of a crucified Lord) and the way it works (by the power of sheer grace to change the heart and produce **faith** and Christian life). In Romans 3.27–30 he speaks of the 'boasting' of Jewish people, including his own former self. They possessed God's **law**, and that (so they thought) made them 'somebodies' over against the **Gentile** 'nobodies'. He says the same thing in Ephesians 2.9. Later in our present letter (3.21) he will apply the point to those who 'boast' about different teachers, himself, Apollos, or whoever.

In this passage, though, he is talking about the classic pagan language that would be used when people wanted to give themselves airs, to become 'somebodies'. This was the kind of social and cultural status that the Christians in Corinth were now so eager to obtain. They are missing the point, he declares. No Christian can boast of the status he or she possesses, because from first to last it is God's work and gift.

In saying all this, Paul is alluding to two Old Testament passages and another biblical theme. In Deuteronomy, particularly chapter 7, the Israelites are reminded that they are God's people, not because they are anything special in themselves, but despite the fact that they aren't. They are called to love and serve the one true God out of gratitude for what he's done for them, not least the 'redemption' from Egypt in the **Exodus**. Paul wants the new Christians to understand themselves as God's new-Exodus people (see chapter 10), with the same understanding of God's grace.

Then in Jeremiah 9, quoted in verse 31, the prophet warns against exactly that kind of 'boasting' which Paul is attacking in this passage. Paul only quotes verse 24, shortening it as he does so; but he clearly has in mind the whole of verses 23 and 24:

> Don't let the wise boast in their wisdom;
> don't let the powerful boast in their power;
> don't let the wealthy boast in their riches;
> but let those who boast, boast in this,
> that they understand and know me, says YHWH;
> I act with steadfast love, judgment, and righteousness
>   in the earth,
> for in these things I delight, says YHWH.

Time and again, Paul quotes the phrase 'the Lord' from the Old Testament, where the word refers directly to **YHWH**, Israel's God, and makes it refer to Jesus the Messiah. So it is here. He is the one 'in whom' Christians possess all the wisdom they need – and the status ('righteousness') of being his forgiven, **justified** people, and the extraordinary privilege of being set apart for his service ('sanctification') in virtue of his 'redemption' of them from the slavery of sin.

The biblical theme which Paul is drawing on here is the theme of 'Wisdom'. In the book of Proverbs, in particular in its great introduction (chapters 1—9), we find Wisdom as a person, the one through whom the world was made, inviting humans to discover who she is and so to become the genuine human beings they were meant to be. Later Jewish writings like Ecclesiasticus ('The Wisdom of Ben Sirach', probably written about 200 BC) and 'The Wisdom of Solomon' (probably early first century AD) developed this idea into the notion that Wisdom is to be found in the Jewish law, or in the presence of YHWH in the **Temple**, and that by following this Wisdom people can be and do what God intended them to be and do in the world. For Paul, Jesus the Messiah is the true wisdom (see, e.g., Colossians 1.15–20 and 2.1–3). Having him – or rather, being 'in him' – means that you are a genuine human being at last, called to live by God's wisdom rather than that of the world.

Exploring what it means to be 'in the Messiah', so that what is true of him is true of you, is the Christian's basic strength and delight. God has vindicated Jesus in his **resurrection**; God set him apart for his own service; God accomplished in him the defeat of the great enslaving powers of sin and death. If you are 'in Christ', a member of the Messiah's family, this 'wisdom, righteousness, sanctification, and redemption' are yours too. And if that doesn't make you 'somebody', nothing ever will.

1 CORINTHIANS 2.1–5

The Powerful Message of the Cross

[1]This is how it was for me, too, my dear family. When I came to you, I
didn't come and proclaim God's mystery to you by means of a supe-
rior style of speaking or wisdom. [2]No: I decided to know nothing in
my dealings with you except Jesus the Messiah, especially his crucifix-
ion. [3]I came to you in weakness, in great fear and trembling. [4]My
speech and my proclamation were not in persuasive words of wis-
dom, but in transparent proof brought home powerfully by the spirit,
[5]so that your faith might not be in human wisdom but in God's power.

Life is full of mystery. The deepest, richest and most complex theories that science can ever come up with only serve to highlight the fact that there is still a depth of mystery which goes way beyond it all. You can study biology and human genetics, and know everything there is to know about fertilization, reproduction, pregnancy, birth and childhood; but when you see your own newborn child, and two eyes meet yours with a look that seems to say, not 'Who are you?' but 'So – it's you!' you glimpse a mystery which no physical explanation can ever begin to explore.

It's the same with music. The physicist can in principle explain what happens when a particular instrument is played. But why Mozart makes us want to laugh and cry and dance, why some music is deeply consoling and some deeply disturbing, remains a mystery.

The deepest mysteries of human life – love, death, joy, beauty and the rest – have for millennia been believed to point to the deepest mystery of them all, the mystery of God. Sometimes in the ancient world people developed whole systems for trying to penetrate this mystery, often in relation to a particular divinity such as Isis or Mithras. People believed that by going through particular initiation rites and disciplines they would get to the heart of the mystery, and would discover things that would change their lives completely.

Most Jews believed that the one true God had already invited them to share his own **life** and purpose, so they didn't go this route. But they, too, knew a strong sense of mystery as they tried to understand the truth about how and why God had made the world, and in particular what his purpose was for them and for the future. Among the writings of ancient Israel, both in the Bible and in other books, there are many which try to penetrate to this truth, to discover what was going on in God's world, and where different people might fit into his purposes.

This is where Paul comes in. He picked up this Jewish tradition and declared that God's past, present and future had at last been unveiled in and through Jesus the **Messiah**. Jesus was the clue to all the secrets of God. Paul spells this out elsewhere, for instance in Colossians 1.26—2.3. And Paul wants the muddled Corinthian Christians to see that, though the **message** about the crucified Jesus is indeed a foolish, scandalous thing in the eyes of the rest of the world, at the heart of the Christian message there is the clue to the deepest mystery of life. In speaking like this, here in verse 7, and elsewhere, Paul may be teasing them a little about the way their culture and philosophy liked to probe into 'mysteries' of the pagan sort. He is pulling them over onto solidly Jewish ground.

One of the reasons, in fact, why the mystery of the **gospel** *is* a mystery is because nobody in Corinth or most other places would ever think of looking for the secret to life, the universe, God, beauty, love and death in a place of execution outside a rebellious city in the Middle East. That is why, as Paul says, not only were the Corinthian Christians themselves, for the most part, neither wise, powerful nor aristocratic, but also he himself, when he announced the message to them, found himself in fear and trembling.

Imagine finding yourself standing up to make a speech in front of an audience of the great and the good, and having nothing to say except some stammering words about a strange thing that happened a few years ago which you know sounds crazy but which you just happen to think contains the secret to everything. You'd watch the faces, and see a lip curl here, an eyebrow lift there, people glancing at one another with knowing looks, shaking their heads not only at the stupidity of what's being said but at the insult to the audience to offer them such rubbish.

And yet there was power in it. We don't know exactly what Paul meant by 'brought home powerfully by the **spirit**', but it may imply that healing **miracles** took place. What was more important, though, is that without Paul using any of the normal rhetorical tricks of the trade, people's hearts, minds and lives were changed. The truth of the gospel carried its own power, and Paul was happy to keep it that way, even though he looked a fool while he was announcing it.

At the heart of the appropriate response to this gospel was '**faith**'. This is central to his vision of what being a Christian is all about. It is important to notice what he says about it. This 'faith', which elsewhere he sees as the sole true mark of Christian identity, is brought about by the power of the spirit at work in the gospel. He doesn't spell out here what this faith consists in, but the places where he does so fill in and clarify this passage. In Romans 10.9 he says that Christian faith means confessing that Jesus is Lord and believing that God raised him from the dead. That ties in closely with his summary of the gospel message itself, the message they 'believed', in 15.3–8 of the present letter. And in 12.3 he says something similar: no one can say 'Jesus is Lord', except by the work of the holy spirit.

But in 15.3–8, where he reminds them of the basic gospel message which he and the other **apostles** all announced, he speaks not only of Jesus' death but also of his **resurrection**. Indeed, he elaborates the resurrection by listing several times when the risen Jesus was seen by different people, including Paul himself. How does this fit in with what he says here, that he decided to know nothing when he was with them except 'Jesus the Messiah, the crucified one'?

He doesn't mean that he only spoke of Jesus' cross and never mentioned his resurrection. Hundreds of people, after all, were crucified in Paul's day; what made Jesus different was that God raised him from the dead. But, by placing proper emphasis on the crucifixion, Paul ensured that nobody could mistake this message for a kind of crowd-pleasing rhetorical stunt, convincing at the time but making no lasting impression. Crucifixion was regarded in the ancient world as so horrible, so revolting, so degrading that you didn't mention it in polite society. Imagine somebody at a fashionable dinner party going on in a loud voice about how he'd seen rats eating the body of a dead dog in the street; that's the kind of impression you'd make by standing up in public and talking about someone being crucified. No self-respecting sophist or rhetorician would dream of doing it. But Paul believed, and the new-found faith and life of the Corinthian Christians bore this out, that this was the clue to the mystery of life.

1 CORINTHIANS 2.6–13

God's Strange Wisdom

[6]We do, however, speak wisdom among the mature. But this isn't a
wisdom of this present world, or of the rulers of this present world –
those same rulers who are being done away with. [7]No: we speak God's
hidden wisdom in a mystery. This is the wisdom God prepared ahead
of time, before the world began, for our glory.

[8]None of the rulers of this present age knew about this wisdom. If
they had, you see, they wouldn't have crucified the Lord of glory. [9]But,
as the Bible says,

> Human eyes have never seen,
> human ears have never heard,
> it's never entered human hearts:
> all that God has now prepared
> for those who truly love him.

[10] – and that's what God has revealed to us through the spirit! The
spirit, you see, searches everything, yes, even the depths of God.
[11]Think of it this way: who knows what is really going on inside a
person, except the spirit of the person which is inside them? Well, it's
like that with God. Nobody knows what is going on inside God except
God's spirit. [12]And we haven't received the spirit of the world, but the
spirit that comes from God, so that we can know the things that have
been given to us by God.

[13]That, then, is what we speak. We don't use words we've been
taught by human wisdom, but words we've been taught by the spirit,
interpreting spiritual things to spiritual people.

When my sister celebrated her 21st birthday, she and I were at university, a long way from home. So a cousin of my father's, who lived nearby, invited the two of us to dinner to celebrate. He and his wife had no children of their own, and were eager to entertain us properly.

We had a wonderful meal and a delightful evening. As it drew towards a close, he produced the final touch. He had a bottle of brandy that was then 100 years old. He had been keeping it for a special occasion. He solemnly opened it, and poured everyone a glass. We sipped it equally solemnly, and told him how wonderful it was. We were truly grateful, but our praise meant nothing; we had neither of us ever tasted brandy before, and would not have been able to tell the difference between the contents of that bottle and a cheap one produced the previous week.

Paul speaks in this passage of a kind of teaching that is only for those who have grown up, who are mature, who have had their palates trained up from childish food and drink to appreciate and value the higher things. Having insisted that his **gospel** was, and needed to be, foolishness to Greeks and a scandal to Jews, he doesn't want them to think that this is all he has to offer. He really does have wisdom in store, deep and rich and many-sided; but it's only for those who can and will appreciate it, who are sufficiently grown-up in their spiritual discernment.

This is not to take back with the left hand what he's just given with the right. He doesn't mean that when converts get more mature he will then give them the same kind of 'wisdom' that you'd get from the sophists and philosophers in the wider world. Far from it. The wisdom he has in mind doesn't belong to 'this age' at all. It belongs to the '**age to come**'; speaking of it to those who aren't already part of this 'age to come' is like speaking of a sunrise to blind people. Only those who have believed in the rising of the **son of God** can even begin to understand what this wisdom is. For the rest, it is as mad as the gospel itself.

Paul here draws on a crucial distinction to which he will return frequently throughout the letter. This, indeed, is one of the main things he wants the Corinthians to learn. World history divides into two 'ages' or epochs. There is the '**present age**', the period of history characterized by human rebellion, sin, despair and death. Then there is 'the **age to come**', the time when the one true God will be king over all the world, bringing to an end the rule of all forces that oppose him. And the point is this: 'the age to come' has already broken in to the present age in Jesus the **Messiah**. His death and **resurrection** form the decisive break, the moment when the great melody of history has begun to be heard in a major key instead of a minor one.

That's why the present age, and its rulers, don't understand this wisdom. They are still playing the tune in the old key, and the notes of the gospel, and the new 'wisdom' that flows from it, simply won't fit. Paul here introduces a theme which will occupy him later in the letter, but which is important as a backdrop for much of what comes in between as well. 'The rulers of this age' are clearly the actual governments of the world. They are the ones, he says, who 'crucified the Lord of glory' (verse 8): in other words, they are the political powers, and the actual rulers, who conspired to put Jesus on the cross. Rome, under the emperor Tiberius, was in charge, acting through the local governor, Pontius Pilate. Judaism, under the rule of the chief **priests**, in an uneasy relationship with Herod Antipas, 'the king of the Jews', played their part by keeping the local people on side with Rome's decision.

Thus, as my teacher, Professor George Caird, used to say, the highest religion and the best government that the world had ever seen got together to execute the Lord of glory – an irony that Paul, too, undoubtedly appreciated. The Bible is always clear that God intends human society to be ruled by appropriate wise and just government; but all government, precisely because it wields power, has the capacity to go bad, to become arrogant, to act in ways that promote its own self-interest instead of true justice, wisdom and truth. That, it appears, is what happened at Jesus' crucifixion. The ruling authorities had no thought that they were doing anything but getting rid of another troublemaker, all in a day's work for ruthless empires from that day to this. But if they'd realized what was going on they would never have dreamed of doing such a thing. Why not? Not simply because they would have respected Jesus and refused to kill him. Rather, because they would have realized that in doing so they were signing their own death warrants.

In Colossians 2.15 Paul speaks, with heavy irony, of the cross of Jesus as the moment when the 'principalities and powers' were led along like a defeated rabble behind the chariot of a conquering general. Here in 1 Corinthians he speaks of Jesus winning the final victory over every rule and power and authority on the day when he finally appears as king (15.23–28). The two moments are closely joined together. What the cross achieves, the final 'appearing' of Jesus will implement fully. And if, as he says, the last enemy to be destroyed is death itself, the rulers of this world have nothing more to say. As every tyrant knows, death is the final threat by which power is exercised in this world.

Paul allows this statement about the ignorance of the present world rulers to hover in the air over what is to come. Their power is already doomed, and Christians are called to live as citizens of God's sovereign rule instead. For the moment, he develops the positive side: God has prepared for 'those who love him' (an Old Testament way of describing God's people) things which not only pass human wisdom and understanding but also imagination itself. (The quotation here is not from the Old Testament itself, but from another ancient Jewish book, known to some in the early church but now lost.) 'Wisdom', it turns out, is not just intellectual information, or even the elegance and beauty of abstract theories; it blossoms like a garden, flows like a mighty river, satisfies human beings at every level in ways we can't even guess at the moment. That is what God has in mind for those who love him.

How do we know? Because God has given us his **spirit**. This is another major theme of the letter, introduced here for the first time. Paul relishes the fact that the spirit who is poured out upon believers, bringing them to **faith** and opening their hearts and minds to the wisdom of the 'age to come', is God's own spirit, not some lesser being. The spirit within a person – the deep innermost **life** where thought, feeling, memory and imagination meet – knows best what the person is really all about. Even so, Paul declares, God's spirit is like that with God; and this spirit is given to all God's people in the Messiah.

This is an astonishing claim. It clearly doesn't mean that Christians automatically know everything about God, or why would Paul bother to write letters? It means that they have open access to God's mind – or, as he says in verse 16, to 'the mind of the Messiah'. But to explore this they must themselves be 'mature' (verse 6). They must themselves be, in some important sense which he will now go on to explain, 'spiritual'.

This tight-packed and challenging passage has many lessons for us, but perhaps the most important is for Christians who have forgotten, or perhaps never known, two truths.

The first is that there is a wealth of knowledge and life-enhancing understanding waiting for us to explore. Christianity is not simply a set of beliefs and a rule book for life, such as anyone could master in a weekend. It is as many-sided as the world itself, full of beauty and mystery and power, and as terrifying and wonderful as God himself. There is always much, much more to learn, to relish, to delight in.

The second is that the Christian message from the very beginning challenged the world of power, including social and political power, with the message of God's superior **kingdom** unveiled in Jesus' death and resurrection. Paul doesn't want the Corinthians to imagine that he is talking simply about a religious experience that won't have anything to do with the real life of politics and government. He wouldn't want us to imagine that either. Let us not settle for a gospel which allows the world's power games to proceed without challenge.

1 CORINTHIANS 2.14—3.4

Spiritual or Merely Human?

[14]Someone living at the merely human level doesn't accept the things
of God's spirit. They are foolishness to such people, you see, and they
can't understand them because they need to be discerned spiritually.
[15]But spiritual people discern everything, while nobody else can dis-
cern the truth about them! [16]For 'Who has known the mind of the
Lord, so as to instruct him?' But we have the mind of the Messiah.

[3.1]In my own case, my dear family, I couldn't speak to you as spirit-
ual people, but as people who were all too obviously merely human,
little babies in the Messiah. [2]I fed you with milk, not solid food, because
you weren't able to take it – and you still can't, even now! [3]You're still
determined to live in the old way! Yes, wherever there is jealousy and

quarrelling, doesn't that mean you're living in the old way, behaving as any merely human being might do? [4]When someone says 'I'm with Paul!', and someone else says 'I'm with Apollos!', are you not mere humans?

Once, during the 'hippy' era in the late 1960s, I sang and played my guitar in a folk club on the west side of Vancouver. I was there a week, and got to know some of the other regular performers quite well. One was a young man with the beginnings of a drug habit. He was quite a good guitarist, and a passable singer. But, some way into the evening, he would take a shot of whichever drug it was he was using at the time.

The effect was revealing. (I had never been remotely tempted to try drugs before, and I certainly didn't want to after watching him.) Once he was 'high', his playing and singing got worse and worse; but he came off stage convinced that he had been absolutely brilliant. Nothing could deter him from taking the drug to enhance his performance, as he thought, even though the rest of us tried to tell him it was doing the opposite.

Paul is now bringing his discussion of wisdom and folly, and spiritual maturity and immaturity, right down to where the Corinthians themselves are. They have been using the drug of sophistry, supposing it makes them more 'spiritual'; and Paul declares that it has made them all the more merely human.

They may by now have become fascinated by what he's been saying. Hearing the letter to this point, they will perhaps have been glad that he seems to have forgotten, or left behind, the issue he started with in 1.10 (the faction fighting in support of different teachers). If they are thinking that, they are in for a shock; because the discussion about wisdom and maturity was all preparing the way to come back to the point. They have been imagining that they had a 'wisdom' which elevated them above the ordinary. They were eager for the kind of teaching the sophists were giving, imagining that by putting together a bit of Christian **faith** with a strong dose of sophistry they were becoming some kind of super-people. But they are deceived. The more they take the drug, the more immature they show themselves to be; and the proof of it all is – their in-fighting about different Christian teachers!

That is the main point Paul is making here, and it bears reflection in today's church as we so easily lapse from serious issues to personality-clashes, and from personalities to mere gossip, while all the time pretending we are still dealing with important matters. But we need to note as well the way in which Paul sets up the problem. The language he uses is complex and appears to be technical. We need to understand it in order to see what he does with it later on.

He begins by making the distinction between 'spiritual' people, the ones he's just mentioned in verse 13, the ones who can understand the deep and spiritual wisdom that as a teacher he longs to share with people, and 'merely human' people, people living on the ordinary level.

The word he uses which we translate 'merely human' is a tricky one. Other writers of the time use it in a variety of ways. Paul may himself be picking it up from things the Corinthians, or others, are saying, in order to turn it back and make it serve his purpose rather than theirs. But the basic difference he is describing is between people in whom God's **spirit** has come to dwell, opening them up to new depths and dimensions of truth and experience, and people who are living as though the world, and human life, was rumbling along in the same old way. They may think they're very sophisticated, but in reality they are 'merely human'.

The word he actually uses could be translated 'soul-ish' as opposed to 'spiritual' – meaning someone who is directed and led simply by the ordinary human interior **life** ('soul') rather than by the fresh, **gospel**-driven wisdom or energy given by God's spirit. Such a person (2.14) simply can't understand what's going on when the talk turns to the deeper things of the spirit. They become like a tone-deaf person at an opera: it's all nonsense to them. Take that picture one step further. Imagine being the only musical person listening to a wonderful string quartet in a large room full of tone-deaf people. That is rather like Paul's picture of being a 'spiritual' person in a world of 'merely human' people.

This could sound as though Paul is setting himself up as some kind of high and mighty spiritual leader, but that's not the point. He stresses first that the 'spiritual' person makes judgments on a different plane to the merely natural one (verse 15), while the judgments that such people make will pass him or her by without effect. The evidence he offers is a quotation from Isaiah 40.13, where the prophet looks at the wider world and asks 'who has known **YHWH**'s mind?', expecting the answer 'no one'. But if the **Messiah** has already become for us 'wisdom, righteousness, sanctification and redemption' (1.30), then it is not a long step to say that we – that is, those who have the spirit – possess the Messiah's *mind*. If that is true, there is no depth of wisdom too deep, no height too high, for us to explore.

But the Corinthians themselves aren't ready for it! Paul shakes his head over them. They may have supposed, listening to the letter as it is read out in their assembly, that he is talking about them as the 'spiritual' ones, but he isn't. Picking up his earlier comment about people being 'grown-up' or 'mature' (2.6), he uses the language many teachers of his day employed to explain the difference between those who were ready for serious teaching and those who were still at the infancy stage. When he had been with them before, he explains, he only taught them the basics: milk, not meat. He may be answering the charge that his teaching had been very basic; the other teachers who'd come in after him had been much more exciting, much deeper, much more gratifying to the Corinthian eagerness for social and spiritual status and pride . . .

. . . which only goes to show, Paul concludes, that you are still babies, even now (3.1–2)! You are driven by all-too-human impulses. Here again Paul uses words which are difficult to translate, but which mean, more or less, 'living on the basis of your created and corruptible nature alone' (verse 1), and 'living as people determined to make that created and corruptible nature alone your guide and rule' (verse 3). There is, in fact, a very subtle shift from 'merely human' (2.14) to 'all too obviously human' (3.1), to 'very determinedly only-human' (i.e. actually resisting the spirit, not merely showing no evidence of it) (3.3). Paul is not suggesting that each of these words refers to a different level of Christian (or sub-Christian) experience, or to a different type of person. He is insisting that all of them alike are 'unspiritual' – and that the Corinthian church, insofar as it is indulging in personality cults, is showing strong evidence of exactly that. This is why he hadn't been able to give them stronger, deeper, richer teaching; they weren't ready for it, and their present factional fighting shows that they still aren't.

What words might Paul use for today's church? For your own church?

1 CORINTHIANS 3.5–11

God's Farm, God's Building

> 5So what d'you suppose Apollos actually is? What d'you think Paul is?
> I'll tell you: servants, through whom you came to faith, each one as
> the Lord gave. 6I planted and Apollos watered, but it was God who
> gave the growth. 7It follows that the person who plants isn't anything
> special, and the person who waters isn't anything special; what mat-
> ters is God who gives the growth. 8The person who plants and the
> person who waters are just the same, and each will receive his own
> reward according to his own work. 9We are God's fellow-workers, you
> see: you are God's farm, God's building.
>
> 10According to God's grace, I laid the foundation like a wise master
> builder, and someone else is building on it. Everyone should take care
> how they build on it. 11Nobody can lay any foundation, you see, except
> the one which is laid, which is Jesus the Messiah!

Was Paul 'the founder of Christianity'?

I found myself embroiled in a debate on that subject a few years ago. From time to time people try to establish a familiar viewpoint: Jesus didn't really begin Christianity, since he was just an ordinary Jewish teacher who would have been appalled to think of a 'religion' being started around him, and what we know as Christianity, and project back on to Jesus, was in fact the invention of Paul. On this occasion, the writer making the case was a well-known journalist, novelist and biographer, trying his hand on early Christian history.

Well, debates come and debates go. This one rumbled on in the newspapers for some time (which was a nice change; normally British newspapers don't take much notice of such things). It became a focal point for much wider questions, to do with Jesus himself and his **resurrection** (if Jesus really did rise from the dead, no one could say that Paul made it all up), and also to do with what sort of religion ordinary people want in our own day (as though what people wanted had anything to do with historical or theological truth). But the present passage gives Paul's own comment on the central question.

There is a sense in which Paul did indeed 'found' churches, like somebody laying the foundation of a building. He was happy to describe his work in that way. But the 'foundation' he put down was Jesus himself, the **Messiah**, the Lord. That, he says (verse 11), is the only 'foundation' that there ever can be. Paul didn't invent Christianity; several other teachers, independent of him, taught essentially the same **gospel** (see 15.11). But in the sense that he 'founded' churches, it was always the case that Jesus himself was the 'foundation'.

The issue he's getting at here isn't about the relationship between himself and Jesus, though that comes into it as well. It's about the relationship between himself and other teachers who came after him. (He mentions Apollos here, but we may assume that he refers to others as well, perhaps including Cephas/Peter.) In addition to the picture of laying a foundation and building on it (verses 10–17), he uses the image of farming or gardening, to make the point that while he did the planting and Apollos (and perhaps others) did the watering of the plants, it was God all along who made the plants grow.

This in turn explains what Paul means in verse 5. He and Apollos are 'servants through whom you believed'. The word 'servant' here, unlike the word 'slave', can mean 'the one who waits at table'; in other words, Paul and Apollos are simply the people who serve the food, while God is responsible for choosing it and cooking it. You shouldn't make a fuss about which waiter brings the food to your table. What matters is that God is in charge in the kitchen.

The question of whether the waiters, the farmers and the builders do a good job or not is something else. Paul will come to that in the next passage, and merely hints at it in verses 8 and 10. Each worker will receive his or her appropriate reward according to the work that they have done. When it comes to building, they should take good care how they go about the job. Paul will shortly discuss the different sorts of materials that they might use; but we might consider, for the moment, the question of what sort and size of building they are putting up.

If you come upon a foundation ready laid, but without any plans for the superstructure, you will have to choose what sort of building to build. Paul's basic answer is that this must be a building for *worship*: a **Temple**, in other words (verses 16–17). That's the question every church worker should ask: is what I'm doing encouraging and enabling people to worship the true and living God, in holiness and truth? If not, am I perhaps being untrue to the foundation that has been laid?

It should be clear from all this, as from 16.12, that Paul has no basic quarrel with Apollos. When he takes serious issue with false teaching, he lets us know in no uncertain terms, as (for instance) in Galatians. What he has a problem with is the idea that anyone might play off him and Apollos against one another, within some personality contest based on the human standards of 'wisdom' and rhetoric. Of course, we may suspect that in any such contest Apollos might have come off best. But that isn't the point. Paul is just as cross about people putting him on a pedestal as he is about anybody else being there. There is only one pedestal in the **kingdom of God**, and only one person to be put on it. But it isn't a statue to be put up as a monument in a town square. It is a cross; and the Messiah who hung and died on it passed judgment on all human fame, celebrity, popularity and reputation. That is the message Paul wants above all to get across. Were he to come to our churches today he might well feel that he had to make the same point to us as well.

1 CORINTHIANS 3.12–17

The Coming Day, the Coming Fire

12If anyone builds on the foundation with gold, silver, precious stones,
wood, grass or straw – 13well, everyone's work will become visible,
because the Day will show it up, since it will be revealed in fire. Then
the fire will test what sort of work everyone has done. 14If the building
work that someone has done stands the test, they will receive a reward.
15If someone's work is burned up, they will be punished by bearing the
loss; they themselves will be saved, however, but only as though
through a fire.

16Don't you see? You are God's Temple! God's spirit lives in you! 17If
anyone destroys God's Temple, God will destroy them. God's Temple
is holy, you see, and that is precisely what you are.

I love sightseeing around ancient ruins. Like many historians who have had the good fortune to travel round the ancient world, I have stood in the Temple of Apollo in Corinth, in the synagogue at Capernaum, in the Forum at Rome, and in many other places where history was made, where events took place which still reverberate today.

But all visitors to ancient sites have to use a good deal of imagination. Even when buildings and monuments have been skilfully restored, they almost always look significantly different to how they would have looked to their first builders. You have to imagine the Elgin Marbles back in Athens, not in the British Museum. You have to 'see' the ancient synagogues with worshippers praying, listening, discussing. When you stand beside the huge Senate building that Julius Caesar put up in the Forum at Rome, you have to imagine it covered, not in the boring brick we see today, but in gleaming marble.

The building materials Paul mentions in verse 12 were things you might use to adorn or build up one particular building: the **Temple**. Solomon's Temple was resplendent with gold, silver and precious stones, and when Herod the Great and his heirs rebuilt the Temple they did their best to make it just as spectacular once again. Though Paul doesn't mention the Temple explicitly until verses 16 and 17, he almost certainly has it in mind throughout this passage. This is the 'building' that he and other Christian workers are putting up.

The idea of the 'Temple' as a community of people, rather than a building of bricks, mortar and suitable adornment, was not invented by Paul. The **Dead Sea Scrolls** speak of their community in the same way. Many Jews in this period believed that the present physical Temple in Jerusalem was under God's judgment, and that God would do a new thing, which might or might not involve a new physical building but which would certainly involve a new community, made up of people transformed by God's saving power. Just as God's own presence dwelt in the Temple (known as the Shekinah, the 'tabernacling presence'), so God's **spirit** dwells, Paul says, within the Christian community, making them the functional equivalent of the Temple within the new dispensation, the '**age to come**' that has already arrived.

The emphasis of the passage is therefore still on those who build up this Temple, and on the danger not just that they will build with the wrong materials (verses 12–15) but that they will actually pull the building down altogether (verse 17). If the building is indeed God's Temple, destroying such a holy place is an act of sacrilege. Faulty builders, as a recent writer has put it, may get away with 'singed eyebrows' when the fire comes. But destroyers may end up being destroyed in their turn.

But what is all this business about fire? Does this have anything to do with the belief made popular in the Roman Catholic Church in the Middle Ages, and still quite widely believed today, about a 'purgatory' after death to make Christians holy and fit for the presence of God?

At one level, the passage has nothing to do with that. It isn't a general statement about all Christians. It's a particular warning to those whose vocation is to work within God's church; in other words, to undertake some aspect of the building up of the community. ('Building up' the church is a favourite picture of Paul's, as we see later in the book, not least in chapter 14.) Paul is warning that it's possible to do such work well or badly, and that one day the results will be made known.

To make the point vividly, he describes two types of building material one might use. The first – gold, silver, precious stones – would all be able to stand up to a fire, while the second – wood, grass, straw – are all notoriously combustible. Into this picture he brings the regular Old Testament warning of a coming fire. Israel had known many times of actual fire, when foreign nations had swept down and wreaked havoc, sometimes even on the Temple itself. The question here is whether the 'building' of the church, the work that he, Apollos and the rest are undertaking, will in the end be seen to be of lasting value. 'The day' which is coming, and which will show what sort of work has been done (3.13), is clearly 'the day of the Lord' about which he spoke in 1.8. Then and only then it will be seen what each one has actually accomplished. Different workers have been at work on the building, using different materials; the 'fire' will burn up some parts and leave others enhanced. Those whose work is burned up will 'suffer loss'. (The word Paul uses for this could refer to the fines that would be levied when a builder was sued for shoddy work.)

Once we have grasped that the picture here is basically about different types of 'building', i.e., working to 'build up' the church, we can also read this passage, by a kind of extension, as indicating something at least of what Paul would say about God's judgment of each person 'according to their works' (see Romans 2.5–11; 14.10–12; 2 Corinthians 5.10). Two points need to be made here.

First, there is no tension between Paul's belief in a future judgment according to works and his doctrine of '**justification** by **faith**' (Romans 3.21–31; Galatians 2.15–21; etc.). The point about 'justification by faith' is that it makes sense within a *sequence*: it brings forward into the present the verdict that God will announce on the last day. Paul always assumes, and often states, that, by the work of the spirit, those who are justified by faith in the present will have that verdict reaffirmed in the future on the basis of the whole life they will have lived in the meantime, be it short or long (Philippians 1.6). Although he is principally speaking of those who work (well or badly) at building up the church, it would be rather odd if the dramatic picture here didn't apply to other Christians as well.

When the 'fire' does its work, he says, builders who have used the wrong material will 'suffer loss', but they themselves will still be saved. This seems to be Paul's way of preserving his view of Christian assurance ('those whom God justified, he also glorified', Romans 8.29), while maintaining also a serious view of Christian responsibility for what one does with the new life which begins, as the spirit's gift, with faith and **baptism**.

Second, then, it is possible to see this image of 'fire' (it is only a picture; Paul is not here talking about a literal fire) as a biblical way of doing what the traditional doctrine of 'purgatory' was trying to do (unhelpfully, in my view). Some leading Roman Catholic theologians have recently returned to this passage and declared that the idea of a single moment of judgment, in which all remaining impurities are burned up, is perhaps what the old doctrine of purgatory 'really meant'. If that had been said five hundred years ago, the Reformation might not have been necessary; because the Reformers, too, believed that death itself, 'the last enemy' (1 Corinthians 15.26), finished the job of purifying the Christian from remaining sin. Paul's imagery here can fit with that perfectly well.

The main point, of course, is the seriousness with which Paul takes the various tasks and responsibilities of Christians, particularly leaders and teachers in the church. We are not playing games. There are serious and lasting issues at stake. It is possible to build wisely, well, and with the right materials. It is also possible to build badly, or with the wrong materials. It is possible actually to pull down the building altogether. God takes these possibilities very seriously. Do we?

1 CORINTHIANS 3.18–23

Everything Belongs to You

18 Don't let anyone deceive themselves. If anyone among you supposes
they are wise in the present age, let them become foolish, so that they
can become wise. 19 The wisdom of this world, you see, is folly with
God. This is what the Bible says: 'He catches the wise in their trickery.'
20 And again, 'The Lord knows the thinking of the wise – and he knows
that it's all a sham!'

21 So don't let anyone boast about mere human beings. For every-
thing belongs to you, 22 whether it's Paul or Apollos or Cephas, whether
it's the world or life or death, whether it's the present or the future –
everything belongs to you! 23 And you belong to the Messiah; and the
Messiah belongs to God.

I remember a wise address given at a graduation ceremony by a respected senior professor. (I was present in order to say the opening prayer.) In his address, the great man said many things, and gave a lot of good advice, but the one thing that stands out in my memory is his description of a humble **faith**. 'It isn't', he said, 'a matter of knowing that you've got it all together; you haven't. It's a matter of knowing that somewhere it *is* all together – and that you're part of it.'

That combination of humility and confidence is hard to keep in balance. The pressure from the world around us is always trying to make us either deny that we know anything or adopt one of those brittle, high-risk, know-it-all positions. Genuine Christian faith isn't like that. It involves learning to be foolish, as Paul says here, in order to become wise; and it involves celebrating that fact that 'all things are yours' while recognizing that 'you belong to the **Messiah**, and the Messiah belongs to God'. What does Paul mean by these astonishing statements?

He is rounding off the central part of his argument about the danger of 'boasting' about human beings – the danger into which the Corinthian church has fallen with a splash. They had been saying 'I belong to Paul', 'I belong to Apollos', and so on, setting up Paul and the other Christian teachers as 'owners' of groups of **disciples**, after the manner of the sophists and 'wisdom' teachers of the day. But, in addition to all the other things that were wrong with their attitude, Paul's word here is that such a position is actually selling themselves short. It isn't that they belong to these teachers; rather, all these teachers belong to *them*! In fact, not only the teachers belong to them, but everything else does as well – excepting only the Messiah, and of course God himself! What can he be thinking of?

It makes sense only within the world of Jewish thought, according to which, as he will say later on, those who belong to God's true people are destined, when the '**age to come**' is fully here, to rule the world in obedience to God. As the book of Revelation puts it, adapting an ancient promise to Israel, God's people are to be 'kings and **priests**' in the new world (Revelation 1.6; see Exodus 19.6).

There were, of course, pagan philosophies which taught people that they were in some sense 'kings' already, if only they could learn to master themselves and discover their true place in the world. But Paul's promise, building on the Jewish tradition, goes way beyond what was on offer in the world at large. The **apostles** belong to you! The apostles don't own the church; instead, as Paul has said a few verses ago, they are the property of the church, 'servants through whom you believed' (verse 5). But it isn't just the apostles; it's the world itself. Paul is no dualist, rejecting the created world as evil; the God who revealed himself in and as Jesus of Nazareth is the same God who made the world, and by belonging to him Christians inherit the world, as Jesus himself declared (Matthew 5.5; Paul says in 1 Corinthians 6.2 that God's people will *judge* the world).

And, if the world, then life and death themselves. Christians are, in other words, already **resurrection** people, because of the sure hope that is theirs through the **gospel** message of Jesus' own resurrection (chapter 15). The present and the future belong to them; that's how important they already are. They are assured, even while the '**present** evil **age**' is continuing, that they belong in 'the age to come'. Nor do they belong in it as 'extras', coming in alongside in a script that is basically about someone or something else. They are the stars of the show.

In short, the Corinthians were like people splashing about in a muddy pool when the ocean itself was right beside them; like people drinking dirty water from a polluted tap when the finest wine, and sparkling mountain water, were theirs to command. Fancy indulging in personality cults, as though you were merely another bunch of squabbling sophists, when the entire cosmos and all its truth, mystery and wisdom were yours for the exploring! Temptations often promise more and give less – sometimes, in fact, nothing at all. Satan offers the moon, and then laughs at you when you don't get it, while God promises you the sun itself.

It is vital to get everything in the right order. Paul develops in several passages a way of talking about the Messiah and God in the same breath. This enables him to declare at the same time, first, that Jesus, the Messiah, is on God's side of the picture over against the whole world and the rest of the human race, and, second, that Jesus remains distinct from the God whom elsewhere he calls 'the father' or 'the creator'. Paul didn't take the time to write a long treatise about how this might all work out philosophically. He didn't need to. Enough to state, again and again as he does, that when Christians look up from the world, and from their own lives, they see, not a distant or unapproachable deity, not a vague divine force that they couldn't know much about, but the God of Israel, the creator God, who has made himself known in Jesus.

The point is that you don't have to understand how it all works. You have to believe – on the evidence of Jesus' resurrection in particular – *that* it works, and that you are called to be part of it. And believing that is itself, Paul would say, the sign that God's **spirit**, the spirit of God's son Jesus, is living within you, making you part of his **Temple**, the people whose primary task it is to worship and praise him.

That's why all human wisdom is overturned by the divine folly of the gospel. Verses 18–20 sum up, and buttress with further biblical quotations, the point Paul has been making from various angles ever since 1.18. And the sharp command which goes with this summing-up, which we need today as much as ever, is this: don't deceive yourself (verse 18). It is easy to do, and the results are sad. And those who think they're not likely to deceive themselves are the very ones who are about to do so.

1 CORINTHIANS 4.1–5

Judgment Then Rather Than Now

> [1]This is how we should be thought of: as servants of the Messiah, and household managers for God's mysteries. [2]And this is what follows: the main requirement for a manager is to be trustworthy. [3]Having said that, I regard it as a matter of minimal concern to think that I should be interrogated by you, or indeed by any human court. I don't even interrogate myself. [4]I don't actually know of anything that stands against me, but that isn't what vindicates me; it's the Lord who interrogates me.
>
> [5]So don't pass judgment on anything before the time when the Lord comes! He will bring to light the secrets of darkness, and will lay bare the intentions of the heart. Then everyone will receive praise – from God.

I stood in the workshop, barely able to see over the workbench as my father patiently whittled away at a piece of wood. I was fascinated and (as befits an eight-year-old) puzzled. What on earth could he be doing? The work seemed to have no purpose, no beauty, no reason. He was just cutting, very slowly, more and more tiny shavings off an already very thin spike. Surely if he went on like that there would soon be nothing left?

I can't remember what I said but it must have sounded critical as well as questioning. He was in any case concentrating hard and didn't need interrupting. 'Shouldn't see a job half done.' Another puzzle, perhaps a tease. What was going on?

A few days later all was revealed. When I came down to breakfast, there, on the table, was a model ship inside a bottle. I had witnessed him carving one of the last spars – a tiny but perfect part of a small but perfect ship, now inserted in the traditional fashion into a bottle and its masts raised, once inside, by pulling the thread that made everything stand up at last. At no stage of the project until that final act (performed when the rest of the family were safely out of the way in bed) could curious eyes have seen how it was going to work out.

There is going to be a final judgment. There has to be if God is a good and just God. It isn't simply that there are wicked people out there who need punishing. It is that the world needs to be put to rights. You can't read the newspapers and watch the television day by day and imagine that all is well in the world (as I typed this sentence, the main evening news came on the television, and it proved the point – more violence, murder, bitterness and injustice). There are some religious systems that try to make out that the world isn't so bad after all, or, alternatively, that what we perceive as evil is just an illusion. But in Judaism and Christianity at least, this much is clear: the world is God's good and lovely world, and evil is a real, powerful and horrible intruder into it. Sooner or later, God must and will put it to rights. Believing in God's final judgment is actually part of believing that God is the good and wise creator, and that his **kingdom** will one day come on earth as in **heaven**. And when that judgment comes it will be seen to be just. It will bring to light everything now hidden, including the thoughts and intentions of people's hearts (verse 5; see also Romans 2.12–16, 29).

But it's very tempting for people to want to put everything right, and to pay off what they see as old scores, ahead of time. We think we know what God should do, and we're eager to give him advice (and to tell others about it too). Once again, Paul is faced with the task of explaining to the Corinthian Christians a basically Jewish and Christian view of the world which he wants them to accept in place of the half-pagan, half-Christian view they hold at the moment. They seem to think that their new status as Christians, coupled with the 'wisdom' they think they've got in the world's eyes, gives them the right to pass judgment on people, including Paul himself. Paul doesn't measure up to what they think a fully fledged Christian teacher should be like; very well, they will pass judgment on him.

Paul's response is: Don't see the job half done. When judgment comes, he seems to imply, it will bring to light a lot of other things as well as his own apostolic shortcomings, if such there be. Maybe it will also show up something about their own intentions.

The point of being an **apostle**, in any case, is not that one should be showy and spectacular; not even that one should be successful. 'Stewards of God's mysteries', say some translations in verse 1; that's fine, but the word 'steward' has been so overused that we may need to find other ways of bringing out the point. Apostles are like household managers, whose job is to look after the silverware and administer the domestic accounts. God's 'mysteries' (see 2.7) are like a rich storehouse of treasures, to be used appropriately. Apostles and teachers don't own the treasure, they merely have to do what they're told with it. What is required is simply that they be faithful with what's been entrusted to them.

Once that is clear, Paul states a remarkable principle: Christian workers should expect to be judged by the Lord himself, and should not regard human tribunals as of any particular importance. Of course, like many Pauline principles, this one would be easy to abuse. Most church leaders will know of at least one or two ministers who have stood on their high horse, refusing all discipline or correction, and have brazenly asserted their innocence when everyone else can see their folly or guilt. But Paul will not back down. It is not up to the Corinthian church, in playing at personality cults and factional squabbles, to evaluate how good an apostle he was and is. As well might the plant evaluate the planter to whom it owes its very life! After three chapters of introduction, we have a sense that here at last Paul has arrived at the real confrontation which needs to take place.

There is a fine balance here both in Paul's own writings – including this one – and in what's needed in our current church practices. Paul is quite clear that in some instances the church must bring forward God's judgment into the present moment, and that not to do so risks the health of the church at large (see below, on chapter 5). When to judge and when not to judge; when to listen to whispers of criticism and when to dismiss them as irrelevant and time-wasting; these are decisions which themselves need wisdom and good judgment.

1 CORINTHIANS 4.6–13

Apostles on Display

6I have applied all this to myself and Apollos because of you, my dear
family, so that you may learn from us, as the saying goes, not to go
beyond what the Bible says – so that nobody gets puffed up in favour
of one person and against another.
7Who is going to concede that you are special, after all? What have
you got that you didn't receive? Well then, if you received it, why boast
as if you didn't? 8Do you really suppose you've already had all the food
you need? Do you think you've already become rich? Do you think
you've already been crowned as royalty, leaving us behind? I wish you
really were already reigning, so that we could reign alongside you!
9This is how I look at it, you see: God has put us apostles on display
at the end of the procession, like people sentenced to death. We have
become a public show for the world, for angels and humans alike.
10We are fools because of the Messiah, but you are wise in the Mes-
siah! We are weak, but you are strong! You are celebrated, we are
nobodies! 11Yes, right up to the present moment we go hungry and
thirsty; we are badly clothed, roughly treated, with no home to call
our own. 12What's more, we work hard, doing manual labour. When
we are insulted, we give back blessings. When we are persecuted, we
put up with it. 13When we are slandered, we speak gently in return. To
this day we have become like the rubbish of the world, fit only to be
scraped off the plate and thrown away with everything else.

We walked down the hill in the bright sunshine. This, our guide explained, is where the Roman generals would come when they returned to the city after winning a great victory. They built massive 'triumphal arches', some of which are still there, through which the procession would pass. There was a religious meaning to this: the soldiers needed purifying after all the terrible things they had had to do to win the victory, and some believed that a solemn ceremonial procession through the arch would have this effect. But there was much more going on as well: a public display of glory, power and victory, a great day out for everyone, a celebration of the fact that Rome had triumphed again.

The whole event, in fact, was called a 'triumph'. In the days before the news media flashed pictures of battles and victories around the world within minutes of their happening, this was how the people back home knew for sure their generals had won the war: they would march in parade through the streets carrying the booty they had captured, and leading a bedraggled and weary gang of prisoners at the back of the procession. Usually the day would end with the prisoners being killed, or sold into slavery.

That's the picture Paul uses to show the Corinthians what the work of an **apostle** is like. This is a sharp passage, another brilliant piece of writing designed to argue that brilliant oratory isn't what matters. He is at last addressing the real problem: rivalry and enmity within the Corinthian church, with different teachers and speakers claiming that their wisdom and skill makes them 'full', 'rich', or even 'kings'. Some philosophers of the time made claims like this. It's likely that these Corinthians were supposing that their Christian **faith**, coupled with their expertise in thinking and speaking, gave them a status nobody could challenge.

Paul challenges it, though, head on. What he's been saying about Apollos up to now is simply for the sake of illustration; he and Apollos (and Cephas, for that matter) have no particular quarrel. The problem lies between the warring factions in Corinth itself. He wants them to think through what he has said about his relationship with Apollos, which he has described purely as an example, and apply it all to their own situation.

This means that they must put together the various biblical themes he has been expounding up to now and realize that they set a strict limit. 'I will destroy the wisdom of the wise' (1.19, quoting Isaiah). 'The one who boasts must boast in the Lord' (1.31, quoting Jeremiah). 'He catches the wise in their craftiness' (3.19, quoting Job). And many more beside – it's worth looking them all up and pondering their cumulative effect. Paul draws them together here to say: scripture itself forbids you to get 'puffed up' in this way. (The word translated 'puffed up' is a favourite in this letter.)

The most obvious argument against boasting of the kind that's been going on is that every gift, talent and skill we possess is a gift from God. You might as well boast about having brown eyes or being left-handed. But the Corinthians are going beyond even boasting of their abilities. They think they have been 'filled', fed with so much spiritual food that they are now complete. They imagine, as did some philosophers, that they are rich and royal – and they expect others to acknowledge the fact. Paul withers this claim with sarcasm: I wish you really *were* on the throne – then I could share it with you!

In fact, the situation is very different. Their own apostle, the one through whom they came to faith and learnt of Jesus and his death and **resurrection** in the first place, is not like a king or victorious general leading a triumphal procession. He is one of the prisoners, the bedraggled and humiliated captives, pulled along in chains at the back. This is a stark and shocking picture of Christian ministry, but Paul is quite consistent on the point, especially in the two letters to Corinth, where the message was particularly needed.

He contrasts his own actual situation with the one they pretend to have. He is, of course, being heavily sarcastic: we are fools, you are wise, we are weak, you are strong, you are celebrated, we are nobodies! Paul's picture of himself, going around the Mediterranean world in and out of trouble, prison, danger and scorn, is designed to shake them out of their complacency. And the underlying point, here as in 1.18—2.5, is clear: do we or don't we follow a crucified **Messiah**?

We should notice particularly how the **message** of the cross comes through in verses 12 and 13, rethought in terms of what it means to be the messenger of such a **gospel**. Philosophers of the time often scorned the ignorant mob. If a Cynic philosopher was insulted, he would hurl insults back again, especially if the person concerned was rich or famous in the world's eyes. If a Stoic was attacked, he might simply try to rise above it, ignoring the event as beneath his contempt. Even within Judaism, the tradition of the martyrs suggested that if you were tortured or threatened with execution, you should threaten your captors that God would condemn and punish them in their turn (see, for instance, 2 Maccabees 7).

But Paul has learnt a different way. When people insult him, he offers blessings; when they persecute him, he bears it patiently; when people tell lies about him, he speaks gently and kindly in return. What sort of a person behaves like this? Only someone who believes that God's wisdom is revealed in the tortured and broken body of his beloved son. When Paul declares that he and his fellow apostles are like the rubbish left over on a plate at the end of a meal, fit only to be scraped off and thrown out, we may be right to hear the echoes of the event a few years before where his master was scraped off the floor of Pilate's torture-room and dragged out of the city to die. And if Paul needed to make this point to the Christians in Corinth, what would he say to comfortable Western Christianity today?

1 CORINTHIANS 4.14–21

Puffed Up or Powerful?

> [14]I'm not writing this to make you ashamed! I am simply treating you as dear children, and putting you straight. [15]You've got a thousand babysitters in Christ, I know, but you haven't got many fathers – because I became your father in the Messiah, Jesus, through the gospel.
>
> [16]So let me appeal to you: copy me! [17]That's why I have sent Timothy to you; he's my child in the Lord, and I love him and trust him. He will remind you how I conduct myself in the Messiah Jesus, just as I teach everywhere, in every assembly.
>
> [18]Some people are getting puffed up, as though I wasn't going to come to you. [19]But I will come to you quickly, if the Lord wants it that way; and then I'll find out, not what these puffed-up people are saying, but how powerful they are. [20]The kingdom of God, you see, isn't about talk – it's about power. [21]What d'you want, then? Shall I come to you with a big stick, or with love, and in a gentle spirit?

We all know the difference between talk and power.

Imagine you are driving along a road, without worrying too much about how fast you're going. All of a sudden a large car with flashing lights overtakes you and motions you to pull over. The police. With a sinking heart you slow down, pull in to the side of the road, and come to a stop.

You get out of the car, and walk towards the policeman who is standing there. Your instinct is probably to talk, to say something, to explain that you weren't going that fast really, that you were going to visit someone in hospital, that the speed gauge in your car hadn't been working too well recently . . .

The policeman doesn't need to say much, except perhaps ask you for your documents. His uniform says it all. He stands there, writing slowly, filling in a form. That's all he has to do. If he started arguing with you, trying to persuade you to drive differently, pleading with you ('How many times have I told you not to go so fast!'), you could handle it. He doesn't need to, and the more you talk the worse it will get.

We can understand that situation; and Paul seems to be referring to the same thing when he says in verse 20 that God's **kingdom** doesn't consist in talk but in power. What does he mean? Is he going to be like a policeman, coming to hand out the spiritual equivalent of speeding tickets? What sort of power has he got to back up his authority?

The tone of voice in this paragraph is all-important. He is serious, but he is making his serious points in a somewhat tongue-in-cheek way. 'You've had thousands of baby-sitters, but you've only got one father!' In Paul's world, the 'baby-sitter' was usually a resident slave in a household, whose job it was to look after the children while the parents were out, and to try – often unsuccessfully – to stop them getting into mischief. That, Paul is implying, is what all the other teachers in Corinth are like. But the father is coming back soon, and then everything will be sorted out. Do they want him to come back home brandishing a big stick, or to come as a father should, with open arms and a big smile (verse 21)? And Paul could surely only ask this question if he knew that they would take it in a friendly, almost teasing, spirit.

But the power which he has isn't simply the 'authority' that he might claim as the one who 'begot' them (verse 15) by preaching the **gospel** to them (he uses this language of 'begetting' someone by preaching the gospel to them elsewhere, for instance in Philemon verse 10, speaking of Onesimus). His power is the power that comes, through prayer and the **spirit**, when he preaches and teaches the gospel. Paul has preached and taught enough by now to know that when he speaks of Jesus, his cross and his **resurrection**, things happen. People's hearts and minds are changed. Those who were rebellious, or clinging to sinful ways, find themselves convicted, conscience-stricken, and eager to embrace the forgiveness and new life which the gospel offers. As Paul says elsewhere (2 Corinthians 13.10, a passage quite similar to this one), God has given him authority within the young Christian communities not in order to pull them down but to build them up. That's what he intends to do.

So, not for the last time in the letter (see 11.1) he urges them to remember the way he himself conducted his life, and to follow the same pattern themselves. One of the things we need constantly to remind ourselves when reading Paul (and when thinking about our own Christian living within a hostile world) is that nobody in Corinth, or any of the other towns outside Palestine, had ever before witnessed somebody living the way Paul lived. Nobody had seen someone giving of himself generously, living a life of self-sacrifice, and refusing to play the power games and the prestige games that were the stock-in-trade, not only of the sophistic teachers who came and went (and made a lot of money), but of the local rulers, the magistrates and civic dignitaries, and those who promoted and ran the new imperial cult. Paul was different, and the difference mattered, because he was modelling the

Christ-life. He hadn't just done it in Corinth; this was how he lived and taught everywhere. If they had forgotten about it, Timothy would remind them; he was probably on his way, as we see in 16.10–11, but Paul wasn't sure how soon he might arrive.

This passage tells us quite a lot – perhaps more than we wanted to hear – about the exercise of authority in the church. For centuries church leaders have copied the models of authority in the surrounding world. Where the surrounding world has been autocratic, the churches have set up parallel (and sometimes intertwined) autocratic structures – popes, archbishops, and so on – who have 'run' the church by telling people what to do and threatening them with dire penalties, such as excommunication, if they refused. Where the surrounding world has been democratic, the churches have set up parallel democratic structures, as though the will of the majority (and all the business of campaigning and soliciting votes that goes with it) was any more likely to indicate the mind of the spirit than the autocratic alternative.

Paul had no intention of telling the Corinthians to take a vote about what sort of a church they wanted. It is quite possible for majorities to be seriously deceived (and if you find that suggestion shocking, ask yourself why). But nor was he going to bully or browbeat them from a great height. His only authority – but it is the most powerful sort – was that of someone who was living and preaching the gospel of Jesus, and acting out the commission which Jesus had given him. He didn't need to say much; he left that to the 'puffed-up' people. His uniform – the life he was living, which he urged them to copy – said all that was necessary.

1 CORINTHIANS 5.1–5

Scandal and Judgment

1Everybody's talking about the sex scandal that's going on in your
community, not least because it's a kind of immorality that even the
pagans don't practise! Well I never – a man taking his father's wife!
2And you're puffed up! Why aren't you in mourning? Why aren't you
getting rid of the person who's done such a thing?

3Let me tell you what I've already done. I may be away from you
physically, but I'm present in the spirit; and I've already passed judgment, as though I was there with you, on the person who has behaved
in this way. 4When you are assembled together in the name of our Lord
Jesus, and my spirit is there too with the power of our Lord Jesus, 5you
must hand over such a person to the satan for the destruction of the
flesh, so that his spirit may be saved on the day of the Lord Jesus.

When I was a boy, studying Greek and Latin classics, the texts we were given to study often had bits cut out. There were lines missing from poems, and sometimes entire sections; in one case (in the Roman writer Juvenal, I recall) a whole poem had been dropped from the edition we used. Naturally, as schoolboys, we used to ask our teachers what was missing, especially once we realized what the answer was likely to be. Almost always the passage in question was about sex – sometimes a sidelong reference, more often a ribald joke, occasionally an entire passage wallowing in material considered too sordid for schoolboys.

Of course today the film industry, along with the producers of videos, novels, plays and poems, has thrown modesty to the winds. Every Western teenager now has access to material that would have shocked Juvenal himself and his still more scurrilous contemporaries. But the point is this. From the perspective of what was considered 'normal' public morality in Britain in the 1950s, and even later, the world of ancient Greece and Rome seemed extremely lax on sexual morality; but it still had its limits. There were taboos. In most towns and villages people would know that, however 'normal' it was to engage in immoral behaviour with prostitutes, or at the orgiastic festivals at some shrines and temples, there were lines drawn in social behaviour and you stepped across them at your peril.

Hence Paul's horror in this passage: the church in Corinth was openly tolerating a situation that no self-respecting pagan would have permitted. A man was living with his own step-mother, presumably his father's second wife. How this situation had arisen we don't know. But it seems that the church had connived at it. The leaders were 'puffed up', convinced (like some amoral 'moralists' today) that they had now passed beyond 'good and evil' into a world where absolutely anything could be done.

This raises two issues for us. We shall be looking at the first from various angles over the next three chapters as Paul moves from one topic to another, mostly involving questions of sex, with the question being: where are the lines to be drawn, and how do we know? The second, which is highlighted dramatically in this passage, is: what kind of discipline is appropriate in cases of severe misbehaviour? What Paul says here is so sharp and striking that we need to stand back, take a deep breath, and see what's going on.

As we do so, we notice that he says the church is 'puffed up' about the situation – actually proud to be part of a community that has been able to leave behind the normal constraints that even Corinthian society (notorious for its moral laxity) would have observed. This tells us that the question at stake here isn't just an isolated moral question. Paul sees it as a further aspect of the issue he's been dealing with throughout the letter so far, the problem that came to a head in chapter 4: some of the local leaders have become proud, and are behaving more like sophists than Christian teachers. In particular – and this, too, we shall meet frequently – they are supposing that throwing moral caution to the winds is a sign of how spiritually grown-up they are, how important their new **faith** and Christian status is. They have left behind, they think, not only the old world of pagan belief but the interlocked world of pagan taboos. They have come of age . . .

Paul doesn't trouble to argue that the particular behaviour in this case is wrong. He knows well enough that most of the Christians will still be sufficiently uncomfortable about it for him only to need to mention it. He moves straight into action. They should, he says, have removed from their midst someone who does that kind of thing; he assumes, in other words, that the community is not simply a free-for-all gathering, but has some coherence about its membership, some lines which it is possible to step over, some control over who comes to worship, who belongs to the community.

This has nothing to do with going back on '**justification** by faith'. As will become clear over the next two chapters, Paul knows that the fellowship of all who believe in Jesus as **Messiah** and Lord can be badly damaged by behaviour which does not acknowledge him as such. In the present case, the offender will still be saved, but, like the person who has 'built' with the wrong material in 3.10–15, this 'salvation', which will be given 'on the day of the Lord', will only be accomplished the other side of judgment on the present behaviour. And, since this behaviour is threatening the very life and witness of the church, this judgment must be exercised through appropriate discipline, namely, ejection from the community.

Paul's description of this ejection is striking and, to us, apparently harsh. 'Hand him over to **the satan**', he says, 'for the destruction of the flesh!' Paul uses the phrase 'the satan' sparingly; it is, of course, a Jewish term for 'the devil', and indicates the one who accuses people of wrongdoing, and entices them to evil so that he will then have something to accuse them of. Paul sees the world outside the church as the sphere over which 'the satan' has unfettered power, so that to put someone out of the community is to expel them from the sphere in which the Messiah saves them, and send them back into the sphere in which the satan's writ runs. Of course, if such a person goes back into his own community, he will find that his own family spurn him for what he has done.

Paul may even mean that such expulsion will result in the man's actual death. So sure is he of the power unleashed through the **gospel**, and at work in the church, not least through its central symbolic actions, that he will speak of people falling sick, and even dying, because of a wrong use of the community's focal meal, the **eucharist** or 'the Lord's Supper' (11.20). That is how seriously he takes the problem of immorality within a Christian congregation.

The means by which he exercises his apostolic authority in this particular case is remarkable, and this tells us something more about what Paul meant at the end of the previous chapter. He envisages such a close spiritual unity between himself and the community that he has already judged the case and found the man guilty. Now, when the community comes together, with Paul himself spiritually present, they must carry out the sentence and solemnly expel the offender.

Most comfortable Western churches have long since given up even thinking of practising discipline – though until quite recently all churches knew, at least in theory, that it was a vital part of community life. Have we too perhaps become 'puffed up', unable to tell the difference between Christian freedom and scandalous behaviour?

1 CORINTHIANS 5.6–13

Get Rid of the 'Leaven'!

[6]Your boasting is no good. Don't you know that a little leaven works its
way through the whole lump of dough? [7]Cleanse out the old leaven, so
that you can be a new lump, the leaven-free lump you really are. It's
Passover-time, you see, and our Passover lamb – the Messiah, I mean –
has already been sacrificed! [8]What we now have to do is to keep the
festival properly: none of the leaven of the old life, and none of the
leaven of depravity and wickedness, either. What we need is leaven-free bread, and that means sincerity and truth.

[9]I wrote to you in the previous letter not to become associated with
immoral people. [10]I didn't (of course) mean immoral people in the
world at large, or greedy people, or thieves, or idolaters. To avoid them,
you'd have to remove yourselves from the world altogether! [11]No; I was
referring to people who call themselves Christians but who are immoral, or greedy, or idolaters, or blasphemers, or drunkards or robbers. You shouldn't associate with them; you shouldn't even eat with a
person like that. [12]Why should I worry about judging people outside?
It's the people *in*side you should judge, isn't it? [13]God judges the people
outside. 'Drive out the wicked person from your company.'

If you've ever been in a Jewish home at Passover-time, you'll know what Paul is talking about in verses 7 and 8. It's a tradition that's been kept for more than three thousand years, ever since the Jewish people came out of Egypt at the **Exodus**. That night, they had to hurry. They were going to be on their way soon, and there wouldn't be time to do the normal domestic things. They would have to bake their bread without the normal leaven they used to make it rise, so that they could cook it quickly, carry it easily, and eat it in a hurry.

The regulations for how to keep Passover turned this non-use of leaven into a central part of the ceremony. To this day, in a Jewish household that is keeping the festival with any degree of seriousness, all leaven is ceremonially cleaned out of the kitchen. There are plenty of good things to eat during the festival, but leavened bread isn't one of them. We sometimes talk of 'the leaven in the lump' in a good sense, meaning the thing that makes something softer and more palatable. In Paul's world, when people spoke of leaven in a metaphorical sense it was almost always a way of talking about a bad influence corrupting something that would otherwise be pure.

That's obviously the way he's using the image here; but it isn't just an image drawn at random. He isn't simply reaching into his mental rag-bag of pictures for a way of saying 'you shouldn't tolerate immorality within the Christian community'. He is pulling out a Passover-image because at the centre of Christianity is a Passover-event, indeed *the* Passover-event. From the very beginning, the early church believed that it hadn't just been a coincidence that Jesus died (and rose again) at Passover-time; this was how God wanted it. The timing explained the meaning.

At the first Passover, each family slaughtered a lamb for their evening meal, and put its blood on the doorposts of the house so that the angel of death would 'pass over' them and spare them, while the firstborn of the Egyptians were killed. When Jews of Paul's day kept the Passover festival, they sacrified lambs in the **Temple**, continuing the tradition and keeping fresh the memory of God's great deliverance. The early Christians saw Jesus' own death as the climax, the culmination, of this whole tradition. He was the real Passover lamb, and his death had won deliverance for the whole world.

The whole Christian life, from this point of view, becomes one long Passover-celebration! That's what it's all about. Every breath a Christian takes is a silent Passover-hymn of gratitude to the God who has acted to save the world through Jesus, the true Passover lamb. Every action a Christian performs is part of the endless ceremonial of the Passover-celebration. And at this Passover there must be no leaven. Paul does not, of course, mean that Christians must not eat leavened bread. It's picture-language. The equivalent of leaven within this new Passover-life that Jesus' people are called to live is the behaviour which goes with the old way of life: 'the leaven of the old life' is the kind of behaviour that pagans engage in before conversion, and 'the leaven of depravity and wickedness' is the kind of behaviour that Christians can be lured back into if they aren't careful.

What they need instead, Paul insists, is the 'unleavened bread' of genuine Christian living. We might have expected him to explain that as 'holiness' or 'purity', but instead he speaks of 'sincerity' and 'truth'. 'Sincerity' doesn't just mean 'doing what you really want to do'; some of the wickedest things in the world have been done by completely 'sincere' people in that sense. No one was more sincere than Adolf Hitler. The word Paul uses speaks of a purity of motive. It isn't just that motive and action must be in tune with each other; that's true of most criminals. Both alike must spring from the purified source of a will realigned to the purity of God himself. The mention of 'truth' indicates that at the heart of all misbehaviour there is a lie: the lie that says God doesn't mind, the lie that pretends this one time doesn't matter, the easy but deadly lie that imagines that this was after all how humans were supposed to behave.

All such 'leaven' is ruled out for Christians, and Paul makes it clear that it is not to be tolerated in the church. Once more, we realize how far many churches in the modern world have travelled away from their roots. Many today have actually elevated moral indifference – on some issues at least – into part of their foundation charter, so that to suggest introducing discipline over (say) sexual misbehaviour would cause a storm of protest, accusations of legalism, Pharisaism, lack of charity, and a host of other nasty things. But Paul is quite clear.

He had already written to Corinth on this subject, in a letter which has not survived. They hadn't understood. They thought he was saying they should avoid all contact with immoral people, and wondered how on earth they could continue to live in Corinth at all! Now he explains: he meant simply within the church. Table-fellowship among Christians, he says, should be the sign of fellowship which is given to those who are living as the **Messiah**'s people should. And, just as Israel was commanded not to tolerate evil in its midst (Deuteronomy 17.7, which Paul quotes in verse 13), so the church must see wickedness for what it is, a cancer which will spread if it is not cut out at the first sign. God will judge those outside the community in his own time and manner. But the Christian community, as he is going to stress in the next chapter, has the God-given right and duty to discriminate between those who are living in the Messiah's way and those who are not.

Once again, we can imagine the howls of anger at such a suggestion in today's church ('Unloving!' 'Intolerant!' 'Judgmental!'). Paul might well have answered: is the doctor unloving or judgmental when he or she tells you that you must have the operation right away? Do we want a doctor who 'tolerates' viruses, bacteria, cancer cells? And if we say that the moral issues Paul mentions in verse 11 are not like diseases, are we so sure? Do these things build up a community, or destroy it?

1 CORINTHIANS 6.1–8

Lawsuits in the Church?

1Can it really be the case that one of you dares to go to law against a
neighbour, to be tried before unjust people, and not before God's
people? 2Don't you know that God's people will judge the world? And
if the world is to be judged by you, are you really incompetent to try
smaller matters? 3Don't you know that we shall be judging angels? Why
not then also matters to do with ordinary life? 4So if you have lawsuits
about ordinary matters, are you actually going to appoint as judges
people whom the church despises? 5I'm saying this to bring shame on
you. Is it really true that there is no wise person among you who is able
to decide between one Christian and another? 6But one Christian is
being taken to court by another, and before unbelievers at that!

7Actually, to have lawsuits with one another at all represents a major
setback for you. Why not rather let yourselves be wronged? Why not
rather put up with loss? 8But you yourselves are wronging and
defrauding people, and fellow Christians at that!

The business was just getting going when one of the customers noticed a strange thing. He had begun bringing his car to this particular garage a few months ago, and had believed that it was doing a good job. People in the community seemed to respect the company, and it appeared to be flourishing. The boss seemed to be in charge; the employees were helpful and efficient.

But then one day this particular customer was in a different part of the town, and he spotted something odd. There, in quite a different garage, was one of the mechanics from the first one. He had brought his own car, not to the garage where he worked, but to a different outfit. And the person he was taking it to wasn't a qualified mechanic at all. In fact, he'd had no training with cars. The customer was anxious. If this mechanic didn't trust his own colleagues to look after his car, why should he do so? What's more, if this man was letting an unqualified operator do the job, it looked as though he didn't know, or didn't care about, the kind of skill required.

This is, more or less, how Paul saw the situation he now deals with. It's guaranteed to make us raise our eyebrows even higher than we did when reading his stern words in chapter 5. Paul really does regard the Christian community – even the small and muddled community in Corinth – as the community of God's people, to whom God will one day entrust the task of judging the world, including the angels! Where on earth has he got that idea from?

The answer is that he's got it directly from the Old Testament, particularly from passages like Daniel 7, where 'the holy ones of the most high' are set in authority over the world. (The word I've translated as 'God's people' in verses 1 and 2 is the same as 'the holy ones' or 'the saints'). Paul will allow nothing to shake his basic **faith**: if Jesus rose from the dead, then he's the **Messiah**; if he's the Messiah, those who belong to him are God's true people; and God's true people will judge the world. If God's true people at the moment look a very unlikely crew to be judging anyone or anything, well then, they must shape up and come into line. They must *become*, through moral reflection and discipline in the present time, the people they actually *are* 'in the Messiah' and in the purposes of God. That's what a good deal of this letter is about.

Paul here faces the unsavoury issue of one Christian going to law – in the regular public courts in Corinth – against another one. Paul's vision of what a Christian community really is doesn't allow for this. The Christian community in any given place is called to be modelling genuine human existence; if it isn't doing that, what's it there for? What *is* it? And part of that genuine human existence is justice – God's justice, the true justice by which the world will one day finally be put to rights. The alternative is Roman justice (Corinth was a Roman colony and prided itself on its Roman legal status and practice); but Paul declares, sweepingly, that its magistrates are actually *un*just, by definition, because they have not been 'justified' by God (verse 1; see 1.30). If you want justice, don't go to the unjust!

He thus issues a double challenge. First, if you must go to law against another Christian, allow the company of Christian believers, the little church itself, to choose people who are competent to try cases. Since all of you are destined to be judges of the world, however unlikely that seems, you should surely be able to find someone who can do the equivalent here and now! There may be a touch of irony here too, though Paul undoubtedly believes in God's future judgment and that God's people will share in administering it. Since some among the leadership are 'puffed up', why don't they do the judging?

Second, though, and still more challenging for us, it would be better that Christians didn't go to law against one another at all. From time to time in our own day it happens that church people, sometimes people in church leadership, are taken to court by one another; the thing gets in the newspapers, and all the gossips have a field day at the church's expense. Nobody minds much who wins; no doubt they will take sides, but that's secondary. What matters in the eyes of the world is that a public dispute between Christians is a sign that Christians are really no different from everybody else. And 1 Corinthians is all about the fact that Christians *are* different from everybody else – and if they're not, they might as well not bother calling themselves Christians in the first place.

Paul's challenge to the church might almost have come from Jesus himself. He, after all, told the rich young ruler to give up all his property and follow him (Mark 10.21). Paul declares that it's better to put up with being defrauded in order to follow the Messiah, in order to show the world that there's a different way to be human. Of course, that's no excuse for allowing fraud among Christians. But the church should deal with it as a matter of internal discipline.

Those of us who live in societies where the public legal tradition itself has been shaped over the centuries by Christianity – not always as much as we might like, but to some extent – and for whom the line between the church and the watching world is far more blurred than it was in Paul's day, may find this whole passage simply perplexing. Yet its underlying message is stark and clear. Those who name the name of Jesus and claim to follow him have an astonishing destiny in the future, which results in an astonishing responsibility in the present. Our life as a community, as Paul says in Philippians 2.14–16, should be like a light shining into a dark world. From time to time this happens, often in unexpected places, and the effect is explosive. We should not allow our natural reactions to a passage like this ('totally unrealistic!' 'sheer fantasy!' – can't you hear it?) to prevent us from asking: where in today's church – in *my* church – are we behaving in such a way that we are shaming the **gospel** in the eyes of the world?

1 CORINTHIANS 6.9–11

Inheriting God's Kingdom – or Not

> [9]Don't you know that the unjust will not inherit God's kingdom?
> Don't be deceived! Neither immoral people, nor idolaters, nor adul-
> terers, nor practising homosexuals of whichever sort, [10]nor thieves,
> nor greedy people, nor drunkards, nor abusive talkers, nor robbers
> will inherit God's kingdom. [11]That, of course, is what some of you
> were! But you were washed clean; you were made holy; you were put
> back to rights – in the name of the Lord, Messiah Jesus, and in the
> spirit of our God.

We stood in line for the ride at the funfair. But as we got closer I saw a sign. This ride was for little people only – for children. Beside the sign was a small wooden archway, and you had to walk through, without stooping, to get to the ride. Only people who could walk through were allowed on. Anybody else simply wouldn't fit. The ride wouldn't be safe for them; if they went on it, it wouldn't be safe for anybody else. Two of my children got on (with an anxious backward glance at me), but I had to stay out.

God's **kingdom** isn't a funfair ride, but the same principle applies. There are certain ways of behaving, certain lifestyles, which just won't fit. To come into God's kingdom while being that sort of person is a kind of category mistake.

This doesn't mean that God is being capricious. It isn't that God (or the church) has made up a list of rules on the back of an envelope, or even on a stone tablet, which are now being applied to everyone on an arbitrary, one-size-fits-all basis. God isn't behaving like old Procrustes, the Greek mythological character who put people on his bed and made them fit it either by cutting bits off or by stretching them. Many today imagine that the moral teaching of Christianity is like that, and they grumble against God, or the church, for such an unfair system. Rather, it's that the creator God has unveiled his genuine model for humanity in Jesus the **Messiah**, and there are certain ways of behaving which just won't fit. If you want to be a truly, fully human being, those ways of behaving have to be left behind. Coming on board into God's kingdom while still being that sort of person is a liability both for the person themselves and for everybody else.

These things have always been contentious in the church. Every generation has its own blind spots, its own sudden enthusiasms for some moral rules and its own angry rejection of others. Feelings run high, particularly where strong human instincts are involved. People are quick to react crossly when something they have assumed is perfectly all right, and perhaps have been told by others is perfectly all right, is then declared to be wrong. But, as all serious moral thinkers know, it is desperately easy to be deceived on issues like this, to fool ourselves into believing that all is well. 'Don't be deceived' is one of Paul's regular warnings, here and elsewhere. Sometimes, when you're driving a car, it's tempting to carry on down the wrong road without consulting the map, because stopping the car, putting on your spectacles, and finding out where you really are is such a bore compared with simply driving on.

Paul warns them that it's possible to be on the wrong road without realizing it. Don't be deceived, he says. Sincerity and conviction are not enough. There is such a thing as being sincerely wrong. Those who killed Jews in the Nazi Holocaust, for instance, often sincerely believed that this was a moral duty, to rid the world of what they had been taught was an evil race. We shudder at such twisted thinking and its horrible results. But we are not immune from making mistakes which, even though not in the same league, are equally ways of failing to discover full, genuine human living.

In the contemporary Western world, as in a pagan city like Corinth, one of the key areas where self-deception could run riot is sexual morality. Where people live in close-knit family structures, sexual behaviour is usually more regulated (though there, too, of course, warped emotions and sexual abuse can occur). But in a society on the move, where people come and go and sit loose to social and family life, as in a port city like Corinth, or many parts of today's world, it's much easier to live irresponsibly, since you won't have to face the consequences of your actions.

But consequences there are, especially when it comes to sex. We humans are so designed, in the fascinating interplay of body, mind, emotions and imagination, that what we are and do as sexual beings affects every other aspect of our lives. There is no such thing as 'casual sex'; sex is far more important than that. To trivialize sex is to trivialize our God-given humanness. To tell lies in that area inevitably sets up a fault line that will run through the rest of our character; or, to look at it the other way round, if there are fault lines elsewhere in our lives, they may well result in distorted or damaging sexual desires and practices.

Many in today's world have drunk so deeply from the 'anything goes' culture that they find the mere suggestion of moral restrictions on sexual behaviour surprising or even offensive. Yet, as every pastor knows, the human devastation that results from sexual permissiveness, especially where it involves breaking marriage promises, is far-reaching and long-lasting.

The terms Paul uses here include two words which have been much debated, but which, experts have now established, clearly refer to the practice of male homosexuality. The two terms refer respectively to the passive or submissive partner and the active or aggressive one, and Paul places both roles in his list of unacceptable behaviour. As with everything else on the list, these are practices that some people find they deeply want to engage in, so much so that in our own day (this is a novelty of the last hundred years or so) we have seen the rise of the words 'homosexual' or 'gay' as an identifying label, a sign of a hidden 'identity' which can be 'discovered' or 'recognized'. Biblical witness and pastoral insight alike suggest that this is deeply misleading – as is the implication that all humans need active sexual experience, of whatever sort they prefer, in order to be complete, to be fully alive.

Paul is not, of course, suggesting that sexual error is worse than any other kind – though the central place of sexuality within the human make-up indicates that we shouldn't take it lightly. But the point he's making, with this as with other distorted ways of behaving, is that they take away from that full humanness which God longs to see come to flower in his creatures, and which will be completed in the final 'kingdom of God' (verse 10). It isn't, to repeat what we said before, that God has an arbitrary list of rules and if you break them you won't get in. It is, rather, that his kingdom will be peopled by humans who reflect his image completely; and behaviour in the present which distorts and defaces that image will lead in the opposite direction. The whole New Testament joins in warning of the real possibility of this happening.

But the whole New Testament also joins in announcing that it needn't – because God has himself provided the way in which people can leave their past, and indeed their present, behind, and move forward into his future. You can be washed clean, whatever has happened in the past. You can be made one of God's special people, whatever you are in the present. You can be '**justified**', declared here and now to be one of God's true people. And this happens 'in the name of the Lord, King Jesus, and in the **spirit** of our God'. The way Paul says this probably echoes the early Christian practice of **baptism**. The point is that when you become a member of the Christian family, with baptism as its mark and **faith** as its inward reality, you receive a new identity, and are launched on to a new lifestyle.

Paul knows, of course, that this new identity and lifestyle doesn't work out automatically. That's why he's writing this letter! But once faith is present and baptism has happened, the way is open to a different lifestyle, a whole new way of being human. It is then up to each Christian, with the help and support of the wider fellowship, to recognize the ways in which the deceitfulness of sin has distorted their thinking and behaviour, and to find the way forward into God's new life.

1 CORINTHIANS 6.12–20

What Is the Body For?

12'Everything is lawful for me' – but not everything is helpful! 'Every-
thing is lawful for me' – but I'm not going to let anything give me
orders! 13'Food for the stomach, and the stomach for food, and God
will destroy the one and the other' – but the body is not meant for
immorality, but for the Lord, and the Lord for the body. 14What's more,
God raised the Lord; and he will raise us, too, through his power.

15Don't you know that your bodies are members of the Messiah?
Shall I then take the members of the Messiah and make them mem-
bers of a prostitute? Of course not! 16Or don't you know that anyone
who joins himself to a prostitute is one body with her? 'The two shall
become one flesh' – that's what it says. 17But the one who joins himself
to the Lord becomes one spirit with him.

18Run away from immorality. Every sin that it's possible for some-
one to commit happens outside the body; but immorality involves
sinning against your own body. 19Or don't you know that your body is

a temple of the holy spirit within you, the spirit God gave you, so that you don't belong to yourselves? [20]You were quite an expensive purchase! So glorify God in your body.

I once knew a student who never bothered to buy a screwdriver. He had a couple of knives that he used instead, one larger and one smaller; and most of the things he needed to screw or unscrew he could do quite well with the point of one of the knives.

The problem was, of course, that it didn't do the knives any good. The ends got bent, and they were harder to use for their proper purpose. Then one day, trying to unscrew a particularly stubborn screw, the knife-blade snapped in three pieces, and cut his hand quite badly. That's what can happen when you use something for the wrong purpose.

This whole passage is about learning to use the human body in the right way, for the right purpose. Paul says several remarkable things about the body in this passage, making it clear that the question of sexual immorality is one of the most serious issues the Corinthians faced. He begins by quoting two slogans which were popular sayings in Corinth, and which some in the church seem to have been repeating to justify their behaviour.

He quotes the first one twice, giving it a quick and memorable answer each time. (Christian teachers should note the technique: find out the catch-phrases that people say that lead them astray, and find ways of providing memorable responses!) 'Everything is lawful for me': I'm a free agent, I can do what I like, moral rules are for other people . . . it sounds fairly contemporary, doesn't it?

Interestingly, Paul doesn't deny the slogan itself. He knows, after all, that the Jewish **law** in particular isn't binding on Christians, so there is a sense in which he agrees with the point in principle. But there are two balancing principles which must be considered as well. Everything may be lawful for me in some sense, but by no means everything is beneficial or helpful. You can use the knife as a screwdriver if you like; you can even use a spoon; but don't expect that when it comes to mealtimes the cutlery will be in good shape for what you now need to do. In particular, precisely because Christianity means freedom, it's important that nothing is allowed to give me orders: not my appetites, not my habits, not the surrounding atmosphere of my culture, with its hardly noticed pressures towards certain styles of life. Paul shifts responsibility back to the individual Christian, to think through and work out what is actually 'helpful', and what practices and habits will gain the mastery over them if they aren't careful.

The second slogan was clearly being used as an excuse for immorality. 'That's what it's made for', they would say: 'food's for the stomach, the stomach's for food', and so by implication 'sex is for the body, and the body's for sex'. Paul doesn't deny that God has made sexual organs for their particular purpose, but he does deny, very strongly, that this purpose is fulfilled by any and every sexual practice. In the next chapter he will speak about marriage itself; but first he must clear out of the way the idea that any sexual practice that takes someone's fancy is as good as any other.

He does so in terms of God's intention for the body, and here we see him starting to develop a line of thought which will continue, one way or another, right through to the long exposition of the **resurrection** of the body in chapter 15. What is the body meant for?

For the Lord! he answers triumphantly. This is a surprise. Somehow Paul envisages the Christian's relationship with the Lord Jesus not simply as a 'spiritual' one, but also a physical one: not of course in the sexual sense, but in the sense that Jesus wants to know us and work through us as fully physical human beings, both here and hereafter. After all (verse 14), God raised Jesus the Lord, and will raise us too; so what you do with your body matters. The resurrection of the body remains a mystery; we don't have the language to do justice to what it will finally mean (15.51). But it certainly means that there will be some sort of *continuity* between the present body and the future one. What you do in and with the present body will have consequences, not just arbitrary rewards or punishments, in the life to come.

Verses 15–17 then develop this in one particular direction: the possibility that a Christian man might use his 'freedom' to visit prostitutes. (Prostitution was often linked to pagan temples, but was much wider as well, especially in a port city like Corinth.) Instead of just laying down a simple take-it-or-leave-it rule, Paul wants Christians to think things through for themselves. If you give someone a rule, you may keep them on track for a day or two, but if you teach them to think Christianly you'll help them to go on making the right decisions on their own.

The point here is that as a Christian you *belong* to Jesus; you are part of his 'body', as Paul will develop at more length in chapter 12. This is a union of '**spirit**' which can be damaged or threatened, it seems, by inappropriate unions of 'flesh'. You cannot belong simultaneously to the **Messiah** and to a prostitute, and, as we saw in the previous section, there is no such thing as a casual sexual encounter. What you do sexually, you do with your whole self, not with one little bit of you. What you are and do as a Christian you are and do as your whole self, not just with the 'spiritual' part of you.

The result (verse 18) is that when faced with sexual temptation there is no virtue, no wisdom, in staying around to argue with it or trying to battle against it. You should cut and run. Paul may be thinking of Joseph in Genesis 39.6–12, running out of the house rather than being seduced by his master's wife. Every person knows where the equivalent moment comes for them. A book that one person may read with profit and appropriate enjoyment can be a temptation to someone else. So too with a movie, a magazine, a website. (There are, of course, plenty of books, movies and so on which are produced solely with the aim of sexual arousal – and with the aim of making money; this is a kind of prostitution at one remove.)

Paul's final argument goes back to foundational Christian beliefs, to the spirit and to the cross. In 3.16–17 he said that the whole church was God's new **Temple**; now he insists that the individual Christian is as well. The point of the Temple was that God lived there; part of the point of being a Christian is that God himself lives in you, in the person of the **holy spirit**. If you are a Christian, it isn't the case that you only have dealings with the spirit when you are praying, or engaged in other more obviously 'religious' activities; the spirit comes to take up permanent residence. You can, of course 'grieve' the spirit (as Paul warns in Ephesians 4.30); but you cannot simply tell him to take a vacation somewhere else while you go off on your own.

Nor can you ever stop being someone who has been bought with a high price. Paul clearly refers to the cross itself, where Jesus paid the price of his own life, his own blood, to rescue human beings like you and me, ordinary sinners, muddled sinners, great and small sinners. If you pay a lot of money for a wonderful book, you don't start tearing pages out to make shopping lists, or writing rude words in the margins. If you pay a lot of money for a lovely house, you don't spray-paint silly patterns on the front door. In the same way, those who have been 'bought' at tremendous cost must remind themselves of what special people they are, and learn to behave accordingly. 'Glorify God in your body'; in other words, discover how to live the truly human life which brings glory to the God in whose image you are made, and whose own unique image, his son Jesus, died to rescue you from all that will stop you being the person he longs for you to be.

1 CORINTHIANS 7.1–7

Life within Marriage

1Let me now turn to the matters you wrote about. 'It is good for a man
to have no sexual contact with a woman.' 2Well, yes; but the tempta-
tion to immorality means that every man should maintain sexual
relations with his own wife, and every woman with her own husband.

[3]The man should give his wife her marital rights, and the woman should do the same for her husband. [4]The woman isn't in charge of her own body; her husband is. In the same way, the man isn't in charge of his own body; his wife is. [5]Don't deny one another, except perhaps by agreement for a period of time, so that you may have more space for prayer. But then come together again, in case the satan might tempt you because of your weakness of will.

[6]I'm not saying this as a command, but as a concession. [7]I would be happy to see everyone be in the same situation as myself. But each person has his or her own gift from God, one this way, another that way.

I was staying for a week in the suburbs of an American city where I hadn't been before. I had some free time lined up, and after a long flight and many hours at a desk I fancied going for a good walk. I asked my host where he would recommend.

'Well,' he said, 'under no circumstances go more than four blocks to the south. Just don't go beyond that, whatever you do. But in the other directions there are a few options. If you want a city walk, with shops and cafés, then head north – though you may find some of them closed today. If you want a nice park, with a lake and plenty of trees, then go east – but I think you'll find that during the afternoons it's so full of joggers that you might not find it too easy to have a relaxed walk. But if you want to see part of the old town at its best, go half a mile west, and then north, and you'll find yourself back in another century. Wonderful old houses, hotels, streets and shops. It's fascinating.'

Perverse creature that I was, I found myself curious to know what would happen if I went too far south – though I was careful to obey his clear instructions, and I didn't find out. But I followed his advice, which was based on long experience and good judgment.

Up to now in 1 Corinthians Paul has been saying things which correspond to the command not to go south. Under no circumstances should the church divide along the lines of personalities or sophisticated rhetoric. Under no circumstances should the church tolerate flagrant immorality, or have lawsuits with one another, or abandon moral restraint, especially in matters of sex. Paul has put up a notice which says 'Danger! Don't even think of going there!' Some, of course, become fascinated with strict prohibitions, and start to wonder what would happen if they went, so to speak, too far south. Paul urges them not even to think about it.

From now on, though, the tone of the letter changes. The Corinthians had written to Paul to ask his advice on several matters which were bothering them and causing difficulties in the church. With these, Paul lays down some firm principles, but much of what he says is more in the nature of wise Christian advice, based on biblical understanding, theological reflection and pastoral experience.

The first discussion, beginning with this passage, is a good example. As often happens, when some in the church were all for casting off moral restraint altogether (chapter 6), others were all for moral severity. In line with some of the well-known philosophies of the time, they were urging people either to celibacy or, if already married, to abstain from sexual relations within marriage. Some teachers strongly maintained that this was the way to new depths of personal holiness and spiritual maturity. So they have quoted another slogan which Paul comments on: 'It's good for a man not to "touch" a woman.' (In the language of the time, 'touch' was a polite way of saying 'have sexual relations with'.)

Now at one level Paul agrees with this. He himself is unmarried (he may have been a widower, or his wife may have left him when he became a Christian, or he may simply never have married – we don't know). He is quite clear that being celibate is a perfectly good state, providing one is in control of one's sexual impulses. Unlike many in our world, he doesn't consider life without active sexual relations to be inferior or deficient. So he doesn't disagree with the sentiment itself – but he does disagree with the use to which he knows it's being put.

He knows, in particular, that in a cosmopolitan city like Corinth the temptations of the flesh are coming at you from every angle. To be married, but to abstain from sexual relations, is to ask for trouble. The intimacy of the shared life without the intimacy of sex stirs up longings which can all too easily be drawn to alternative outlets. So his comment in verse 2, developed in verses 3 and 4, is clear: every married man should have regular sexual relations with his wife, and vice versa.

Here, too, Paul uses a polite expression, often misunderstood. He says that every man should 'have' his own wife, and every woman should 'have' her own husband. This doesn't mean 'everybody must get married'; 'have' is another way of saying 'have sexual relations with'. He isn't saying, as some of the older translations imply, that 'marriage is necessary because of fornication'. He is saying that married people who don't engage in sexual relations are in danger of being tempted to immoral pursuits elsewhere. Some have even suggested that part of the problem in chapter 6 – Christian men visiting prostitutes – may have been caused by Christian wives deciding to abstain from sex in order to develop their spiritual lives more fully.

Verses 3 and 4 make clear what he has in mind, in a striking statement of mutual equality between husband and wife. Many people still think Paul was a woman-hater, reinforcing male dominance, but a passage like this makes us pause and wonder. He mentions first the husband's obligation to the wife, then the wife's to the husband. Then he stresses that, just as the wife doesn't have authority over her own body, because the husband does, even so the husband doesn't have authority over *his* own body, because his wife does! That was daring at the time, and is challenging still. Working out what it means in the day-to-day and year-to-year rhythms and routines of family life, especially when one or both partners are under pressure at work or with children, is part of what the joy and discipline of married love is all about. But the main guideline is quite clear.

Paul doesn't deny that there may be a time when couples need to abstain from sex for a while in order to spend more unhurried and unpressured time in prayer. He doesn't suggest that abstention itself raises them to a higher level of spirituality, merely that a short-term agreement to abstain will give both partners the freedom to focus their thoughts and prayers. In the modern world, we might think of someone going on retreat, or preparing in prayer for a particular task; they may need some space for a few days or even a few weeks. But even though abstention may have benefits, it shouldn't become permanent. That gives the enemy a chance to attack (verse 5).

Paul is clear that this is advice, not a command like the previous chapters (verse 6). He knows that God enables people for the lifestyle to which they are called, whether married or single. But he has had enough experience of working with young Christian communities for his advice to be heeded. And there is no reason to suppose that it has gone out of date.

1 CORINTHIANS 7.8–16

Marriage and Divorce

> 8To unmarried people, and to widows, I have this to say: it's perfectly all right for you to remain like me. 9But if you don't have power over your passions, then get married. Much better to marry than to have desire smouldering away inside you!
>
> 10I have a command, too, for married people – actually, it's not just from me, it's from the Lord: that a woman should not separate from her husband. 11If she does, she should remain unmarried or return to her husband. So, too, a man should not divorce his wife.
>
> 12To everyone else I have this to say (this is just me, not the Lord). If a Christian has an unbelieving wife, and she is happy to live with him, he shouldn't divorce her. 13If a woman has an unbelieving husband, and he is happy to live with her, she shouldn't divorce him. 14The unbelieving husband, you see, is made holy by his wife, and the unbelieving wife is made holy by her husband; otherwise your children would be

impure, whereas in fact they are holy. [15]But if the unbelieving partner wants to separate, let them separate; a brother or sister is not bound in a case like that. God has called you in peace. [16]If you're a wife, how d'you know whether or not you will save your husband? If you're a husband, how d'you know whether or not you will save your wife?

Divorce has swept the Western world like a plague. When I was young, nobody I knew, in our street, my school, anywhere, was divorced. There were occasional mentions of marriage breakdown well outside our close family and friends, but it was assumed that such things were as rare, and as tragic, as a suicide. Within the last fifty years all that has changed, and now every street, every family, every school, and even every church has some people who have been through divorce, often more than once. Some countries where divorce was almost unthinkable a generation ago (including some largely Roman Catholic societies where it was more or less impossible) have seen divorce statistics shoot up.

The world in which Paul's converts lived was more like the Western world today than like that of the mid-twentieth century. Especially in the upper levels of the social scale, divorce and remarriage was common; and there was strong social pressure, sometimes even legal pressure, for divorced or widowed people, especially women, to remarry quickly. We must not make the mistake of thinking that the late twentieth century was the first time such a situation arose, and that Paul lived in a world that was more like the world of our parents and grandparents! Different societies had different customs and rules. With increasing mobility on the one hand and the huge changes brought about by the Christian **gospel** on the other, church members must have found themselves faced with a bewildering array of moral questions and difficulties, made harder by pressures from some Christians themselves to say that sexual relations, even within marriage, were a poor second best to a life of abstinence. This is the minefield Paul is picking his way through in this passage, and as we watch him do it we can learn a great deal that will help us in facing the minefields that we ourselves are called to walk through in our own day.

He divides his comments into three areas: a message for people who have been married but now aren't (verses 8 and 9), a message for married people (verses 10 and 11), and a longer message for people in the tricky situation of being married to someone who is not a Christian (verses 12–16).

The first of these is the closest Paul gets to revealing his own situation, which the Corinthians themselves will have known. The word

I've translated 'those no longer married' can simply mean 'unmarried', but it's quite likely that Paul is referring to widows and widowers. (He gives advice later in the chapter, in verses 25–38, to people who have not yet been married.)

Paul is walking on a tightrope here, between the social pressures towards remarriage on the one hand and the pressures from some 'spiritual' teachers towards permanent celibacy on the other. He wants them to be free from the pressure to get married again; there is much to be said for them, both men and women, being able to choose either to remarry or not, without outside forces influencing their choice. This was quite a socially subversive, even shocking, thing to suggest in his world. But equally he wants them to be comfortable, and not ashamed in the face of those advocating abstinence, to admit to themselves that their sexual desires are still powerful and will be a nuisance, and a temptation, if they do not marry.

This is almost certainly the meaning of verse 9. The older translation ('better to marry than to burn') used sometimes to be interpreted as meaning 'to burn in **hell** because of sexual misconduct', but this is probably not the point. Far more likely that Paul means 'to be on fire with passion and to have no legitimate means of dealing with it'.

In these matters, he is giving guidance and advice, not strict rules. When it comes to divorce, though, he is quite clear, referring (most unusually for him) to a specific command of Jesus himself, presumably the one we find in Mark 10.9 and similar passages. Divorce never was God's intention for his children, and is not now. Ever since God created male and female together in his image (Genesis 1.26–28), there is something about that union and bond which reflects God's image into the world, and back in worship to God himself. Anything which breaks that image is therefore dishonouring to God, and (as almost all divorced people will admit) damaging to the humans involved. Paul is not, of course, discussing the problems that can arise within a marriage. We can be sure that, given more time and space, he would urge married couples to be sure that the sort of behaviour likely to lead to divorce – anger, unkindness, bitterness, abuse, long separation, infidelity – are nipped in the bud before they start.

Already, however, he discusses an exception: a woman who has separated from her husband should remain unmarried (very unusual, as we have seen) or should return to the husband. This then opens the door to a larger discussion of whether or not divorce should be allowed in a case where one party is a non-Christian. This must often have been the case in the early church, where one partner would hear and believe the gospel while the other one did not. (Paul urges in verse 39, and in 2 Corinthians 6.14, that Christians should only marry other Christians.) Some have even suggested that this was one of the main ways by which the Christian gospel spread in the ancient world; but many Christians at the time might not have seen it that way. Having come from the pagan world where the old dark gods and goddesses were worshipped, and where strange practices of all kinds were encouraged, they may well have felt strongly that they had passed from darkness to light. How could they then continue living with someone who was still in darkness?

Paul's response is a striking example of how the Christian gospel stands the old negative codes of purity on their heads. As with Jesus' healings, in which he touched **lepers** and other unclean people and, instead of being infected with their diseases, infected them instead with God's new **life**, so Paul believed that holiness could be more powerful than uncleanness. The relationship would not need to be damaging for the Christian. The unbelieving partner would be regularly within the reach of God's love in **Christ**, shining through the believing partner. (This is the ideal; of course, actual events might be very different, as Paul knew well.) The Christian partner should not therefore initiate a split. There is always the possibility, through God's grace and help, that the unbelieving partner may be won over.

So, too, he says, one Christian parent makes the children 'holy' as opposed to 'unclean'. Presumably this means that the children, in coming under the influence of one Christian parent, are within the sphere of God's love and the power of the gospel, not that they are automatically Christians. The verse says nothing about the practice of infant **baptism**, though part of the logic behind that practice is contained here by implication.

If, however, the non-Christian partner wanted to separate (as many might; not everyone would want to be associated with this strange, bizarre new movement), the Christian should not try to oppose the split. At this point Paul has felt able to introduce an important modification into the teaching of Jesus. He has done so, however, not by treating Jesus' words as mere good advice, but by applying them in detail to a new situation Jesus never faced. We who live in many different situations never envisaged by either Jesus or Paul need wisdom, humility and faithfulness to apply their teaching afresh in our own day. And we certainly need those same qualities when thinking through what the church's marriage discipline should be in a culture that seems increasingly at odds with the gospel.

1 CORINTHIANS 7.17–24

Stay the Way You Were Called

[17]This is the overriding rule: everyone should conduct their lives as
the Lord appointed, as God has called them. This is what I lay down
in all the churches. [18]If someone was circumcised when he was called,
he shouldn't try to remove the marks. If someone was uncircumcised
when he was called, he shouldn't get circumcised. [19]Circumcision is
nothing; uncircumcision is nothing; what matters is keeping God's
commandments!

[20]Everyone should stay within the calling they had when they were
called. [21]Were you a slave when you were called? Don't worry about it
(but if you get the chance of freedom, seize it!). [22]The one who is in
the Lord and called as a slave is the Lord's freedman, just as the one
who is called as a free person is the Messiah's slave. [23]You were bought
at a high price; don't become the slaves of human beings. [24]So, broth-
ers and sisters, let each person remain before God in the state in
which they were called.

I once sat in an entranced audience as one of the leading comedians of the day told a very long, very funny, story. The story itself was clever, witty and amusing in all sorts of ways; but what fascinated me was the way he would keep breaking in to his own long story with other, shorter ones, sometimes just one-line asides, sometimes small stories in themselves. On at least one occasion he had a small story within a middle-sized story within the large story; and somehow he kept the whole thing together so that nobody lost the thread of where he was really going.

The danger with breaking up a chapter like 1 Corinthians 7 into smaller pieces is that we can easily lose the thread of where Paul is going, particularly when he starts to talk about important issues that still get people excited today. This passage looks as though it's about two things, **circumcision** on the one hand and slavery on the other; and so it is. But why is Paul talking about these things here, in the middle of a chapter on marriage and sex?

The answer is that he's using them to illustrate the larger point he's making, which we find repeated three times here: don't try to change the status you had when you became a Christian. He says this in verses 17, 20 and 24, and the point for the larger discussion is obvious, namely that you shouldn't feel under any pressure either to get married if you're single, or to separate from a spouse if you have one.

But why has he chosen these two parallel examples? And what do we learn about the small stories (circumcision, slavery) when we see them in themselves, and also as illustrating the larger one?

In Galatians 3.28 Paul lays down one of his basic principles of living within the Christian family: there is no longer Jew or Greek; there is no longer slave or free; there is no 'male and female'; you are all one in the **Messiah**, Jesus. Our present chapter is about how 'male and female' is to work out in the Christian community, and to illustrate it Paul chooses precisely the other two pairings, 'Jew and Greek' and 'slave and free'. Two of these divisions, 'slave and free' and 'male and female', ran through the entire ancient world; for a Jew, the 'Jew and Greek' distinction was even more important, while for a Greek the line might have been 'Greeks and barbarians' (barbarians being everybody who wasn't Greek). And Paul's point is that social, cultural, ethnic and even gender distinctions are as nothing compared to the new life in which, through the **gospel**, all Christians are brought together into one.

That is why Christians should not allow social pressures of whatever sort to force them into thinking that the most important thing they could do was to change their status into something else. That would undermine the very thing he had been urging in the first two chapters. God chose the nobodies of the world; if the nobodies then decide they want to become somebodies, aren't they accusing God of making a bad job of it? Many Jewish men in Paul's day were under pressure to pretend they were **Gentiles**, and some even tried surgery to make it look as though they were uncircumcised after all (Greeks went naked when they took exercise, or used public baths, so Jewish identity was all too obvious). Likewise, as Paul knew from the Galatian situation and elsewhere, Gentile men who either attached themselves to the synagogue or became Christians might come under pressure from Jewish groups to get circumcised.

Paul sweeps aside all such social and cultural pressures with a wonderful statement: neither circumcision nor uncircumcision matters at all, since what matters is – keeping God's commandments! Paul knew as well as any other Jew that circumcision was itself one of God's commandments, and I think he meant verse 19 to be deliberately and provocatively amusing. Somehow, he is saying (in ways which we need the letter to the Romans to explain), there is a new sort of 'obedience to the commandments' which has come into being through the Messiah and the **spirit**. That's what counts; so don't let yourself be pressured into seeking to change your social status one way or the other. In the Messiah you already have all the status you will ever need.

This may seem fair enough. The second part, though, is where today we find our hackles rising. One of the great achievements of the nineteenth century, largely the work of devout Christians, was the abolition of the slave trade (not that it doesn't continue in other forms; but the conscience of most of the world has been educated to realize that slavery is evil). Surely Paul isn't saying that slavery doesn't matter? Some have even used this passage to suggest that Paul gets his moral teaching so badly wrong that we can't trust him on other matters either.

But his point is, again, that even the slave/free distinction, central though it was to all ancient society, doesn't matter compared with the status you have in the Messiah. If you were a slave when you became a Christian, you shouldn't be constantly seeking to become free as though everything depended on it. Likewise, if you were free, you shouldn't enslave yourself to someone. That may sound an unnecessary prohibition, but in fact people did sometimes sell themselves into slavery to escape problems of debt and similar situations. It is, though, far less common than slaves seeking their freedom; Paul's warning against self-enslavement in verse 23 is not a true balance to his comment about slaves in verses 21 and 22.

People still argue over what exactly Paul is saying in the second half of verse 21. Some think he's saying 'Even if you have a chance of gaining your freedom, you should instead try to use your present situation as a way of serving the Lord'. I think it's more likely that he means what I've put in the translation: if you get the chance of freedom, grab it with both hands! The point is that the slave shouldn't be spending all his or her waking hours worrying about how to become free; but if the chance suddenly comes (as a gift from the owner, as often happened, or by some other means) one should take it.

Slavery in the ancient world was in fact a many-sided thing. It was and is an evil idea that one human being could 'own' another. Yet many masters and mistresses treated slaves fairly and kindly, and many slaves gained a fine education and often rose to positions of considerable responsibility and authority, with more actual status and prestige than many poor but free people. Equally, many slaves were treated brutally and callously. But slavery was woven as deeply into the ancient world as, say, electricity and cars are in the modern world. Though some small parts of our world (such as the Amish communities), recognizing the potential for evil of such modern inventions, manage to do without them, most of us accept the compromise of polluting our planet for the sake of getting things done. Paul is, in any case, not writing an essay on slavery, but making a brief point in order to illustrate a different theme. Even in the letter to Philemon, where he appeals for the converted slave Onesimus to be pardoned and set free, he doesn't set out the case in any detail.

His point here, then, is that God's calling through the gospel, the 'call' through which people come to **faith** and enter the Messiah's people, is far more important than social or cultural status. Christians should resist the subtle and not-so-subtle pressures that are put on them to make a change of status their overarching goal. He is now in a position to return to the subject of marriage and sex and address the next aspect of it that presents itself. But before we move on we should pause and ask ourselves: in our churches and fellowships, are we clear that the status we have, through belonging to the Messiah, is more important than the social or cultural status we hanker after for ourselves, or try to force others to adopt?

1 CORINTHIANS 7.25–31

On Remaining Unmarried

25Now when it comes to unmarried people, I have no command from
the Lord, but I give my opinion as (thanks to the Lord's mercy!) a
trustworthy person. 26This, then, is what I think is for the best: just at
the moment we are in the middle of a very difficult time, and it's best
for people to remain as they are. 27Are you bound to a wife? Don't try
to dissolve the marriage. Have you had your marriage dissolved?
Don't look for another wife. 28But if you do marry, you are not sin-
ning, and if an unmarried woman marries, she is not sinning. But
people who go that way will have trouble at a human level, and I
would prefer to spare you that.

29This is what I mean, my brothers and sisters. The present situation
won't last long; for the moment, let those who have wives live as
though they weren't married, 30those who weep as though they were
not weeping, those who celebrate as though they were not celebrat-
ing, those who buy as though they had no possessions, 31those who
use the world as though they were not making use of it. The pattern
of this world, you see, is passing away.

I remember a cartoon from my childhood days. A young man sits in an office. He is talking on the telephone, but standing beside him is a huge figure with a bristling moustache, staring at him angrily: obviously the boss. The young man is saying, in a half-whisper, 'Of course I still love you! It's just that it isn't very convenient to discuss it right now . . .'

The present passage is dominated by the thought that certain things are 'not very convenient right now'. But what is going on for Paul and the Corinthians? Why is 'right now' so inconvenient – sufficiently inconvenient, it seems, to prevent them living the normal kind of life they might otherwise have expected, not least pursuing the right and proper practice of going ahead with plans for marriage?

It has often been supposed – and many translations reflect this – that Paul believes the present world is bound to disappear before very long. The **kingdom** will come, and the present world will pass away altogether. For that reason, he says, you shouldn't get entangled in matters of the world; don't enter into marriage if you haven't done so already; don't even give a thought to what would otherwise be pressing matters, grief or celebration or business. Live 'as if not' (verses 29–31), as if you were not in fact doing what you are in fact doing. None of it matters; the Day of the Lord is almost upon us!

Now there may be an element of truth in this way of reading the passage. Paul certainly does believe that the time will come when 'the trumpet will sound, the dead will be raised, and those of us who are left alive will be transformed' (15.52). He assumes, when he's writing this letter, that these events will happen within his own lifetime–though by the time he writes 2 Corinthians he has faced the probability that he will die ahead of that time. But though this final crisis may be in the back of his mind as he writes the present passage, there seems to be something even more urgent in the front of his mind.

Paul left Corinth, most likely, in AD 51. Right around that time, and for a few years afterwards – exactly the period between his leaving and his writing this letter – there was a severe shortage of grain, the most basic foodstuff, around the Greek world. Other people writing at the same time mention it. Many Roman citizens and colonists – and many in Corinth were both–had taken it for granted that the great Roman empire would keep them safe, sound and well fed. Suddenly the food had run out. A great question mark hung over the whole imperial world. Was everything going horribly wrong? The poor in particular – and most of the Christians in Corinth were poor (1.26) – would be feeling the pinch. It was a time of great distress, as much because people were anxious that it would get worse as because of the immediate effects of the crisis.

I think Paul is referring *both* to this immediate crisis *and* to the fact that it points forward to the ultimate crisis, the time of the Lord's return (4.5). He is using the second of these to colour in the warnings which apply to the first; even if the present crisis suddenly passes, if wonderful crops and plentiful food again flood the markets of Corinth and everywhere else, there will still be the final crisis to face. There will never be a time when Christians can settle down and treat the world as though it's going to last for ever. But his particular advice (and it is only advice, strongly worded though it may be) relates most specifically to the social distress caused by near-famine. Verse 29 doesn't necessarily mean that world history has only a short time left; it may well be better taken to mean, as I've translated it, that the present crisis can't last for ever, so that it's better to do nothing drastic for the moment.

In that situation, engaged couples may well want to think hard about postponing their marriages. That seems to be what's at stake in these verses and in verses 32–38, which follow immediately. Again, some have imagined that the passage goes on addressing the question of people contracting a kind of sexless marriage, for the sake of spiritual advancement; but in fact it seems that Paul is now dealing with a somewhat more straightforward issue. Couples would often be betrothed at an early age, frequently through arranged marriages; girls were often married immediately at puberty, around the age of twelve, and had frequently been 'promised' to someone well before that.

Christians in Corinth would be facing all kinds of pressures: the natural desire of a betrothed couple to consummate their marriage and get on with building a life together; the huge social pressure on young women in particular to get married and bear children; the anxiety about the present food shortages (do you really want to start a family if you can't feed yourselves, let alone extra mouths?); and in and through it all was the real desire to serve the Lord Jesus and live in a way that is pleasing to him. Paul wants to help them through this present time, and is now building on the previous verses (17–24) in order to say: who you are as a Christian matters much more than changing your social status, so don't be worried about whether you may need to postpone your marriage. It's not a problem.

The passage resonates out from first-century Corinth into all kinds of situations in subsequent periods of history and other parts of the world. The Christian is not to be alarmed by the various turbulent things that happen in the world, nor to be distressed if troubled times mean putting off, for a while or for ever, the kind of life and social status that one might otherwise have expected to enjoy. But looming up behind all this as well is a point Paul wants to make to the Corinthians over and over again, because as we shall see in chapter 15 in particular they still needed to rethink their whole view of the world to take account of it. The present world will one day give way to the world that is to be, the world in which Jesus will have completed his kingly work of defeating all hostile powers, including ultimately death itself.

When that moment arrives, it won't matter that you followed or didn't follow some social order or pattern in the way that your family and friends all assumed you would. What will matter is that you were faithful to the Lord in whatever strange circumstances you found yourself. And that is the main point Paul is now going on to make.

1 CORINTHIANS 7.32–40

Divided Loyalties

32I want you to be free from worries. The unmarried man worries
about the things of the Lord, how to please the Lord; 33but the married
man worries about the things of the world, in other words, how to
please his wife – 34and he is pulled in both directions. So too the
unmarried woman or girl worries about the things of the Lord, how to
be holy both in body and spirit; but the married woman worries about
the things of the world, in other words, how to please her husband.
35I'm saying this for your own benefit. I'm not placing restrictions
on you; my aim is that nothing will get in the way of your appropriate
behaviour and steady devotion to the Lord.
36If anyone thinks he is behaving improperly towards his fiancée – if
he finds the situation overly stressful, and matters reach a point of
necessity – then let him do as he wishes, he won't be sinning: let them
marry. 37But the man who settles it firmly in his heart and is not under
necessity, but in control of his own will, and has made his judgment
in his own heart to keep her as his fiancée, will do well. 38So the one
who marries his fiancée will do well; and the one who holds back
from marrying will do better.
39A woman is bound in marriage as long as her husband lives. But if
the husband dies she is free to marry anyone she likes, only in the
Lord. 40But in my opinion she is happier if she remains as she is. And
I think I too have the spirit of God.

He came to see me both excited and distressed. He was one of the brightest students I had ever taught at that time; but he was also passionately involved in the plight of some of the poorest people in the world. Most of his fellow students were doing their academic work for between five and eight hours a day, and whiling away the rest of their time in music, sport and a rich variety of student social life. But he was squeezing his work – the work he'd come to university to do – into two or three hours a day, and then spending every other waking moment working, campaigning, writing letters, raising money, doing everything he could to help the people whose plight had touched his heart. And of course his academic performance was going downhill fast.

He was torn down the middle. I respected both halves of who he was, but it was my job to tell him that he had to make a decision. He couldn't do both things at once. Either he should follow his course of studies and get the degree he was capable of; or he should give it up and work full-time on the projects his heart was aching over. Of course, some students might have been able to combine academic work and worldwide social concern; but the things in his heart and the things in his mind were both too strong, at that moment, to admit of compromise. I respected the decision he eventually made (I won't tell you what it was). But he was simply an extreme example of the problem Paul highlights here: the problem of divided loyalties.

This is one of the passages that has gained for Paul the dubious reputation of being opposed to marriage, except as a concession if people really can't control themselves. How this could be maintained in the face of his clear commands to married couples in verses 2–5 it's hard to understand; but in any case the present section is not about marriage in general, but continues Paul's urgent advice to a church pulled this way and that by conflicting social and personal pressures.

Paul clearly doesn't think that it's impossible simultaneously to serve both the Lord and one's marriage partner. He knows many married Christians, including most of the other **apostles** (see 9.5), and he doesn't imagine for a moment that the two callings are mutually exclusive. But there was a famine on. Times were hard, particularly for newlyweds, who would rightly be eager to build up their marriage relationship by pouring themselves into thinking what would make their newly acquired spouse happy.

Paul does not look down on that aim. It is right and proper. Indeed, we find in Ephesians 5.22–33 that the self-giving love of husband to wife, and the answering love of wife to husband, are themselves things richly pleasing to God, gloriously reflecting his image. But in times of social and economic distress it may simply be impossible to do both things well – to find out and do what will please the Lord, working for the **gospel** in whatever way one is called to do, and to find out and do what will build up a new marriage relationship. And if that's the choice, Paul is clear: one's service to the Lord belongs first.

As in most of the chapter, Paul is not laying down hard and fast rules. He is trying to teach the Corinthians to think clearly, wisely and above all Christianly about delicate issues where there is no absolute right and wrong. In our own day there are many who have ignored his wise advice and have rushed ahead into marriage and into a new sphere of Christian work or service, assuming that because God has brought them together the complex business of learning to work for the gospel and the complex business of learning to live as a couple will somehow fall into place. This simply can't be assumed. The sorry story of marriage tensions and breakups among Christian workers in recent times bears witness to the dangers.

Standing at the head of the passage is Paul's stated aim: to keep Christians free from anxieties. Sometimes he simply tells people to put anxieties away, trusting the Lord for everything, as in Philippians 4.6. But maybe part of that 'trusting the Lord for everything' will involve taking steps to make sure that one is not placing unnecessary burdens of anxiety upon oneself – and upon those to whom one is bound in ties of human love. This isn't a way of saying that the Lord helps those who help themselves. But it is a way of reminding God's people that when we pray for something, part of the answer to the prayer may be some action that lies in our own power to do or not to do. There is no point in praying for safety on the road while continuing to drive dangerously.

Paul is very emphatic in all of this that he is not opposing marriage itself. (He here addresses the man, although elsewhere in the chapter he is careful to speak to both man and woman; perhaps this reflects the social situation in which the engaged man was responsible for arranging the wedding.) On the contrary; if the man finds that his desire for his fiancée is getting stronger, putting him in an impossible position (compare verse 9), then they should marry; that is perfectly all right. But they should be prepared then to face the difficulties that will accompany the early days of a marriage, even and perhaps especially a Christian one, when life for other reasons is in any case hard.

Paul concludes the discussion with a short word of further advice – once again, not a command – to widows. A widow is free to marry again, though only 'in the Lord', i.e. to another Christian. But Paul sees, once again, that there may be reasons for resisting the social pressure that would otherwise hurry such women into a further marriage as soon as reasonably possible. 'I think I too have God's **spirit**,' he says, perhaps venturing a gentle comment on some in Corinth who were claiming great spiritual wisdom. He isn't saying that his advice is binding in all cases. But he is saying that it must be taken seriously.

Christian teachers in each generation need to learn how to give wise and spirit-led advice while recognizing that in some matters there may be room for disagreement. Happy the church where both pastors and flock know how to live with that balance.

1 CORINTHIANS 8.1–6

Meat Offered to Idols

[1]Now when it comes to meat offered to idols, we know that 'We all
have knowledge'. Knowledge puffs you up, but love builds you up!
[2]If anybody thinks they 'know' something, they don't yet 'know' in the
way they ought to know. [3]But if anybody loves God, they are 'known' –
by him.

[4]So when it comes to food that has been offered to idols, we know
that 'idols are nothing in the world', and that 'there is no God but one'.
[5]Yes, indeed: there may be many so-called 'gods', whether in heaven or
on earth, just as there are many 'gods' and many 'lords'. [6]But for us

There is one God, the father,
from whom are all things, and we live to him and for him;
and one Lord, Jesus the Messiah,
through whom are all things, and we live through him.

There is a restaurant in Rome which is built around the ruins of an old temple. Two of the pillars are still visible. The restaurant makes a feature of them, and is proud of the ancient origins of the building where they now serve excellent pasta, great local cuisine, and fine Italian wines.

But what people don't normally realize is that in the ancient world the temples normally *were* the restaurants. Each town or city had plenty of shrines to local gods and goddesses, to the great divinities like Apollo or Venus, and, in Paul's day, more and more to the Roman emperor and members of his family. And what people mostly did there was to come with animals for **sacrifice**. When the animal was killed, it would be cooked, and the family (depending on what sort of ritual it was) might have a meal with the meat as the centrepiece. But there was usually more meat than the worshippers could eat, and so other people would come to the temple and share in the food which had been offered to the god.

Even that would often fail to use up all the sacrificed meat. So the temple officials would take what was left to the market, where it would be sold in the normal way. In fact, most of the meat available for sale in a city like Corinth would have been offered in sacrifice.

For that reason, some Jews in the ancient world, in places where they couldn't or didn't have a butcher of their own, refused to eat meat at all. They didn't want to be involved, even at one remove, in the worship of idols, of man-made gods and goddesses. They knew, after all, that there was one God and only one: **YHWH**, the Lord, the creator of the world, the God who had made a special **covenant** with Israel. They were reminded of this in their regular daily prayer: 'Hear, O Israel: the Lord our God, the Lord is One; and you shall love the Lord your God with all your heart, **soul** and might.'

This situation was always likely to present problems for the newborn Christian church living in the pagan world. But there was an additional element as well. Some teachers had been saying things which effectively gave Christians permission to eat meat that had been offered in sacrifice – not only to buy it in the market, but actually to go to the temples themselves and eat there as though they, too, had been worshipping whichever god or goddess it might be. To cap it all, around this time, as part of the emperor-worship which was springing up all round the Roman empire, Roman citizens in Corinth had a special right to share in meals connected with imperial festivals. If they didn't go along with it, people would notice, and there might be trouble.

Paul is going to take his time about setting out the issues and dealing with them. He has to build up gradually to the central discussion, but he won't reach it until the middle of chapter 10. There is much to find out on the way as he sketches out the principles of Christian living in a pagan world before he applies them to this problem in particular. We who live in an increasingly pagan world today can learn a good deal from him. But this quick-fire opening discussion, once we see what's going on, sets up the terms for what is to come. In doing so, it shows where the foundations really are for Paul: in the reality of who God actually is. This is one of Paul's most astonishing statements on that most central topic.

The Corinthian teachers, as before, had coined slogans to sum up what they were saying. 'We all have knowledge' – in other words, all true Christians have inside them a deep, secret 'knowledge' of the real truth, so this can't be affected by anything so trivial as eating food that's been offered to an idol. 'Idols are nothing in the world', in other words, they don't have any real existence, they're just man-made nonsenses, so going into their temples or eating their sacrificial meat really doesn't matter. 'There is no god but one' – which they might have meant in the Jewish sense, but they might also have meant, as many ancient teachers would have put it, that all the beings which people think of as gods or goddesses are really manifestations of the one and only god which lies behind them all. That's a very un-Jewish idea; the God of Israel stood over against the pagan gods and showed them up as dehumanizing delusions.

Paul responds to these slogans with answers which are almost as dense and cryptic as the sayings themselves. Knowledge, indeed (verses 1–3)? That just puffs you up (his regular charge against the Corinthian teachers); what you need is not knowledge but love – the point he will eventually spell out in detail in chapter 13. And in any case what matters is not *your* knowledge about this or that, or even about God and the gods; what matters is *God's* knowledge of you, and the way you will be aware of that is by the love you find for this true God deep in your own heart and mind. This already hints at the point which, for Paul, stands behind the whole thing: Christians must work out in practice what that ancient Jewish prayer means, about loving the one true God with everything we have and are.

So he responds in verses 5 and 6 to the second and third slogans. It may be the case that no idol has any real existence, but there are certainly a lot of would-be, so-called, 'gods' and 'lords' out there in the world. Some of them are in **heaven** (the traditional gods); some of them are on earth (the imperial cult being the obvious example).

And the Jewish-style one-God worship (the technical term is 'monotheism') to which Christians remain committed stands over against all these gods and lords, whether they have any real existence or not. You can't simply assume that because you're a monotheist therefore all worship offered to all imaginary gods and lords somehow counts as worship offered to the true God.

The true God is different, and the Christian **gospel** shows just how different. Our God, says Paul, is the God of Abraham, Isaac and Jacob, the God which the ancient Jewish prayer celebrates, the God we are summoned to love. But Paul has glimpsed the astonishing truth that this one true God is now to be *known as* 'the father'; that this one true Lord is now to be known as 'Jesus the **Messiah**'. Somehow, within the very being of the one God, we learn to see *both* the world's creator, the one from whom everything comes into being, to whom we owe our all, *and* the world's redeemer, the man Jesus, Israel's Messiah, the one through whom everything came into being (Paul here echoes the Jewish language about 'wisdom'), the one through whom we ourselves have come to be God's people.

This is mind-blowing today, and must have been even more so in Paul's own day. Paul is not content with offering simple rules, a set of dos and don'ts to guide the Corinthians through the difficulties of living as people of the true God in a world full of other gods. He wants them to be able to think through the issues for themselves, and that means thinking hard about just who the true God is, and what it means to love and serve him. That remains as urgent a task today as it was in the first century.

1 CORINTHIANS 8.7–13

Respecting Weak Consciences

7The problem is that not everybody has this 'knowledge'. Some have been accustomed up to now to eating idol-food with the assumption that it really does belong to the idol. This has left them with a weak conscience, and now that conscience will be polluted. 8But the food we eat won't recommend us to God. We won't be any worse off if we don't eat, and we won't be any better off if we do.

9But you must take care in case this official right of yours becomes a danger to the weak. 10Look at it like this: if someone with a weak conscience sees you, a person with 'knowledge', sitting down to eat in an idol-house, that conscience of theirs is likely to make up its mind actually to eat idol-food, isn't it? 11And so, you see, the weak person – a brother or sister for whom the Messiah died! – is then destroyed by your 'knowledge'. 12That means you'll be sinning against your brother

or sister, and attacking their weak conscience; and in doing this you'll
be sinning against the Messiah. [13]So, for this reason, if food causes my
brother or sister to stumble, I will never ever eat meat, so that I won't
make my brother or sister trip up.

I never found out what had really been wrong, but it could have been serious. I was leading a party of walkers in the Scottish highlands, and we found ourselves high up among the crags when the mist came down. I got out the compass, checked the map, and started to navigate towards the next point on our route. But it quickly became apparent that we weren't where we should be. There were steep rocks and gullies where there should have been a flat bit of grass and heather. Rather than carry on, we looked at a different compass. Mine had been malfunctioning. We used the other one and were quickly back on track.

Paul sees the 'conscience' like a sort of internal compass, telling each person what is right and wrong. But the human conscience, like a compass, is a sensitive instrument, and it can easily malfunction. It can get trapped in magnetic fields that pull it off course. It can allow itself to be set in a particular pattern even though it's inappropriate. It often can't tell the difference between social custom – 'the way things are done' in this town, this country, this college, this family – and actual issues of right and wrong.

Paul knows that human consciences can get things wrong, and can be re-set and re-educated. But he also knows, from years of pastoral experience, that re-educating someone's conscience takes time and patience. It won't do simply to tell people to give up the deep inner ideas they have at the moment and adopt some other ones instead; even if they go along with you, their conscience – the very thing you were trying to re-educate! – will be deeply troubled, will be telling them they're in the wrong place. So, although Paul himself has a robust conscience when it comes to eating meat, and doesn't need to ask where it's come from, he is well aware that not all Christians are like this, and that he can't force them overnight to change what their conscience is telling them.

But the individual conscience really matters for the Christian. This is one of the key ways in which each individual maintains responsibility before God for his or her own actions. Keeping a clear conscience before God is part of basic Christian living. If one Christian behaves in a way which shocks or distresses another, or leads them to do something their own conscience is telling them is wrong, they are taking away their responsibility, and forcing them to disobey what they are convinced is God's will for them. At that point, the 'stronger' Christian is actually making the 'weaker' one sin. And at that point we should all realize that something has gone badly wrong.

This isn't an excuse for people with small minds and badly educated consciences to prevent the rest of the church doing things that are harmless in themselves. Sometimes people from a very narrow background, full of rules and restrictions which have nothing to do with the **gospel** itself and everything to do with a particular social subculture, try to insist that all other good Christians should join them in their tight little world. But in a case like that the rule-bound Christians are in no danger of having their consciences damaged. They are not being 'led astray'. They are quite sure of their own correctness. Paul is dealing with a very different case.

The problem he's facing is that several of the Christians in Corinth, before their conversion (which was after all quite recent), had been regular worshippers in the shrines of the idols. They knew what went on there – the dark sense of mystery and fear, the sense that in feasting at the god's table you were really eating and drinking the god himself, taking his life to be your own life; and then the drink, the sense of casting off moral restraint, the girls and boys waiting round the back to do whatever you wanted in return for a little extra payment to the god . . . And once you had shared in that dark but powerful world on a regular basis, perhaps for many years, it would be difficult, in your memory and imagination, to separate part of it from the whole thing. Now that you had become a Christian you would feel you had been rescued from the world of darkness and brought out into the light. True worship wasn't like that; truly human living wasn't like that. You had escaped. You were free.

And, looking back, you wouldn't be able to split that old world up into different bits. You wouldn't be able to say that this bit was all right while that bit was wicked. The very smell of the meat that you used to eat in the temple, with the priests chanting and the drink and the prostitutes waiting for you, would bring it all back. It would be natural and right that your conscience could not, without some years of teaching, prayer and wise help, cope with any element of the old package deal, even if Christian friends who perhaps hadn't had that background had no problem with one aspect of it, namely the meat. And Paul is concerned, deeply concerned, for such people. He doesn't want their consciences to be troubled.

In fact, because he sees all Christians as 'members of the **Messiah**', part of the 'body' in which the Messiah's life is now expressed in the world (see chapter 12), he sees any attack on the conscience of a 'weak' Christian as an attack on the Messiah himself (verse 12). What he insisted on earlier in the chapter was that 'knowledge' puffs you up, but love builds you up; and it's love that he's appealing to now, as part of the foundation of his argument. You may, he says, have the 'right' to eat meat offered to idols. He may even be referring to the 'right' that Roman citizens in Corinth possessed to attend great imperial festivities. But you must be careful in case this 'right' of yours leads you to do things which will lure the 'weak' brother or sister back into the old life. The language of 'rights' needs to be held up to the light; and the light in which we can see clearly what it should and shouldn't mean is the light of love.

1 CORINTHIANS 9.1–12a

The 'Rights' of an Apostle

1I'm a free man, aren't I? I'm an apostle, aren't I? I've seen Jesus our Lord, haven't I? You are my work in the Lord, aren't you? 2I may not be an apostle to other people, but I certainly am to you; in fact, you are the authorized stamp of my apostleship in the Lord.

3This is the defence I make to anyone who wants to bring a charge against me. 4Do we not have the right to eat and drink? 5Do we not have the right to take a Christian wife with us on our travels, as the other apostles do, as the Lord's brothers do, as Cephas does? 6Or are Barnabas and I the only ones who don't have the right to be set free from the need to work? 7Who serves in the army at their own expense? Who plants a vineyard and doesn't eat its fruit? Who looks after animals and doesn't drink the milk?

8I'm not just using human illustrations to make the point; the law says the same thing, doesn't it? 9This is what is written in Moses's law: 'You must not muzzle a threshing ox.' God isn't concerned for oxen, is he? 10Doesn't it refer completely to us? Yes, it does – because it's written that the one who ploughs should do so in hope of the produce, and the thresher should thresh in hope of a share in the crop. 11So if we have sown spiritual things among you, is it such a big thing that we should reap worldly things? 12If others have that kind of right over you, don't we have it even more?

One of the great moral gains of the second half of the twentieth century is the belief, shared by most people around the world, that all people are to be respected and valued. All people, not just some. Weak people, poor people, little people, hungry people, frightened people, people of different colour, people of either sex – they all matter; and the strong, rich, big, well-fed, confident, socially advantaged people in the world have no right to do what they like with them.

This has often been expressed by talking about 'human rights'. That phrase has become common in a way that wasn't true a hundred years ago. It has become a way of saying that we, the worldwide community, won't stand for tyranny and oppression, won't tolerate the bullies who exploit people for their own ends. We say that people have 'rights' in order to say that other people don't have the 'right' to abuse or exploit them.

Whether the worldwide community yet knows how to move from talking about all this to doing something about it remains to be seen. But, in any case, talking about 'rights' as a way of making the point has its own problems. It can be a way of standing up for the weak; but it can also be a way of asserting all kinds of other things about people being independent, being able to do what they like or want in every sphere of life . . . in fact, about having the 'right' to be arrogant, selfish, greedy or whatever.

Paul faces the problem of 'rights' in dealing with the question of meat offered to idols, which he's been discussing in chapter 8, and to which he will return in chapter 10. Some of the Corinthians have been stressing that they have the 'right' to eat whatever they like. This may be because, as 'strong-minded' Christians, they know that a piece of meat is just a piece of meat, and what's happened to it before it gets to your plate is irrelevant. Or it may be that they are reminding Paul that as Roman citizens they have the 'right' to join in the imperial celebrations. And Paul agrees with them! He, too, is a 'strong-minded' Christian. He, too, is a Roman citizen, and is prepared to make use of that 'right' when it's appropriate (see, for instance, Acts 16.37–39; 22.25–29; 25.11–12).

But his whole point is that 'knowing your rights' is only one side of the story. It's not enough to say that you have the right to do something and so you're going to go ahead and do it. There may be occasions when the correct thing to do is *not* to act on your 'rights'. How is Paul going to make this point clear? By describing, at some length, the 'rights' he has as an **apostle**, and by showing, dramatically, that he is deliberately not making use of these 'rights'. He wants the Corinthians to see that there can be something more than 'rights'; that 'rights' by themselves can lead to arrogance, the cure for which is to think about the demands of the **gospel** itself.

So the present passage, describing Paul's view of what being an apostle is all about, is designed as an example of the rights someone has which they are then prepared not to use. At the same time, it tells us a great deal about how Paul saw the calling of an apostle. This, too, was a matter of some dispute in Corinth, as we saw in chapter 4 and will see more fully in the second letter. That, I think, is why this passage has quite a different tone of voice, full of rhetorical questions, almost teasing.

So how did Paul understand apostleship? What did it involve?

For a start, it meant that he had seen Jesus, the risen Lord (verse 1). The Corinthians had had all kinds of wonderful Christian experiences, but not this one. As Paul says in 15.5–8, the risen Lord appeared to several people, but he, Paul, was the last in the list. The 'apostles' were those who had seen Jesus, alive again after his death, and who therefore could tell the world first-hand of the **good news** that the one true God had broken the power of death, and with it all the other powers that enslave humankind. So Paul was an apostle, and even if the rest of the world didn't think of him like that, the Corinthians certainly should, because it was through his witness that they became Christians themselves, experiencing the power of the good news through his announcement of it.

But Paul hasn't behaved like the other apostles have. They – Cephas (Peter) and the rest, including the actual brothers of Jesus himself – have set a standard of how apostles should live and work. The task of announcing the good news, with all the hardships and dangers it brought, was to be seen as an occupation deserving of support. Those who became Christians were to fund the continuing work of the apostles, their food and drink and family needs (verses 4–5). It was only Paul and Barnabas who had not made use of this right.

He explains the point with three examples from ordinary life. The soldier, the vineyard worker and the farmer all expect to get their living by what they do (verse 7). And he even draws in a passage from the Mosaic **law** (Deuteronomy 25.4) in support, backing it up with another from a later Jewish writing, the book called Ecclesiasticus or Ben Sirach (verse 10, quoting Sirach 6.19). He wants to make it quite clear, not for his own benefit but for all Christian workers thereafter, that announcing the good news of Jesus is an activity that deserves the material support of those who benefit from it.

This point is important at a time when in many parts of the world clergy and preachers are paid at a minimal rate. True, there are other places where their work is honoured, valued and rewarded (that brings other problems, of course, but at least it shows that people are taking the principle seriously); but there are many places, including some reasonably affluent countries, where it is considered good for clergy to be paid badly, in case they 'do it for the wrong reasons'. Paul would have had no time for such an attitude. If Christian people are giving as they should, he might have said, a congregation of ten people can support a minister at the same level of their own average income. How many churches take that challenge seriously?

But, having made the point about the rights of an apostle (and, by implication, those who continue the same work in the next generation), Paul comes to the crunch of his argument. His hearers might have thought he had changed the subject, and was about to say 'so isn't it time you began to pay me at last?' Not a bit of it. Remember, he is setting them an example; and the example consists in the fact that, though he has these rights, and hasn't forgotten he has them, he has not made use of them. He will now explain why.

1 CORINTHIANS 9.12b–18

Giving Up Rights for the Gospel

12bBut we haven't made use of this right. Instead, we put up with eve-
rything, so as to place no obstacle in the way of the Messiah's gospel.
13Don't you know that those who work in the Temple eat the Temple
food, and those who serve at the altar share in the food from the altar?
14In the same way the Lord has laid it down that those who announce
the gospel should get their living from the gospel.
15But I haven't made use of any of this. I'm not writing this in order
to make it happen like this for me. It would be better for me to die
than . . . Nobody's going to deprive me of my boast! 16If I announce
the gospel, you see, that's no reason for me to be proud. I'm under
compulsion! Woe betide me if I *don't* announce the gospel! 17If I do it
willingly, I have a reward; if I do it unwillingly – well, this is the com-
mission that's been entrusted to me! 18So what is my reward? Just this:
that when I announce the gospel I should give it away free of charge;
that I shouldn't make use of my rights in the gospel.

A haunting song by Joni Mitchell describes a clarinet player standing by the side of the road in a busy city. He wasn't like ordinary buskers, playing mediocre music in a bored sort of way and hoping for enough small change from passers-by to make it through the next day or two. He was brilliant. He stood there, with music pouring out of the instrument, seeming to come from his very **soul**. And he wasn't collecting money. He was doing it for free.

Mitchell contrasts this with her own life as a professional musician. She is used to singing in concert halls, with a large car to take her to and fro, and plenty of money coming in from people who pay to hear her perform. The fact that the clarinet player is playing without any intention of earning a reward shows her an authenticity which, she fears, her own work may be starting to lack. He is playing 'for free'; and maybe, she implies, his music is echoing, embodying, celebrating, a deeper freedom as a result.

Paul was announcing the **gospel** 'for free'. He cherished and guarded this privilege, as he says in verse 15, as though his life depended on it. He would rather die than accept payment.

Why? Isn't he being stubborn? Wouldn't it be easier for him, better practice for his churches, more productive for the work of the gospel itself, if he could give up having to earn his living? (He hasn't mentioned what work he did, because the Corinthians knew well enough. He was a tent-maker. They'd all seen him at it.)

Well, part of the reason he does it is because he's aware of the need to present a role model for Christians to follow. In this case, he is offering a model of how one may have certain rights but may have to give them up for particular reasons. But it goes deeper than that as well.

For a start, as we have seen earlier in the letter, Paul is determined to make clear the difference between being a worker for and in the church of Jesus the **Messiah** and being a travelling teacher of wisdom, sophistry and rhetoric. Such teachers always asked for money, and when people showed a special interest in their work they invited them into more intimate classes, for which there was of course a higher fee. That wasn't how the gospel of Jesus worked. It was for everybody, not just for those who could afford it.

It may have had something to do, as well, with Paul's sense of utter indebtedness to Jesus himself. He had, after all, been a persecutor of the young church, as he reminds them in 15.9. And when Jesus had, none the less, rescued him from the angry and bitter life he had established for himself, it was so as to commission him to announce the **message**. Paul had no choice. He wanted to obey, out of the love that welled up in him, answering the Messiah's own love (see Galatians 2.19–20). But he knew that even if he hadn't wanted to, or if one morning he woke up and didn't want to, he had no choice. He had been set free in order to do this, and do it he must.

His own peculiar position, therefore – the only one of the **apostles** who needed to be stopped in his tracks as a persecutor and turned round in the opposite direction – had to be embodied in a particular practice, of making the gospel free of charge. His reward was – that he didn't get a reward! The paradox of that embodied the paradox of Paul's whole apostleship, the sheer oddity of who he was and what he was doing.

He uses one more illustration to make it clear just what it is he's giving up, and this time it's not just an illustration taken from spheres of work and life at some distance from what he's talking about. This time it's much closer in. Those who work in the **Temple**, he says in verse 13, eat the food from the Temple. I don't think he's referring here to the local temples in Corinth. When Paul spoke about the Temple in the singular, it was the same as when he spoke about God in the singular. He meant, I think, the Temple in Jerusalem. And Paul has already reminded the Corinthians that the church as a whole, and individual Christians one by one, are God's Temple (3.16; 6.19). The **holy spirit** lives within them, as Jews believed the presence of the living God made his dwelling in the Temple. It isn't just a parallel, then (as with Temple workers, so with gospel workers). Paul believes that the gospel, which works through the power of the spirit, creates Christians individually and corporately as God's new Temple. So the ministry of the gospel is actually an extension, or rejuvenation, of the ministry of the Temple. His point about the rights of gospel workers is thus grounded in the same dramatic view of the church that he has appealed to in chapters 3 and 6.

He refers, as well, to an actual command of Jesus – something that he had 'laid down' as a principle. This seems to be the saying we find in Matthew 10.10 and Luke 10.7: the worker deserves his (or her) hire. Even while Paul is anxious to explain that he does not and will not make use of this right, he is equally anxious – in case anyone in the church should suggest anything else – to make it clear, from the Bible, from the precedent of other apostles, from the close link with Temple-practice, and finally from a word of Jesus himself, that 'those who announce the gospel should live by the gospel' (verse 14). All too often the church has taken the exception and made it the rule, and taken the rule and made it the exception.

1 CORINTHIANS 9.19–23

The Apostle's Freedom – to Be Enslaved to Everyone

> [19]The reason for all this is as follows. I am indeed free from everyone;
> but I have enslaved myself to everyone, so that I can win all the more.
> [20]I became like a Jew to the Jews, to win Jews. I became like someone
> under the law to the people who are under the law, even though I'm
> not myself under the law, so that I could win those under the law. [21]To
> the lawless I became like someone lawless (even though I'm not law-
> less before God, but under the Messiah's law), so that I could win the
> lawless. [22]I became weak to the weak, to win the weak. I have become
> all things to all people, so that in all ways I might save some. [23]I do it
> all because of the gospel, so that I can be a partner in its benefits.

One of the greatest thinkers and statesmen of the Roman world a century before Paul was Cicero. He was a sophisticated philosopher, a brilliant lawyer, a politician, and above all a passionate believer in the glory of Rome. He argued that Rome was naturally free; other cities and nations were by nature slaves, but Rome was by nature free. Rome had a fine republican system of government; her citizens were free people; other nations should be grateful when Rome came in and took them over. Rome was sharing the gift of freedom. As a backhanded compliment to him, one of his political rivals managed to get him exiled, and in his absence had a gang of thugs destroy his house and build a statue of the goddess Liberty where it had stood.

Cicero's boast didn't last long. He came back after his brief exile, but he died in the civic purges that swept through Rome after the death of Julius Caesar. He was considered too dangerous to be allowed to live. He might start criticizing the new regime that was coming to birth. The new regime, having got him and many others out of the way, was quick to declare that 'freedom' had been restored. It's what every regime wants to tell its subjects, not least when it is in fact enslaving them.

As well as their 'rights', the Corinthian teachers prided themselves on their 'freedom'. This had several aspects. They were 'free' because Corinth, as a Roman colony, had freedoms and rights that other cities didn't. They were 'free' because, in the popular philosophies of the day, people who had true knowledge and wisdom (as they thought they had) had discovered true human freedom. And now they were 'free' because, as Christians, those who had previously been 'under' the Jewish **law** were now free from it, and all of them were now free from the corruption of the world as a whole. So now they could do what they liked. Or could they?

In the chapter so far, Paul has argued that he has 'rights' as an **apostle**, but has chosen not to make use of them. But he began the discussion by saying (9.1) that he was 'free'. He returns to this theme by pointing out, again in order to serve as an example to them, that he is 'free' in all the important senses, but has made himself 'slave of all', again for the sake of the **gospel**. His overall point is to make them see that Christian freedom is not freedom to do what you like, but freedom *from* all the things that stop you being the person God really wants you to be, which is freedom *for* the service of God and the gospel.

All this is still only an example of his main point. But once again what he says shines a light on what he does as an apostle, and the reasons why he does it. His statements together build up a picture of his many-sided vocation and work, and of his self-understanding.

His opening line is a familiar paradox: free from everything, and now a slave to everyone! As he said in 7.22, the Christian slave is the Lord's freedman, and the Christian free person is the **Messiah**'s slave. Freedom is important, but in Christian terms it is never the freedom of a subatomic particle, to whizz around in all directions in an apparently random fashion. It is always freedom *for*: for the Messiah, for God's people, for those who need the gospel.

Paul describes the ways in which he has become 'slave to all' – the ways in which, in other words, he has happily curtailed his own complete 'freedom' for the sake of the gospel. The point is that there are people out there, beyond the present Christian fellowship, who need to be 'won' – a word he uses five times in this passage, before finally changing it to 'save' (verse 22). The word is used not so much of winning a prize, but of making significant profit on an investment: God has 'invested' everything in the gospel, including his own very self in the person of Jesus his son. Now he wants to 'gain' something back from it, namely the people of all sorts and conditions whose lives will be 'won' through the gospel.

Paul begins, astonishingly, by describing how he had become 'as though a Jew to Jews' – astonishing, because of course Paul *was* himself a Jew, and was capable of making quite a point of this on occasion (e.g. Romans 11.1). He could not have put it like this if he regarded Christianity as simply a sub-branch of Judaism; it is a new thing, a fulfilment, no longer bound by ethnic or geographical identity. But what does he mean by saying that he *became* 'as though a Jew to the Jews'? Presumably, that he has continued to go to the synagogue and take part in the prayers and liturgy, using the opportunity to tell them about Jesus as the Messiah. That, indeed, is the only explanation for why he continued to be beaten, accepting the official discipline of the synagogue for the sake of the opportunities it afforded (2 Corinthians 11.24). Had he not gone, the beatings would not have occurred; synagogue authorities had no right to beat someone not under their discipline.

His next line is similar, but more focused: 'to those under the law, I became as one under the law, even though I am not myself under the law'. This means, more specifically, that while presenting the gospel to Jewish people and groups he was prepared to observe customs and key commands of the law, presumably meaning by this that he would keep the **sabbaths** and the food laws. Paul knew that his **justification**, God's regarding him as part of his true people, didn't depend on these observances. If anyone tried to suggest that they did, Paul would have been ready with the entire argument of the letter to the Galatians. That's what he means when he says that he is not himself 'under the law'. But once that was clear, Paul was ready to submit to any restrictions upon his liberty in the Messiah if it would bring the gospel to more people, and 'win' them for God's **kingdom**.

He then turns the point around in verse 21: there are many people, indeed the majority of the human race, who are without God's law (see Romans 2.12–14). That is the natural condition of the **Gentiles**; and Paul has become like one of them, living alongside them without regard for the regulations of the Jewish law which would have set him apart from the very people he was called to speak to most particularly. Just as he was quick to comment in the previous verse that he was not himself 'under the law', so he is quick to say here that he is not a 'lawless' person himself in God's eyes. He is under a new kind of 'law' altogether, the 'law' which consists of the Messiah and his whole way of life (see Galatians 6.2).

Finally he comes to the point which, we may suppose, has been in his mind all along, the point he really wants to rub in for the sake of those in Corinth who want to use their 'rights' and their 'freedom' to do whatever they like, irrespective of the conscience of other people in the church. 'To the weak I became weak, to win the weak.' If people had 'weak' consciences, in the sense he set out in 8.7–13, he would happily go along with them. Anything for the sake of the gospel, and the people it was meant to be 'winning'.

This leads him to the famous statement (verse 22b): 'I have become all things to all people, so that in all ways, or by all means, I might save some.' Paul's rights, his freedoms, are as nothing; what matters is whether people are being won for God, being saved from the corrupting wickedness around and within them, being rescued from darkness and brought into the light. This statement has sometimes been understood as though it meant that Paul was a mere pragmatist, a spin-doctor, twisting his message this way and that to suit different audiences. That's not what he's saying. The **message** remains constant. It is the messenger who must swallow his pride, who must give up his rights, who must change his freedom into slavery. Woe betide those who trim the message so that they don't have to trim themselves.

1 CORINTHIANS 9.24–27

The Christian Athlete

> [24]Don't you know that when people run on the race-track everybody runs, but only one person gets the prize? Run in such a way that you'll win it. [25]Everyone who goes in for athletics exercises self-discipline in everything. They do it to gain a crown that perishes; we do it for an imperishable one. [26]Well then: I don't run in an aimless fashion! I don't box like someone punching the air! [27]No: I give my body rough treatment, and make it my slave, in case, after announcing the message to others, I myself should end up being disqualified.

Last night on the television news I saw a sight which might have been funny if it hadn't been so revolting. People, it seems, are getting bored with ordinary sports and games; so someone has had the bright idea of persuading (and presumably paying) people who are famous or notorious for quite other reasons to put on boxing kit and fight one another. First there were two men, former professional sportsmen long past their prime. Then, to my horror, there were two women, both of whom had been in the news because of something unpleasant or unsavoury. Needless to say they were hopeless boxers; they flailed around to make a spectacle, not to hurt each other. Male boxing is at best a sport that borders on ugliness and brutality. Female boxing seems to me quite abhorrent. Female boxing between two people whose only claim to fame is that they have been in the news for all the wrong reasons seems to drag entertainment down to . . . the level it was at in Paul's day.

Of course, there were serious athletes in the world Paul knew. People went into training, worked out techniques, developed particular skills and gained fame for it. But there was also a good deal of very low-level entertainment, involving fighting, often wounding, frequently killing. Sometimes it was humans against humans; sometimes it was humans against animals. Often the humans in question were criminals; this was a way of punishing them while making some entertainment for the crowds at the same time. Have we really advanced that far in the last two thousand years?

So Paul and his audience would have known the difference between those who box like serious professionals and those who box without any idea of what they're doing. That's the image he calls up in verse 26: of someone landing great punches, but none of them on the opponent's body – all of them on thin air. No, he says; the discipline of the Christian life requires strenuous moral effort. You have to learn how to play this game. It's no use just getting into the ring and hoping it'll all work out.

And the point is that the body needs to be brought into submission, into 'slavery' (verse 27). That's where the argument is going. All the much-boasted 'freedom' and 'rights' that some in Corinth were so keen on must give way before the needs of the work of the **gospel**. This will mean that many things the body wants to do, has a right (in theory) to do, and is 'free' to do, must be denied.

This message, we may well imagine, was about as popular in Corinth as it is today, that is, not popular at all. Western culture still tells its own story as the story of developing freedoms, and any attempt to speak of discipline, self-denial or the necessary abandonment of 'rights' is shouted down as a return to 'the dark ages' or 'the Middle Ages' (not that those doing the shouting often have much idea what those periods of history were actually like). The difficulty of saying what Paul needs to say here, and will go on to say in the chapter which immediately follows, may explain why he has taken so long to build up to it; but now that he's got to this point, he's determined they will hear it as strongly as he can say it. *The gospel will demand that you give up some of your 'rights' and 'freedoms', even if this feels like going into hard, athletic training.* Paul doesn't want to end up himself, and doesn't want his churches to end up, like people in a boxing ring who are simply waving their arms around. Far too much Christianity is like that today, and Paul saw the danger already: people making a lot of fuss about some things but doing none of the hard and demanding moral (or for that matter intellectual) work that would actually advance the gospel in their own lives and the world.

The other athletic image in this passage (verse 24) reinforces the point. There's no point entering the race unless you are going to go all out to win. And, says Paul, all they get when they win is a wreath that gathers dust and eventually moulders away! Compare that with the wreath you'll get if you go into proper training for the athletic contest of Christian living in a hostile pagan environment. Here we see, emerging from under Paul's argument, one of the major thrusts of the whole letter, which will eventually come into the spotlight in chapter 15: athletes, he says, go into training to win a *corruptible* wreath, but we do it to obtain an *incorruptible* one. He has his sights on nothing less than the renewal of all creation, the conquest and abolition of death itself. The Christian is called to live in the present as someone who will inherit that incorruptible, deathless new body when God makes the whole world new.

If we just read these verses by themselves, we might imagine that Paul thought the human body was a bad or wicked thing, perhaps even that the true God didn't make it. Some translations have Paul speaking in verse 27 of 'punishing' the body, which looks as though it's saying that sort of thing. But the word that appears as 'punish' in some translations simply means 'treat roughly'; it goes with Paul's picture of a boxing match, and the point of boxing is not to 'punish' the opponent in any legal sense. And from the rest of the letter we know that Paul doesn't mean the body is bad, however popular that idea became in some quarters after his time. The point of it all is not to get rid of the body, but to glorify God in it (6.20), and to prepare it for its true destiny, its union with the Lord, its **resurrection** (6.13–14; 15.35–49). But for this to happen the Christian cannot simply rely on the rhetoric of 'rights' and 'freedoms'. Paul's point here is that Christian obedience will often mean giving up supposed 'rights' and 'freedoms' in order to become the person God means us to become.

1 CORINTHIANS 10.1–5

The First Exodus

[1]I don't want you to be ignorant, my brothers and sisters, that our
fathers were all under the cloud and all went through the sea. [2]They
were all baptized into Moses in the cloud and in the sea. [3]They all ate

the same spiritual food [4]and drank the same spiritual drink. They
drank, you see, from the spiritual rock that followed them, and the
rock was the Messiah. [5]But God wasn't pleased with most of them, as
you can tell by the fact that he laid them low in the desert.

As you drive on the main road through central Northumberland, between Newcastle upon Tyne and the Scottish border, you see frequent signs saying things like '150 Accidents Last Year On This Road,' and 'Number of Speeding Fines Last Month: 37'. The message is clear: think about what happened last time – last year, last month, whenever – and make sure you don't become part of the next lot of statistics yourself.

Paul isn't concerned with statistics, but he is very concerned with history repeating itself. One of his main aims throughout this letter, coming to a climax in chapter 15, is to get the Corinthians to realize where they are on God's timetable. They are like actors who have blundered on to stage in the middle of a performance and don't even know which act they're in. They need to discover what's happened so far, how the plot is working out, and how the people who played these characters in previous acts managed to get things wrong.

So he tells them the story of the **Exodus** from Egypt. At least, he tells them certain selected highlights, carefully phrased in such a way as to say 'and you, of course, are in more or less the same position now'. He has already spoken of the **Messiah** as the 'Passover lamb', the one whose death has brought about the final, true Exodus from the slavery of sin and death (5.7). Now he develops the idea that Christians are the true Passover-people, the true Exodus people. But will they learn the lesson?

The four elements he draws attention to in the Exodus story are the cloud, the sea, the food and the drink. It will presently become obvious why he does this, but let's look inside the story for a minute and discover what's going on.

When the children of Israel left Egypt, they were led by a pillar of cloud by day, which turned into a pillar of fire by night. It was a symbol, and more than a symbol, a strange embodiment, of the presence of **YHWH**, their redeeming God, with them all the way, guiding, protecting and leading them to their inheritance. It led them through the waters of the Red Sea, which parted to let them through and closed again over the Egyptians who were chasing them. The cloud and the sea spoke of the presence of the living God and the passage from slavery to freedom.

No early Christian would have had much trouble decoding what Paul was saying. In case they did, he describes what happened like this, in verse 2: they were all 'baptized into Moses in the cloud and in the sea'. People didn't normally speak of the Exodus as a '**baptism**'; Paul is clearly telling the story so as to make his own point. And then we get the message: the cloud and the sea for the children of Israel are like the **spirit** and the baptism-water for Christians. Just as Jesus in John's **gospel** spoke of being born again 'by water and spirit' (John 3.5), so Paul can speak in this letter of the washing and the spirit (6.11) or baptism in the spirit (12.13). What he wants to say is that Christians are enacting the same drama as the children of Israel did.

It isn't just a parallel, as though similar events happen over and over again. It is also a sequence. The first Exodus established Israel as God's people, but Israel's story led to the decisive, one-off events concerning the Messiah, Jesus. Now Jesus' people are God's renewed Israel, and all those previous events are coming true in a new way in and through them. Or at least, they are supposed to be; but nothing happens automatically in the Christian life. Part of the way the fulfilment will be worked out is by the Christians realizing what part they are supposed to be playing and making sure they play it properly.

The children of Israel, then, were 'baptized into Moses', as Christians are 'baptized into the Messiah'. The foundational events of the cloud and the water, the presence of God and the crossing of the Red Sea, made the Israelites 'Moses's people', somewhat as baptism and the spirit make Christians 'the Messiah's people'. But then Paul adds the obvious third and fourth elements: they all ate the same food and drank the same drink – the 'spiritual' food and drink that God provided for them in the wilderness. This doesn't of course mean that the food and drink weren't real. Rather, it means that they were provided by God through the spirit. They didn't just 'occur naturally'. And once we realize that Paul, in verse 2, is drawing the parallel between the crossing of the Red Sea and Christian baptism, we should have no difficulty in realizing that in verse 3 he is making the similar parallel between God's provision of special food for his people on the journey to their inheritance and God's provision of the food and drink of the special Christian meal, the 'Lord's supper', the **eucharist**.

The point Paul is working towards then comes into view. All the Israelites had these experiences, just as all you Corinthians have had. *But God was displeased with most of them.* It is a terrible warning not to presume on God's kindness.

Why is Paul saying this at this point? Because he is preparing the ground for his double appeal, which finally emerges in verses 14–22 and 23—11.1. Like someone constructing a great building, he has to do quite a bit of work on the foundations, which won't look anything like the building itself, so that when the building itself goes up it will stand firmly in place. The building he wants to put up is his challenge to the Corinthians to appreciate the privilege they have in sharing the bread and the wine of the eucharist, and the responsibilities that go with that. And part of the foundation of that building is the earlier Exodus-story in which the privileges Israel received were not, alas, matched by responsible behaviour. God was displeased with them, and he laid them low, or 'overthrew' them, in the wilderness.

In other words, you must not presume that because you are baptized Christians, sharing in the community life where the spirit is known and present, and eating and drinking the bread and wine of the eucharist, you have automatically reached a level that requires no further moral effort or restraint. Paul has a strong view of baptism and the eucharist: baptism really does bring you into the Messiah's family, and the eucharist really does let you share in the life of the crucified and risen Jesus (verse 16). But Christian sacraments are not magic. They don't automatically make you holy in all other respects. They don't automatically bring you salvation. On the contrary; precisely because they are huge privileges, they carry corresponding responsibilities. Just as the children of Israel went slack on their responsibilities and so lost the privileges – almost all of them failed to reach the promised land – so Paul is anxious that the Corinthians who are insisting on their 'rights' and 'freedom' may slide back into paganism and so fail to make real for themselves the full Christian inheritance they have been promised. If even Paul himself needs to engage in a boxing match with his own body, in case he might find himself disqualified from God's **kingdom** after having announced the **message** to others, how much more must the Corinthians be prepared to live out the life to which baptism and eucharist point.

Two striking features of this little passage demand a further note.

First, in verse 1, Paul describes the Israelites as 'our fathers'. He understands the church, the Messiah's people, composed as it was mostly of ex-pagan **Gentiles**, as the 'children' of the Israelites. The church has not 'replaced' Israel in God's purposes; the Messiah fulfils and completes what Israel was called to be, and all those who belong to the Messiah are now God's people, heirs of Abraham, Isaac, Jacob and the people of the Exodus.

Second, Paul speaks in verse 4 of the 'spiritual rock' that followed the Israelites in the wilderness, and declares that 'the rock was the Messiah'. Although the biblical story only records two incidents where water came out of the rock for the people to drink, some Jewish writers imagined that a rock, filled with water, had followed the people all the way. Paul, simply in order to make his point, that Christians are those who share in the food and drink which is the Messiah's gift of his own self, goes along with this fanciful reading of the text, but insists that what was really going on was the hidden presence of the Messiah himself, the goal of all Israel's wanderings, and their refreshment on the way. As always, what Paul most badly wants is for Christians to realize, and live up to, all the blessings which are theirs because they belong to the Messiah.

1 CORINTHIANS 10.6–13

Don't Make the Same Mistake Again!

6Now these things were patterns for us, so that we should not start to
crave for wicked things as they did. 7Nor should we commit idolatry,
as some of them did – as the Bible says, 'The people sat down to eat
and drink, and got up to play.' 8Nor should we become immoral, like
some of them became immoral, and twenty-three thousand fell on a
single day. 9Nor should we put the Messiah to the test, as some of
them put him to the test, and were destroyed by serpents. 10Nor
should we grumble, as some of them grumbled and were destroyed by
the destroyer.

11Now these things happened to them as a pattern, and they were
written for our instruction, since it's upon us that the ends of the ages
have now come. 12As a result, anyone who reckons they are standing
upright should watch out in case they fall over. 13Every test that comes
upon you is normal for human beings. But God is faithful: he won't let
you be tested beyond your ability. Along with the testing, he will provide the way of escape, so that you can bear it.

We got on a bus in a strange city the other day, and to our horror it started to go in quite the wrong direction. Since we don't speak much of the language it was difficult to ask other passengers, still less the driver, what was going on, but we decided to sit tight and see what happened. What we didn't know was that there was a street fair blocking the main road we had expected to go down. Once the bus had gone a mile or so out of its normal route it gradually began to work back towards the destination we expected. Familiar landmarks began to appear. Finally we ended up where we had hoped, only about ten minutes later than would have normally been the case.

Paul is now working back to the destination of his argument, the long discussion that began at the start of chapter 8; and this is where one or two familiar landmarks begin to appear. The key thing is the mention of idolatry in verse 7; this is the first problem he names that needs watching out for. Everything else hinges on this. The problem of chapter 8 was the relationship Christians should have with pagan temples. Paul has agreed in principle that the food offered to an idol is no better or worse than any other, and he will come back to that point at the end of the chapter; but the real issue for him is whether the 'strong' Christians in Corinth, who insist on their rights and freedoms and look down on those with tender consciences, are going to find themselves drawn back into paganism itself.

We should notice, as we look at this issue from all angles, that for Paul the behaviour which a Christian should avoid is not simply a matter of disobedience to a few rules. It is deeper than that (though rules can often help to focus the issue). It is a matter of desires that well up from inside a person and reach out to objects, and styles of life, which reflect and copy forces, powers and even divinities other than the one true God made known in Jesus the **Messiah**. This comes out clearly in Paul's introductory comment: the story of Israel in the wilderness serves as a pattern for us, so that we should not become 'evil-cravers', people who yearn and hanker and lust after things which don't honour God and won't do us any good.

The four things he mentions are all things which 'some' of the Israelites did (as opposed to the 'all' he mentions in verses 1–4). Idolatry, as we saw, heads the list, though at first sight the quotation Paul uses from Exodus 32.6 doesn't seem to mention it. The word 'play', however, is the key; that word was used as a polite way of referring to the kind of orgy which the Israelites engaged in on that occasion, and which Paul knew was all too frequently the habit around pagan temples and festivals. And the point he is making is the basic one for his whole argument: whatever else you do or don't do about meat that has been sacrificed, it must be clear that idolatry itself, and the behaviour which regularly accompanies it, is completely off limits. (See the next passage as well.)

Within the subculture of idolatry, sexual immorality is one of the most obvious features, and that's the next thing he mentions. Notoriously, the Israelites engaged in large-scale orgies with Moabite women (Numbers 25). This in turn led them to worship the Moabite deities, with the result that a large number of them were killed. Paul has already had a fair amount to say by way of warning against sexual immorality in chapters 5 and 6, and does not need to elaborate further at this point.

The Israelites' tendency to go off after other gods resulted in them appearing to stage a contest between **YHWH** and his apparent rivals, almost as a trial of strength. Was YHWH really capable of looking after them? Since Paul, as we saw in verse 4, believed that the Messiah himself was strangely present with the people in the wilderness, he can express this as 'putting the Messiah to the test' (verse 9); he seems to have Numbers 21 in mind, since that is the time when the Israelites complained that YHWH could not look after them, and were attacked by serpents for their pains. Paul will come back to this point in verse 22: we must not, he says, create situations where we are placing the Messiah on a trial of strength. We might not like the results.

Finally, in verse 10, he warns (as in Philippians 2.14) against the kind of grumbling which the Israelites regularly engaged in, wishing they'd never left Egypt in the first place and suggesting they might go back there. This is of course the point Paul is getting at. Having escaped from paganism by being embraced by God's love in the **gospel**, do you really want to exercise your 'freedom', your 'rights', to do anything at all – including, metaphorically speaking, going 'back to Egypt'? Of course not.

He draws the discussion together by reminding them that the biblical stories are not just interesting illustrations of moral and religious truths. They are the earlier parts of a long narrative that has now reached its climax in the Messiah and in the people who have come to belong to him through the gospel. They – we! – are the people 'upon whom the ends of the ages have come', the people who live in the strange period of history when God's long-awaited fulfilment has begun to appear, in Jesus and the **spirit**, even as the old age rumbles on to its close.

But living in this overlap period has its dangers, not least that the 'freedom' which comes within the now-appearing new age can be confused with the 'licence' that drags you back into the old. This produces times of testing, in which there is no room for pride. At any moment the great hero of **faith**, the man or woman who has won battles in prayer, the person who has given their all for a particular venture of the gospel, may be suddenly and horribly vulnerable. 'Anyone who thinks they are standing should watch out in case they fall over.' As the old age and the new grind against one another like two tectonic plates, those who think they are standing firm one minute may find a moral earthquake happening all around them, and if they're not careful they'll end up flat on their faces.

Paul's wonderful promise in verse 13, though, reaches out to all who face severe testing and temptation (the two English words reflect different aspects of Paul's single word). The temptations you will run into are the common lot of all human beings. *But God is faithful!* – words to be carved in letters of gold on the memory and imagination of all Christians. He will make a way of avoiding the temptation.

The question facing Paul was: will the Corinthians avail themselves of this God-given way out, when they need it? And the question facing us, in the increasingly pagan atmosphere of our contemporary world, is: will we?

1 CORINTHIANS 10.14–22

The Table of the Lord and the Table of Demons

[14]Therefore, my dear people, run away from idolatry. [15]I'm speaking as
to intelligent people: you yourselves must weigh my words. [16]The cup
of blessing which we bless is a sharing in the Messiah's blood, isn't it?
The bread we break is a sharing in the Messiah's body, isn't it? [17]There
is one loaf; well, then, there may be several of us, but we are one body,
because we all share the one loaf.

[18]Consider ethnic Israel. Those who eat from the sacrifices share in
the altar, don't they? [19]So what am I saying? That idol-food is real, or
that an idol is a real being? [20]No: but when they offer sacrifices, they
offer them to demons, not to God. And *I don't want you to be table-partners with demons.* [21]You can't drink the cup of the Lord and the
cup of demons. You can't share in the table of the Lord and the table
of demons. [22]Surely you don't want to provoke the Lord to jealousy?
We aren't stronger than him, are we?

'Christianity', declared the great Archbishop William Temple, 'is the most materialistic of all religions.' He had in mind the commitment of genuine Christianity to the **faith** that God really became human in Jesus of Nazareth, and all that follows from that in terms of the Christian's commitment to bringing the **kingdom of God**, as Jesus taught us to pray, on earth as in **heaven**. But in the present passage we see another aspect of just how 'materialistic' the Christian faith really is. Some may find it worrying, and it's no bad thing to ask why.

What Paul wants to get across above all else is that there is real danger for Christians in having anything to do with idolatry. As he said about sexual immorality in 6.18, the best course is not to argue with it, not to examine it to see whether it's really as bad as you thought, but to get out and run. Treat it as if it were an infectious and deadly disease – as indeed, in a sense, it is. And, again as with sexual morality, people have a tendency to think that because Christianity is about things of the **spirit**, what they do with their body doesn't matter.

Paul had to make it clear in chapter 6 that there is no such thing as casual sex. That's not how God's world works. Human bodies are not toys; they are vehicles, expressions, of an entire person, made in God's image. Now, in the present passage, which in some ways is parallel to chapter 6, he has to make it clear that there's no such thing as casual worship. The material world, including food and drink, isn't just useful to sustain human and animal life. It can become the vehicle, the expression, of the god or goddess, or the God, you are worshipping in eating it.

Paul seems to be arguing this somewhat cautiously, because he says in verse 15 that they will need to think through what he's saying. No doubt he could have said more, and those of us who try to think and teach about the meaning of the Lord's supper or **eucharist** wish he had. But we can still learn a good deal from what he does say.

His argument is that because in the Lord's supper we really do share in the body and blood of the **Messiah**, making us a united body in him, and because in national or ethnic Israel those who worship at the **Temple** really do become 'sharers in the altar', which seems to mean 'people who share the very life of God', then by analogy those who worship, including eating and drinking, in the temple of an idol may well be becoming 'partners', 'sharers', with the idol itself.

Paul knows that this is difficult to grasp. Didn't he agree earlier that 'an idol has no real existence' (8.4)? Yes; but now he warns that, though the 'god' in the shrine is nothing more than a man-made statue of gold, silver, or whatever, there are evil forces, demonic powers, that use the worship offered to the non-gods in order to gain power over both the worshippers themselves and the world around. And the crunch of his argument is that those who sit at the Messiah's table and share in his **life**, the life, that is, of the human embodiment of the one true God, cannot and must not flirt with the possibility of sharing the life of the powers, the malevolent 'forces' as we call them, that twist and distort God's world and God's image-bearing human children.

To use your 'freedom', your 'rights', to switch to and fro between the Messiah, in whom the world is rescued from evil, and evil forces that are trying to claw it back again, is sheer madness. At the very least, it amounts to doing what Israel did in the wilderness, 'putting the Messiah to the test' (verse 22; see verse 9). Nobody in their right mind should doubt that in a trial of strength between the Messiah, through whom death itself was defeated in his **resurrection**, and the dark forces that still try to win back some hold on the world, the Messiah would come out best. Paul declares in ringing tones (15.23–28) that that is indeed what will happen at the end. But nobody in their right mind would want to become, in their own person, the battlefield on which that trial of strength will be acted out.

We should pause here for a moment and reflect on the significance of what he's said, in three areas in particular.

First, when he speaks of '**demons**' as being involved when idols are worshipped, he doesn't think of such beings as somehow equal and opposite to God or the Messiah. These are semi-personal spiritual 'forces' or 'powers'. To see them still at work today you only have to look at what happens when people allow money, or war, or sex, to drive them in directions they would never ordinarily dream of going. Some recent writers have pointed out that large corporations or businesses have a sense of a 'force' that's driving them, imposing its will, despite the fact that most of the people sitting behind desks may not really intend to go that way. Once you invoke the powers, they may well take over.

Paul is careful not to say too much about these powers. He doesn't want the Corinthian Christians to get too interested in them, and doesn't claim to know all that much about what precisely they are. Enough to know, as we are rediscovering in our own day even in the secularized Western world, that there are evil forces, that it's possible for humans to give them power by worshipping them, and that the whole subculture of idol-worship, drunken orgies and the like is the kind of seedbed in which that power grows best.

Second, we notice once again, as we did in verses 1–5, that Paul's argument in verse 18 depends on 'ethnic Israel' being contrasted with a different Israel, presumably the fulfilled people of God in the Messiah. Paul does not say, in this letter, much more about how the identity of God's people is worked out, but what he says is enough to drive us to read Romans 9—11, the passage where he goes into most detail about it, to find out more.

Third, we should not miss the importance of what Paul says about the eating and drinking of the bread and wine in the Lord's supper or eucharist. He will say more about it in chapter 11; indeed, the order in which he's dealing with topics throughout the letter is not accidental, but rather provides a set of building-blocks, so that by discussing one necessary topic he is preparing the way for the next. But already we can see that Paul really believes that the material elements of the Christian family meal, the bread and the wine, do become vessels or vehicles of the personal life of the Messiah himself. 'The cup of blessing which we bless, it's a sharing in the Messiah's blood, isn't it? The bread which we break, it's a sharing in the Messiah's body, isn't it?' That, of course, is why those who share this cup and loaf become one body, the Messiah's body; they are all together nourished by his own personal life. One of the greatest tragedies in the history of the church is that, because of all the doctrinal disputes that have taken place over the central Christian meal, many teachers and preachers have thought it best not to say too much about what it means, and hence have not educated people into the full enjoyment of a central part of their birthright.

1 CORINTHIANS 10.23—11.1

Do Everything to God's Glory

[23]'Everything is lawful', but not everything is helpful. 'Everything is lawful', but not everything builds you up. [24]Nobody should seek their own advantage, but the other person's instead.

[25]Eat whatever is sold in the market without making any judgments
on the basis of conscience. [26]'The earth and its fullness', after all,
'belong to the Lord'. [27]If one of the unbelievers invites you to dinner,
and you want to go, eat whatever is put in front of you without mak-
ing any judgments on the basis of conscience. [28]But if someone says
'This was offered in sacrifice', then don't eat it – because of the person
who told you about it, and because of conscience, [29]by which I don't
mean your own conscience, but your neighbour's. For why should my
freedom be condemned by someone else's conscience? [30]If I eat my
share gratefully, why should someone else speak evil of me because of
something I've given thanks for?

[31]So, then, whether you eat or drink or whatever you do, do every-
thing to God's glory. [32]Be blameless before Jews and Greeks and the
church of God, [33]just as I try to please everybody in everything, not
pursuing my own advantage, but that of the great majority, so that
they may be saved.

[11.1]Copy me, just as I'm copying the Messiah.

Some birds seem to spend all day in tiny, small-scale activities. They busy themselves with making nests, grubbing for food, and squawking to each other within a small space. They seem to be severely practical: everything they do has an immediate object, another little detail in the mosaic of their daily lives.

Other birds seem to spend all day in great, soaring, wide-ranging flight. You can watch them sometimes, riding thermal currents by a cliff or a hill. No doubt they sometimes stop for food, nesting and rearing their young. But for much of the time they seem to be simply taking delight in their ability to float in leisurely fashion over miles of countryside, seeing more of the world with a single glance of those sharp eyes than the average house sparrow sees in a month.

Some people are more like sparrows; others are more like eagles (or perhaps vultures). And some teachers are like the one, or like the other, too. Some teachers are always giving more and more practical details, a wealth of little bits and pieces which you're meant to fit together into the mosaic of truth you're trying to learn. Other teachers give you soaring great platitudes, big general truths that sound fine and inspiring. The trouble is, of course, that the house-sparrow type of teacher often never gets round to giving you the big picture; if you come upon a problem you've not been told about, how will you know what to do? And the eagle/vulture type of teacher, too, may never get round to showing you how the great truths work out in practice when you leave the classroom and walk out onto the street.

It is a mark of Paul's genius that he knows how to be both kinds of teacher, and both types of teaching are right here in this conclusion to the discussion that began in chapter 8. The middle bit of the passage (verses 27–30) deals with the little details: what's likely to happen at a dinner party, the different reactions people may have, how to handle the situation, how to work out priorities. But this is held in place by the basic principles he states in verses 23–26, which can be applied in all sorts of ways, and by the grand conclusion to the section in verses 31–33 and the first verse of chapter 11. (The chapter-divisions in the Bible were, of course, added centuries after the books were written, and here as in some other places they are misleading. The first verse of chapter 11 is the end of the present discussion, not the start of the next one.)

Look at the house-sparrow detail first. Paul imagines a dinner party given by a non-Christian in Corinth. Ancient houses, especially when parties were given, were more open than modern ones; it was quite easy for people to walk in off the street and make comments. Paul wants the Christians to be free to eat whatever is put in front of them without fussing about where it's come from. This is the 'strong' position, based on the principles of verses 25 and 26, which we'll come to in a moment. But if someone else – another Christian, we presume – points out anxiously that the meat had come from an idol-temple, and was thus (in their eyes) tainted, reminding them of the idol-worship they used to take part in, then, says Paul, you should have respect for that person's conscience, and abstain from eating. But in the second half of verse 29, and in verse 30, he is quite clear that you can't legislate for all cases on the basis of the scruples of conscience that some people still have. As a general rule, saying a prayer of thanks to the one true God indicates that the food on the table is morally fit for a Christian to eat. The same point is made in 1 Timothy 4.4–5.

This is clearly a moral halfway house. Paul would prefer it if all Christians could be educated to the 'strong' position. But, as we saw when looking at 8.7–13, consciences aren't like that. You can't re-educate them overnight, or by a simple order. As with many things, the Christian is called to live in a world where there are some great moral absolutes and some grey areas in between. Problems arise not just when people get confused over which is which but when people who like absolutes try to eliminate grey areas, and people who like grey areas try to eliminate absolutes.

But absolutes there are, and we meet them at either end of this passage, rising above the mists of difficult cases. To begin with, Paul repeats the slogan-and-answer format from 6.12. All things are lawful, but not all things are helpful, and not all things 'build up' either the individual or the church. This remains fundamental. You can't argue from your own theoretical freedom to a freedom-to-do-anything-at-all. For a start, it is constrained by your overriding obligation to your neighbour (verse 24). But when that is taken into account the vital principle can be stated (verses 25–26): eat anything that is sold in the meat market; don't raise questions about it; because, as the wonderful Psalm 24 declares, the earth and everything in it belongs to the Lord. This is classic monotheism, Jewish-style, at its best: robust, intelligent, wholehearted. God made everything and he made it good. As with holiness and pollution in 7.12–16, God's holiness doesn't need protecting. Goodness is, after all, more powerful than evil.

But we shouldn't miss the point. In verses 14–22 he was quite clear that Christians should not go near idol-worship. No eating in temples, then. Now he says you may buy and eat anything sold in the meat-market. That's the difference: as one recent writer puts it, it's the difference between venue and menu. The place is off limits, the food isn't.

The great conclusion sums up everything a Christian needs to know about a holy life before the watching world. Whatever you do, do it to God's glory! At the same time, do not give offence, in so far as that is possible, to any of the three categories into which the world is now divided: Jews, Greeks and God's church. Easier said than done, someone will reply (to Paul, and no doubt to me). Yes, but once you've seen the grand sweep, the eagle's-eye view, you are then welcome to swoop down and look at the details of application.

To help his readers do that, Paul reminds them of the basic rule of life which he knew he was giving them when he was with them. He always tried to do what was best for others, not for himself, and in that he had been copying the **Messiah** himself (see Romans 15.2–3). They must now learn to copy him. If all Christian teachers had it in mind that their hearers were also observers, and that the lessons they learned with the eye would be the ones that would go deepest, the **gospel** might have advanced further and faster.

1 CORINTHIANS 11.2–16

Male and Female in the Worshipping Church

[2]I congratulate you that you are remembering me in everything, and
you are keeping the traditions as I handed them on to you. [3]But I
want you to know this: that the Messiah is the 'head' of every man,
and the husband is the 'head' of every wife, and God is the 'head' of
the Messiah. [4]Every man who prays or prophesies while wearing
something on his head brings shame on his 'head'; [5]and every woman
who prays or prophesies with her head uncovered brings shame on
her 'head'. It would be just the same if she had her head shaved. [6]For
if a woman isn't covered, then she should be shaved; but if it's shame-

ful for a woman to have her hair cut off or her head shaved, then let her be covered.

[7]A man ought not to cover his head, you see; he is the image and glory of God. But a wife is the glory of her husband. [8]For man was not made from woman, but woman from man. [9]And man was not created for the sake of woman, but woman for the sake of man. [10]That's why the wife must have authority on her head, because of the angels. [11]However, woman is not apart from man, nor man apart from woman, in the Lord; [12]for just as woman came from man, so now man comes into the world by means of woman. And everything is from God.

[13]Judge the matter for yourselves. Is it really appropriate for a woman to pray to God with her head uncovered? [14]Doesn't nature itself teach you that if a man has long hair, it is shameful to him, [15]but if a woman has long hair, it's her glory? Her hair is given her, you see, instead of a covering. [16]If anyone wants to dispute this, we have no other custom, nor do the churches of God.

Many years ago I was lecturing as a guest in a college in the United States. After my lecture I was told that several of the students had been studying St Paul; would I be happy to answer questions about particular passages and topics? I readily agreed.

What I hadn't realized was that many of the women students had been taught that Paul was a woman-hater, and that this present passage was the most obvious example of his prejudice. Now I have to admit that I didn't understand this passage then, and I'm not sure I've understood it yet. But I think we can see the main point Paul wanted to make, even if the reasons why he's put it like this may still be puzzling.

Paul wasn't, of course, addressing the social issues we know in our world. Visit a different culture, even today, and you will discover many subtle assumptions, pressures and constraints in society, some of which appear in the way people dress and wear their hair. In Western culture, a man wouldn't go to a dinner party wearing a bathing suit, nor would a woman attend a beach picnic wearing a wedding dress. Most Western churches have stopped putting pressure on women to wear hats in church (Western-style hats, in any case, were not what Paul was writing about here), but nobody thinks it odd that we are still strict about men *not* wearing hats in church.

In Paul's day (as, in many ways, in ours), gender was marked by hair and clothing styles. We can tell from statues, vase paintings and other artwork of the period how this worked out in practice. There was social pressure to maintain appropriate distinctions. But did not Paul himself teach that there was 'no male and female, because you are all one in the **Messiah**' (Galatians 3.28)? Perhaps, indeed, that was one of the 'traditions' that he had taught the Corinthian church, who needed to know that Jew and Greek, slave and free, male and female were all equally welcome, equally valued, in the renewed people of God. Perhaps that had actually created the situation he is addressing here; perhaps some of the Corinthian women had been taking him literally, so that when they prayed or prophesied aloud in church meetings (which Paul assumes they will do regularly; this tells us something about how to understand 14.34–35) they had decided to remove their normal headcovering, perhaps also unbraiding their hair, to show that in the Messiah they were free from the normal social conventions by which men and women were distinguished.

That's a lot of 'perhaps'es. We can only guess at the dynamics of the situation – which is of course what historians always do. It's just that here we are feeling our way in the dark more than usual. But, perhaps to the Corinthians' surprise, Paul doesn't congratulate the women on this new expression of freedom. He insists on maintaining gender differentiation during worship.

Another dimension to the problem may well be that in the Corinth of his day the only women who appeared in public without some kind of headcovering were prostitutes. This isn't suggested directly here, but it may have been in the back of his mind. If the watching world discovered that the Christians were having meetings where women 'let their hair down' in this fashion, it could have the same effect on their reputation as it would in the modern West if someone looked into a church and found the women all wearing bikinis.

The trouble is, of course, that Paul doesn't say exactly this, and we run the risk of 'explaining' him in terms that might (perhaps) make sense to us while ignoring what he himself says. It's tempting to do that, precisely because in today's Western world we don't like the implications of the differentiation he maintains in verse 3: the Messiah is the 'head' of every man, a husband is the 'head' of every woman, and the 'head' of the Messiah is God. This seems to place man in a position of exactly that assumed superiority against which women have rebelled, often using Galatians 3.28 as their battle-cry.

But what does Paul mean by 'head'? He uses it here sometimes in a metaphorical sense, as in verse 3, and sometimes literally, as when he's talking about what to do with actual human heads (verses 4–7 and 10). But the word he uses can mean various different things; and a good case can be made out for saying that in verse 3 he is referring not to 'headship' in the sense of sovereignty, but to 'headship' in the sense of 'source', like the 'source' or 'head' of a river. In fact, in some of the key passages where he explains what he's saying (verses 8, 9 and 12a) he is referring explicitly to the creation story in Genesis 2, where woman was made from the side of man.

The underlying point then seems to be that in worship it is important for both men and women to be their truly created selves, to honour God by being what they are and not blurring the lines by pretending to be something else. One of the unspoken clues to this passage may be Paul's assumption that in worship the creation is being restored, or perhaps that in worship we are anticipating its eventual restoration (15.27–28). God made humans male and female, and gave them 'authority' over the world, as Ben Sirach 17.3 puts it, summarizing Genesis 1.26–28 and echoing Psalm 8.4–8 (Ben Sirach was written around 200 BC). And if humans are to reclaim this authority over the world, this will come about as they worship the true God, as they pray and prophesy in his name, and are renewed in his image, in being what they were made to be, in celebrating the genders God has given them.

If this is Paul's meaning, the critical move he makes is to argue that a man dishonours his head by covering it in worship and that a woman dishonours hers by *not* covering it. He argues this mainly from the basis that creation itself tends to give men shorter hair and women longer (verses 5–6, 13–15); the fact that some cultures, and some people, offer apparent exceptions would probably not have worried him. His main point is that in worship men should follow the dress and hair codes which proclaim them to be male, and women the codes which proclaim them to be female.

Why then does he say that a woman 'must have authority on her head because of the angels' (verse 10)? This is one of the most puzzling verses in a puzzling passage, but there is help of sorts in the **Dead Sea Scrolls.** There it is assumed that when God's people meet for worship, the angels are there too (as many liturgies, and theologians, still affirm).

For the Scrolls, this means that the angels, being holy, must not be offended by any appearance of unholiness among the congregation. Paul shares the assumption that the angels are worshipping along with the humans, but may be making a different point.

When humans are renewed in the Messiah and raised from the dead, they will be set in authority over the angels (6.3). In worship, the church anticipates how things are going to be in that new day. When a woman is praying or prophesying (perhaps in the language of angels, as in 13.1), she needs to be truly what she is, since it is to male and female alike, in their mutual interdependence as God's image-bearing creatures, that the world, including the angels, is to be subject. God's creation needs humans to be fully, gloriously and truly human, which means fully and truly male and female. This, and of course much else besides, is to be glimpsed in worship.

The Corinthians, then, may have drawn the wrong conclusion from the 'tradition' that Paul had taught them. Whether or not they could follow his argument any better than we can, it seems clear that his main aim was that the marks of difference between the sexes should not be set aside in worship. At least perhaps.

We face different issues, but making sure that our worship is ordered appropriately, to honour God's creation and anticipate its fulfilment in the new creation, is still a priority. There is no 'perhaps' about that.

1 CORINTHIANS 11.17–22

Rich and Poor at the Table of the Lord

> [17]What I have to talk about now isn't a matter for praise. When you
> meet together, you make things worse, not better! [18]What I mean is
> this: to begin with, I hear that when you come together in the assembly
> there are divisions among you. Well, I believe it – at least partly. [19]There
> are bound to be groupings among you; that's how the genuine ones
> among you will stand out, I suppose! [20]So when you gather together
> into one meeting, it isn't the Lord's Supper that you eat. [21]Everyone
> brings their own food to eat, and one person goes hungry while
> another gets drunk. [22]Haven't you got houses to eat and drink in? Or
> do you despise God's assembly, and shame those who have nothing?
> What shall I say to you? Shall I praise you? No, in this matter I shan't!

The school groundsman was working to get the sports field ready for the big match the next day. The same pitch had been used for both hockey and football, and he needed to be sure that it was now marked out afresh with the right lines for tomorrow's football game.

But early on he made a small mistake and crossed from one line to the other. His eye was so firmly fixed on the ground ahead of him, marking the lines straight, that he didn't realize. Only when he had finished, and stood up and looked at the whole field, did he realize what he had done. He had rubbed out the lines he should have been drawing more clearly, and he had drawn more clearly the lines he should have rubbed out.

Paul now has to tell the Corinthians that, if they have been blurring the lines between male and female which should have been clearly marked (11.2–16), in another area they were marking out clearly a line which should have been obliterated altogether. When they are coming together to celebrate the Lord's meal, the 'supper' or '**eucharist**', they are reinforcing a social distinction which has nothing to do with God's intention in creation, and nothing to do, either, with God's achievement of salvation through the **Messiah**. This is the division between rich and poor, which ran like an ugly line through ancient society as much as in our own if not more, and which threatened to deface the very celebration at which the church's unity in the Messiah ought to have been most apparent.

He begins, as in chapter 1, by commenting that there are divisions among them when they meet together. He isn't surprised at this, he says; there are bound to be different groups within the church. It isn't clear whether he intends verse 19 at face value, or whether he is speaking sarcastically. It has often been taken as a serious comment, in which case he means that, whether we like it or not, there are some in the church who are genuine Christians and some who aren't, and the genuine ones will seek each other out. But I'm inclined to think he means it sarcastically: 'Oh, yes, I'm sure there are parties in your church – after all, you'll want to make sure the really important people stand out, won't you!' This does not, in other words, look like a comment on the same parties and groups that he was talking about in chapters 1—4. It's a wry statement about the sort of divisive attitudes he might have known he could expect from people of the sort that the Corinthians, under their oh-so-wise leaders and teachers, were in danger of becoming.

The present problem was coming to light when the church met for the particular act of worship which Paul refers to here as 'the Lord's meal', or, more literally, 'the meal that has to do with the Lord'. If it wasn't for this passage and the next one, and verses 16, 17 and 21 of chapter 10, we wouldn't have known anything about Paul's views on this meal, or even that his churches practised it; but what he says here reveals that 'the Lord's meal' was a central and vital symbolic action in the churches he founded, based on traditions going back to Jesus himself, and already carrying a substantial and serious theological meaning.

In almost all churches today, the eucharist has remained central, and these passages are our earliest written witness to what was believed and taught about it. The **gospels**, though telling stories about Jesus himself, were almost certainly written down some time after Paul's letters. Of course, Christians have developed different names for this meal: 'holy communion', 'the mass', 'the Lord's supper', as well as 'eucharist'. These names all have their place and point, but if we become divisive over them we miss exactly the point Paul is making.

When you go to church today for this service, you almost certainly won't get a whole meal. The normal practice for centuries has been to provide a *token* or symbolic meal, a small piece of bread or wafer, and a small sip of wine. (In some churches, only the clergy drink the wine.) But to begin with, as with the Last Supper itself, the meal took place in private houses, not in a special 'church' building. And there was a full meal served, during which special words were said over a particular loaf of bread and a particular cup of wine. The problem in Corinth was that this full meal had become a sign of the social divisions that ran through the church.

Imagine going on a picnic with a large group of friends. Suppose when you get to the picnic spot some people get out elaborate hampers with expensive cutlery and glass, and serve themselves delicious and lavish food and fine wines, while other people sitting alongside them have brought a couple of small sandwiches and a bottle of water. Even at a picnic that wouldn't seem right. How much more when you're meeting for worship, and the people you're with are not just friends, they are your brothers and sisters, members of your family; because all those who belong to the Messiah form a single family, indeed, as Paul will shortly explain, a single body. 'One goes hungry while another gets drunk!' (verse 21). Is that really an expression of what God's people actually are?

This problem will have been reinforced by the social customs of the time. Many rich people in the ancient world prided themselves on showing hospitality to those less well off, but they often did so in a way which let the others know they were inferior, and even made them feel ashamed. Sometimes they had a small main dining room for themselves and their closest friends, where excellent food and wine would be served, and another room, or a sequence of rooms, with food and drink of poorer quality. It seems that in Corinth the rich hosts whose houses were large enough for a Christian meeting were continuing this social practice at 'the Lord's supper' itself.

Paul sees this as doing two things. First, it shows contempt for God's church, God's assembled people, regarding this assembly as a mere convenience, a point at which one's own spiritual (and social!) advantage may be furthered, but with little significance beyond that. Second, it shows not just contempt for those who have nothing, but actually, whether intentionally or not, a desire to put them to shame. Rich people, alas, are all too often ready, in little ways or great, to send the signal that they are a superior form of human life to the poor – when often it is the merest accident of birth, or of being in one place at one moment rather than another, that has brought riches to the one and poverty to the other.

Paul will go on in the next passage to explain more about what the eucharist actually is, and why such behaviour is completely out of line at it. But already we should have food for thought about the church's life and its meeting for worship. We don't usually have services at which a whole meal is served, and if we do we normally make sure everyone has the same. But do we have other ways, in our churches, fellowships and assemblies, in which we allow wealth and poverty to send the same signals that they send in the rest of society? If so, what are we going to do about it?

1 CORINTHIANS 11.23–34

Recognizing the Body

[23]This, you see, is what I received from the Lord, and handed on to you. On the night when the Lord Jesus was betrayed, he took bread, [24]gave thanks, broke it, and said, 'This is my body; it's for you! Do this in remembrance of me.' [25]He did the same with the cup after supper, and said, 'This cup is the new covenant in my blood. Whenever you drink it, do this in remembrance of me.' [26]For whenever you eat this bread and drink the cup, you are announcing the Lord's death until he comes.

[27]It follows from this that anyone who eats the bread or drinks the cup of the Lord in an unworthy manner will be guilty of the body and blood of the Lord. [28]Everyone should test themselves; that's how you should eat the bread and drink the cup. [29]You see, if you eat and drink without recognizing the body, you eat and drink judgment on yourself. [30]That's why several of you are weak and sick, and some have died. [31]But if we learned how to judge ourselves, we would not incur judgment. [32]But when we are judged by the Lord, we are punished, so that we won't be condemned along with the world.

[33]So, my brothers and sisters, when you come together to eat, treat one another as honoured guests by waiting for each other. [34]If anyone is hungry, they should eat at home, so that you don't come together and find yourselves facing judgment. I will put the other matters in order when I come.

I once witnessed a moving reconciliation scene, and the most moving thing about it was that no words were necessary. A lay minister had been storing up resentments against the clergyman who was the senior pastor in the church where they both worked. All sorts of issues had increased the tension, and there was a real danger of a complete and damaging break. But through various means, including prayer, the resentments were dealt with, and at the appropriate moment in the service one Sunday morning the layman, in front of everyone, went to the clergyman and gave him the sign of peace; not just a formal handshake, but a huge hug that went on a long time. Nothing needed to be said. Doing it said it.

There are of course many occasions in ordinary life when doing something makes a powerful statement. A handshake at the end of a business deal. The 'black power' salute given by some athletes at the Olympic Games when racial tension was at its height. A president getting out of his formal car and mingling freely with the crowds. We talk these days of actions which 'send symbolic messages', and we have come to learn that those messages are often the ones which really count, the ones which tell you what's really going on, underneath whatever words may or may not be spoken. And at the heart of this passage is Paul's explanation of the symbolic message that is sent when Christians meet together to eat the bread and drink the cup in obedience to Jesus' command.

This is, of course, the earliest written record of what happened on the night Jesus was 'handed over' to his death. The **gospels** were written up later, but they, like Paul, looked back to very early 'traditions' (verse 23) which the church told and retold as the foundation of their common life. The story of Jesus' last meal with his followers is simple, but Paul wants to draw a particular lesson from it, which comes in verse 26. When you *do* this – eating the bread, drinking the cup – you are *announcing* Jesus' death to the world. Paul doesn't mean that the central Christian meal, the **eucharist** or Lord's supper, is a good opportunity for preaching about Jesus' death; that may or may not be the case. He means that when you enact the meal you announce Jesus' death. Doing it says it.

Often when Paul states a principle which he's then going to apply in a particular direction, the principle itself sends off echoes into all kinds of other areas of Christian thinking and living as well, and that is certainly so here. As the following verses make clear, he sees the eucharist not simply as an occasion for Christian devotion and fellowship, but a powerful statement to the world at large, and perhaps particularly to the 'rulers and authorities' who put Jesus on the cross, not realizing that this would bring about their own downfall (see 2.7–8; 15.23–28). It is the announcement of Jesus' death; and through Jesus' death the powers are defeated, and people who were enslaved to them are rescued. No wonder the interpretation and practice of the eucharist has been so controversial in church history. It's an action which speaks louder than words. Some have used it as a weapon of power to boost their own prestige. Others have appeared afraid of it, and have downgraded or sidelined it.

But what Paul is doing is *going to the heart* of it, to explain why the Corinthians' shameful practice of allowing the rich/poor divide in society to spill over into church life is totally out of line. He has already said that their divisive meals cannot actually be 'the meal which relates to the Lord' (verse 20). Now he explains, reminding them of the traditional story of the Last Supper, that when the meal is celebrated the Lord himself is there, not simply absent, away in the past, or longed for at his coming in the future, but present through this 'memorial'. The eucharist is the moment at which the past event comes forward to live again in the present, and the future moment of the Lord's return comes backwards in time to challenge us in the present. That's the point of verses 27–32. Misbehaving in relation to this meal is misbehaving in relation to the Lord himself.

This enables Paul to set up a kind of court scene to explain not only why the Corinthians' way of sharing their common meal is scandalous but how to interpret strange events in the community, including some Christians falling sick and others dying. We may find this strange, but Paul believed passionately that all of life was interlocking, and that individual and social behaviour, belief and practice could and did have results in other areas of human experience, including health.

This is how the court scene works. There will be a future judgment at which those who refuse the gospel (Paul here calls them 'the world' in a negative sense, verse 32b) will be condemned. Part of the strange privilege of being a member of God's people is to have one's judgment in advance, as it were, so as not to be judged on the last day. So (verse 32a) when the Lord judges us in the present time the result is discipline: things happen to us which are to be understood as both punishments and warnings. And because the eucharist is a moment in Christian living when the future comes to meet us in the present, this judgment and discipline is brought into focus there, giving us a choice. Either examine and 'judge' yourselves, making sure your behaviour is appropriate at this meal, or face the scrutiny and judgment of the Lord himself (verses 27–31).

In the middle of this passage (verse 29) Paul explains that the way to incur judgment is to eat and drink without 'discerning the body'. He has already spoken of the church as a single body (10.17), which he is about to explain at length as 'the **Messiah**'s body' (12.12–31). But in chapter 10 this was closely linked to the 'sharing in the Messiah's body' which takes place through the bread of the eucharist. In the present passage, the 'body' of the Lord has been spoken of in reference to the bread itself (verses 24, 26, 27). Somehow, for Paul, the two come together, and that's the point: doing it says it. If, when you break the bread, all share it in the same way, that declares powerfully that you are all one body. If you divide the room, and the guests, into different groups, that powerfully makes the opposite point. The 'body' which is to be recognized is *both* the presence of the Lord in the eucharistic elements *and* the unity of the church that shares the bread. The two belong together.

Paul's closing command therefore goes back to verses 17–18, where the discussion began. When you come together, you should treat all alike as equal guests. (Some translations say 'wait for each other', as though the problem was to do with people starting a meal before everyone had arrived, but the word can mean 'receive or welcome as a guest', and that makes more sense of the problem Paul has described.) If someone wants a larger meal than can be shared with everyone else, they should eat it at home, not in front of the other Christians who may not be able to afford it. Otherwise the solemn moment when past and future come together in the present may bring judgment, not blessing.

Paul finishes by saying he will set the other things straight when he arrives. This is tantalizing for us; we wish we could listen in on some of his other instructions as well! But it is also a challenge. Paul has left some things unsaid, but we can be sure he would deal with each problem in the same way, and on the same basis, that he has used for the things he has written about so far. We need to think through other areas of church life and practice, as well as the ones he has dealt with here, with the same shrewd clarity and on the same theological principles.

1 CORINTHIANS 12.1–11

The Same Spirit at Work

1Now: about things relating to the spirit's work, my brothers and sisters, I don't want you to remain ignorant. 2You know that when you were still pagans you were led off, carried away again and again, after speechless idols. 3So I want to make it clear to you that nobody who is speaking by God's spirit ever says 'Jesus be cursed!'; and nobody can say 'Jesus is Lord!', except by the holy spirit.

4There are different types of spiritual gifts, but the same spirit; 5there are different types of service, but the same Lord; 6and there are different types of activity, but it is the same God who operates all of them in everyone. 7The point of the spirit being revealed in each one is so that all may benefit. 8One person is given a word of wisdom through the spirit; another, a word of knowledge by the same spirit; 9another, faith through the same spirit; another, gifts of healing by the one spirit; 10another, the working of mighty deeds; another, prophecy; another, the ability to distinguish spirits; another, various kinds of languages; another, the interpretation of languages. 11It is the one spirit, the same one, whose work produces all these things, and the spirit gives different gifts to each one in accordance with the spirit's own wishes.

One of the most exciting experiences of my teenage years was playing in an orchestra at school. I had learned the piano for a year or two, but you normally play that without other musicians joining in. Now I began the trombone. Of course, when you start an instrument you have to learn and practise by yourself. You make your mistakes, and try out scales, arpeggios, and small solo pieces, in private. But then, one day, you get to sit with forty or fifty others, and discover that though you're all playing different instruments, and most of you are playing different parts, it all fits together and – if everyone is doing what they should! – it makes a wonderful combined sound.

I quickly discovered that there are class distinctions within an orchestra. The strings consider themselves superior to all others; they are the senior section, they carry the tune in many classical works. Within the strings, the violins consider themselves superior; ask anyone who plays the viola or double bass. But within the wind section, too, there are distinctions. The flutes and oboes consider themselves superior to the brass, and within the brass the trumpets definitely regard themselves as superior to the trombones. The only form of animal life lower than a trombone, it seemed to me then, was the tuba, the triangle and the timpani.

All this is normally meant in good fun, but it does create a strange hierarchy among musicians. Of course, there are sudden moments when everybody depends on instruments that are normally looked down on: you can't start Mozart's opera *The Magic Flute* unless the trombones are on good form, and you couldn't think of playing Dvořák's *New World Symphony* unless you had a first-class cor anglais player. Sooner or later, as you work your way through the repertoire, the instruments have to acknowledge that they all need each other if the music is to be complete.

The problem Paul now confronts in Corinth is that within the Christian orchestra (so to speak) there were some who considered themselves superior to others, and there was a danger as a result that the whole symphony might be played out of balance and even out of tune. Paul writes this section of the letter, in fact, almost as if it's a symphony in itself: chapter 12 is the opening movement, with an introduction (the present passage) leading to a great statement of the central tune (verses 12 and 13), which is then explored from several angles (verses 14–26) before the theme is restated (verses 27–31). Then there comes a second 'movement', a lyrical, gentle but very powerful section, the poem about love in chapter 13. This is so well known that people often forget it was originally written to be the centrepiece of a longer section. Finally in chapter 14 there comes the extensive 'third movement' where Paul takes the theory of chapter 12, seen in the light of chapter 13, and applies it to the real problem, which is the tension between those who possess and practise different 'spiritual gifts'.

For the moment, then, he is concerned to state some first principles. In terms of the illustration we've used so far, we could put it like this: yes, there are indeed different instruments, but all require the same musicianship; there are different styles of playing, but they're all following the same conductor; and there are different tones and volumes of playing, but it's the same composer who wrote the piece and whose music must come through in the performance.

The illustration doesn't work completely here, because nothing in human experience corresponds precisely to Paul's picture of God. But in verses 4, 5 and 6 Paul does something striking at exactly that level. At the very moment when he's wanting to say that the various gifts that different Christians have are all to be seen within a unity, the unity which is God himself, he expresses that unity in three closely related ways: **spirit**, Lord and God. Paul doesn't get into abstract philosophical language here about how these three relate to each other, but from this point there is a straight line into the explorations of the Trinity that later theologians would undertake.

That is the main thing Paul wants to say here, but the way he leads into it is a little more complicated. To begin with, the word he uses in verse 1, which is sometimes translated 'spiritual gifts', doesn't really mean that; it's just 'spiritual things'. Paul changes it for the word 'gifts', which is usually understood as 'spiritual gifts, gifts from God through the working of the spirit', in verse 4, but to begin with he seems to be responding to questions they have raised which they have expressed in terms simply of 'spiritual things'. (When we get to verses 27–31, we will look in more detail at the particular gifts he mentions.)

In the light of the way this word is used elsewhere in the letter, we should probably understand that some at least in Corinth, in line with their other tendencies, were regarding people who possessed some of the 'gifts' as more 'spiritual' than the others – a danger which recurs in the church from time to time. Paul faces a problem which the modern Western world faces a lot: the confusion in people's minds between something that's *spiritual* and something that's *Christian*. In a world (my world, and that of many of my readers) that's been starved of 'spirituality', it's easy to suppose that anything which seems to be in touch with something 'spiritual' or 'supernatural' must be from God. In a world (that of the Corinthians) where people were sometimes labelled 'spiritual' to set them apart from ordinary mortals, experience of the sort of gifts that the spirit gives to different Christians could lead people to suppose that those who received them were thereby promoted to a class above all other Christians. Paul's answer to them is also an answer to us.

He reminds them (verse 2) that in their pagan life ('when you were **Gentiles**,' he says, literally; this reminds us that Paul saw Christians as 'neither Jew nor Greek', but a new entity altogether) their worship of speechless idols sometimes carried them away into ecstasy. Nothing particularly 'Christian' about 'spiritual experience', then! After all, the point of being in touch with the things of the spirit is not in order to have exciting experiences but so that you will be loyal to Jesus, the risen Lord.

That's why he sets out a test: supposing somebody were to say, either because this was the conclusion they'd come to or because they were carried along by some spirit or other, that 'Jesus is cursed'; such a person couldn't be inspired by the true spirit of the true God. This is puzzling, since, perhaps not surprisingly, we don't know of anyone who actually said this in the early church. It may be that some, in Corinth or elsewhere, were wanting to go beyond Jesus into new forms of spiritual experience, or, perhaps through Jewish influence, regarded him as cursed because of his crucifixion (see Galatians 3.13).

Instead, Paul declares, nobody can say 'Jesus is Lord' except by the **holy spirit**. This is a very important statement. 'Jesus is Lord' is one of the most basic statements of Christian **faith** (see Romans 10.9; Philippians 2.11). This means that every Christian has already said it; every Christian, therefore, according to Paul, has already been brought to this point by the holy spirit. This fits with what Paul says elsewhere, that the spirit works through the preaching of the **gospel** to bring people to faith and **baptism** (see e.g. 1 Thessalonians 1.5; 2.13).

In addition, anyone who said 'Jesus is Lord' in Paul's world, especially in a Roman colony like Corinth, would know that part of what this meant was 'and Caesar isn't'. As the church in subsequent centuries would discover, those who pursue their own spirituality for the sake of the experience may well be able to create a safe sphere in which they can have an exciting time without engaging with the real world. (This may have been another reason why some might have wanted to say 'A curse on Jesus'; a century later than this, people were burnt at the stake for refusing to say that.)

But those who name Jesus as Lord, experiencing the power of God's holy spirit in doing so, are thereby brought into the social and political battlefield. The Corinthians were in danger of looking at spirituality as an area of personal growth and experience. Paul wants them to see it as the place where the one true God, known in the three ways he outlines in verses 4–6, equips people to advance his **kingdom** in the face of the principalities and powers of the world.

1 CORINTHIANS 12.12–20

Many Members, One Body

[12]Let me explain. Just as the body is one, and has many members, and
all the members of the body, though they are many, are one body, so
also is the Messiah. [13]For we all were baptized into one body, by one
spirit – whether Jews or Greeks, whether slaves or free – and we were
all given one spirit to drink.

> [14]For the body, indeed, is not one member, but many. [15]If the foot were to say, 'Because I'm not a hand, I'm not part of the body', that wouldn't make it any less a part of the body, would it? [16]And if the ear were to say, 'Because I'm not an eye, I'm not part of the body', that wouldn't make it any less a part of the body, would it? [17]If the whole body were an eye, where would the hearing be? If the whole body were the sense of hearing, what would happen to the sense of smell? [18]But as it is, God has organized the members, placing each one individually in the body according to his wishes. [19]If all the parts were one member, where would the body be? [20]So the result is this: there are many members, but one body.

Paul uses one of his most spectacular and famous illustrations in this and the following passage. It would be gilding the lily to introduce it by another one of our own, so we may as well jump straight to the point.

But the point isn't precisely what many people think when they read what he says about the foot and the hand, the ear and the eye. Many people have supposed that the main thing he's saying is simply that all Christians have gifts which they must contribute to the overall life of the church, and particularly that no Christian must look down on another because they don't share the same particular gifts. More positively, it has been assumed that he is simply painting a picture of the church as a place where every member has something important to contribute. This is true as far as it goes. Paul would have been shocked, possibly even amused in a sad sort of way, at the idea which has prevailed in much official Christianity, that 'ministry', or 'Christian work or service', is something engaged in only by those who are in full-time paid church employment. The phrase 'every-member ministry' would have rung bells with him. In fact, the word 'member', which we often use without thinking where it's come from, owes its place in Christian thinking and speaking not least to this present passage, where the word means 'limb' or 'organ'. The word started out as part of a metaphor – a single body, many 'members' – and has become flattened out into a more general word, 'people who belong'.

All of this is true as far as it goes. But what Paul is saying goes much further. There are three things here in particular.

For a start, he isn't simply choosing this as one 'illustration' at random. (In our last passage, I used the illustration of the orchestra like that – simply as an example of a sphere of life where everybody does something different and it's all supposed to work together.) When he talks about a human being, a human body, he is writing as a Jewish thinker for whom, with Genesis 1 and 2 in the background (and we know from elsewhere in the letter that he had them very much in mind), the question of God creating a new, true humanity in and through the **Messiah**, Jesus, was all-important. In chapter 15 verse 27 he will quote from Psalm 8, the passage in which God declares that human beings are put in authority over the world, and he will declare that this has now happened in Jesus the Messiah. So for him to choose the image of a human body to express what those who belong to the Messiah have now become, and how they are to live, is deep with significance. The church is to be the place where, together, we learn how to be God's genuinely human beings, worshipping God and serving him by reflecting his image in the world.

Second, it is significant that he doesn't speak of the church as the body of *Jesus*, but of *the Messiah*. In some Jewish ways of thinking about Israel's king, we find the belief that the king, and particularly God's ultimate king, the Messiah, would represent Israel, would sum them up in himself, so that what was true of him would be true of them. (Think of David *representing* Israel when he fought with Goliath on Israel's behalf in 1 Samuel 17.) Already in this letter Paul has several times hinted at what he makes clear in other writings, that those who belong to Jesus as Messiah, those in whom the **holy spirit** lives, are the true people of God, the renewed Israel. He has already declared that the people who came out of Egypt at the **Exodus** are 'our fathers' (10.1). He has reminded the Corinthians that they used to be pagans, but now are not any more (12.2). He has even spoken of ethnic Israel as 'Israel according to the flesh' (10.18), hinting at a contrast with a different 'Israel', the one the Corinthians themselves now belong to.

How is he best to express this? Well, the great renewal which God has accomplished in the Messiah was achieved when Jesus was put to death in his 'flesh' – his corruptible, mortal body, that was capable of dying and did indeed die – and brought to new life in his **resurrection** 'body', with the dead flesh transformed by God's act of dramatic new creation. Paul will return to this in chapter 15. So here, speaking of Christians as part of 'the Messiah's body', Paul has chosen a way of addressing their particular problems (how to exercise spiritual gifts) while showing where the foundations of his thought about them lie. The most basic thing about the church is its identity as God's true people, defined over against both paganism and non-Christian Judaism.

Third, Paul must have known that many non-Christian and non-Jewish writers had already used the metaphor of the 'body' as a way of talking about social, civic and political life. There were political theorists in his own day who could speak in that way of the state, or the empire, or the cosmos, as a single body, perhaps with the emperor as its head, but certainly with the different citizens all having their own parts to play. Here and elsewhere Paul is marking out an identity for the Christians as a new and different sort of community, owing allegiance to a new and different 'Lord' (see verse 3). What this means in practice Paul hints at at various points in his letters. Here, though his surface-level meaning is to do with the danger of one Christian looking down on another, he is concerned to speak about this problem within the echo-chamber of his whole view of the Christian family as the true humanity, the true Israel, the true world empire.

The most striking thing in this remarkable passage is the way he introduces it in verse 12. We might have expected him to say 'as the body is one and has many members . . .so also is *the church*,' or at least 'so also is *the body of* the Messiah'. He doesn't. He simply says 'so also is *the Messiah*'.

We have to tread carefully here. Some have said that God, or Jesus, 'has no hands but our hands' with which to work in the world today; that (thank God) is not true. Others have supposed that what he means is that when the fleshly body of Jesus died on the cross, what rose on Easter day was not that same body, but simply and solely the church, the community of the faithful. Dozens of passages in Paul make it clear that that's not what he means, not least chapter 15 of the present letter. No: what he means here by 'the Messiah', as in Galatians 3.16 and elsewhere, is 'the Messiah as the one who represents his people, in whom his people are summed up'.

But how do people come to belong to this community of the Messiah-and-his-people? Here, as elsewhere (e.g. Romans 6.2–11; Galatians 3.27), Paul sees **baptism** itself as the means of entering the family. Sometimes people have taken his phrase 'baptized in one spirit' to refer to a special experience of being filled or equipped with the spirit, at some time after one has come to belong to the Messiah's people (through the ordinary baptism in water). The only thing to be said for this is that sometimes in Acts the phrase seems to be used for a second stage of initiation, but this doesn't seem to be how Paul is using it here.

Paul is precisely not talking about a special experience in which some Christians join a superior class, leaving other Christians behind. That was the danger he was anxious to avoid. He had stressed earlier on, in verse 3, that nobody could say 'Jesus is Lord' (the basic baptismal confession) except by the holy spirit. His point here is expressed in two parallel ways; Paul, as ever, is happy to mix his metaphors! First, the spirit is at work to introduce people into the Messiah's family in the first place ('by one spirit we were all baptized into one body'); second, the same spirit is at work to sustain Christians day by day in that membership ('we were all given the one spirit to drink'). Plunged in the spirit to begin with, drinking from the spirit day by day: that is how Paul sees all Christians alike. And, again as in Galatians 3, he insists that this experience cuts clean across the great social divisions of his day, Jew and Greek, slave and free. If we can get straight on this we will be ready for the more explicitly practical points he now wants to make.

1 CORINTHIANS 12.21–26

The Responsibilities of Each Member

> [21]The eye can't say to the hand, 'I don't need you'; and, again, the head
> can't say to the feet, 'I don't need you'. [22]No: the parts of the body
> which seem to be weaker are all the more necessary, [23]and we give
> much greater honour to the parts of the body we reckon more dishon-
> ourable, so that the parts we hide in shame have a far greater dignity
> [24]which our more presentable parts don't need. In fact, God has made
> the body a single, organized whole; he has given greater honour to the
> lesser part, [25]so that there won't be any division in the body, but that
> all the members may have the same concern for one another. [26]If one
> member suffers, all the members suffer with it. If one member is
> exalted, all the members celebrate along with it.

Two weeks ago, I woke up in the night with a sharp and throbbing toothache. Nobody who has ever had that experience will need to be reminded just how all-consuming such pain can suddenly become. I took some painkilling tablets but they didn't help. I walked round and round the house hoping that by exercising other parts of the body the tooth would settle down. I tried to read an exciting book to take my mind off it, but of course I couldn't even think about what the book was saying. When, finally, the painkillers took effect and I went back to sleep, it was as though my whole body, not just the wretched tooth, had given an enormous sigh of relief.

This obvious example shows what Paul meant when he said that 'if one member suffers, all the members suffer with it'. It isn't difficult to think of examples of his other point, about one member being 'exalted' – the word literally means 'glorified', but within his continuing picture he presumably thinks of a part of the body experiencing pleasure instead of pain. The ear enjoys music, but it seems as though our whole self is caught up in it. The face enjoys warm sunshine, but it seems to penetrate through the entire body. And so on.

Paul's eagerness that the Corinthians should understand how every single member in the Christian family matters as much as every other one is leading him to lay deep foundations for the practical application of all this in chapter 14. And in doing so he has taken the metaphor of the body, which was well known in the ancient world as a picture for civic society, and has made it do quite a new sort of job. This is a typical example of Paul picking up an idea current in his society and making it dance to a different tune.

In some famous examples where Roman orators declared that the whole society was like a human body, the point they were making, as well as the interdependence of the 'body politic' as we say, was that the different jobs involved a difference of *status*. Some, quite simply, were more important than others: more high-profile, more honourable, carrying more dignity, more valuable to the common good. Others, by contrast, were dishonourable, fit for people of a lower sort, more dispensable. (This attitude, of course, was sadly not confined to pagan Romans; it has recurred throughout history. Every generation needs to hear 1 Corinthians afresh.)

Here, by contrast, Paul undermines any actual or potential boasting in the church by insisting that every single member of the body is just as indispensable as any other. Never let one part say to another, 'I don't need you!' In fact, when Paul does agree that some parts of the body are less presentable than others – that there are some parts (the sexual organs, obviously) that we cover up and are ashamed to expose in public – he turns the argument around and insists that these parts are thereby given a greater honour.

What does he mean by this? Perhaps he is thinking of the way in which, in a great imperial household, the person with greatest honour is the person who is normally protected from view. The emperor himself does not come out and appear to everyone walking past on the street. Only the minor officials do that. From this point of view, the 'shame' which covers up certain parts of the body should not imply that we wish we did not possess such things. It should imply, rather, that these things are far too important for every passer-by to glance at.

Perhaps also, underneath this argument, is Paul's deeply Jewish sense, already evidenced in 11.2–11, that the male/female distinction, marked of course by the sexual organs, is one of the creator's most important signs in our human nature, in which male and female together reflect God's image (Genesis 1.26–28, despite the strange passage in 11.7 of the present letter). Some philosophies despised the body, and the sexual organs in particular, as dirty, shabby and potentially or actually evil. Paul, by contrast, celebrates them as God-given.

This is what enables him, as he makes his own use of the common picture, to insist on equality between different functions, leaving no room for social, cultural or 'spiritual' elitism or snobbery within the church. The examples he uses in verses 21–22, leading to the point about the parts of the body of which we are ashamed, are actually rather strange. In what sense is the head or the foot, or the eye or the hand, 'weaker' than its fellow member? Paul seems to be echoing here the language of the 'weak and the strong' from chapter 8, and anticipating his practical conclusions about the way in which different members of the church regard themselves and one another.

Paul clearly has the life of the local congregation in mind. He wants every Christian in Corinth to value every other Christian, and to care for him or her, just like the hand comes to bandage the injured foot, or the foot hurries to take the injured head to hospital. That remains enormously important in every Christian fellowship, congregation and church the world over. But we in our age have been given, through instant electronic communication, a far more detailed picture of the worldwide church than any previous generation has ever had; and shall we restrict our sense of being members of the **Messiah**'s body simply to the people we see every week? Should we not also rejoice with, or grieve with, all Christians around the globe who celebrate or suffer?

1 CORINTHIANS 12.27–31a

Gifts and Ministries

> [27]Now you together are the Messiah's body, and individually you are
> members of it. [28]In the church, God has placed apostles first, then
> prophets, then teachers, then powerful deeds, then gifts of healing,
> helpful deeds, organizational gifts, different types of languages. [29]Not
> everyone is an apostle, are they? Not everyone is a prophet! Not eve-
> ryone is a teacher! Not everyone does powerful deeds! [30]Not everyone
> has gifts of healing! Not everyone speaks with tongues! Not everyone
> interprets!
>
> [31]You should be eager for the better kinds of gifts.

Bishop Lesslie Newbigin, in his autobiography, *Unfinished Agenda*, tells how he served as secretary to the committee that was drawing up, during the 1940s, the constitution for the newly united Church of South India. The chairman raised the question: what shall we do about canons, deans, archdeacons and the like? 'I paused,' said Newbigin, 'with my pen ready to write down the decision of the committee. Nobody said anything for a while; then a single voice said "Abolish them." Since nobody challenged this proposal, I wrote down the one word: Abolished.'

That cheerful iconoclastic approach to 'offices' held by some within the ordained ministry of the church was a response to the needs of a new situation. The newly formed body saw no need to perpetuate the kinds of subtle distinctions that had gradually come to be taken for granted in the older churches which were joining together. And, though Paul clearly envisages the need for something we can call 'offices' within the church (see the 'bishops and deacons' in Philippians 1.1, for instance), he seems to go out of his way to avoid giving us the same list twice, just in case we should suppose that he had an actual hierarchy in mind – which is of course what this chapter is intending to rule out.

In verses 8–10 of the present chapter, which we didn't discuss at that point because we were saving it for now, he lists nine activities which the **spirit** enables within the church: words of wisdom, words of knowledge, **faith**, gifts of healing, working of power, prophecy, discerning of spirits, kinds of languages (or 'tongues'), the interpretation of tongues. Here, in verse 28, he lists eight: **apostles**, prophets, teachers, powerful works, gifts of healing, helpers, organizers, different kinds of tongues. When he lists them again in verse 29, to ask rhetorically whether every member of the church fits any one of these categories, he goes through the list in the same order, but omits helpers and organizers and adds 'the interpretation of tongues' at the end.

The lists have some things, but by no means everything, in common with two other lists: Romans 12.6–8 and Ephesians 4.11. In the Romans passage Paul lists prophecy, ministry, teaching, exhortation, giving, presiding and showing mercy; of these, only prophecy overlaps with the lists in 1 Corinthians 12. In Ephesians, he lists apostles, prophets, evangelists, and pastors and teachers (it isn't quite clear whether these last two are different people or the same ones). Apostles, prophets and teachers overlap with 1 Corinthians 12.28 and 29, but again the lists diverge after that.

When we put all this raw material together, what do we get? A muddle, some might be tempted to imagine. No, Paul would say: the rich, diverse life of God's people. Obviously Paul has not felt under any constraint to say on every occasion the complete sum total of everything he could have said. Equally obviously, there are some fixed points, and we do well to ponder them as we think about how to apply his teaching in today's church. And one of the applications might well be that the church as a whole should be flexible, and not feel under an obligation to insist on exactly the same forms of ministry on all occasions and in all places.

The fixed points, though, should be clear. Paul considers as spiritual gifts *both* those gifts that mainstream churches have seen as central, not least those which involve teaching, building people up in the faith, *and* those gifts normally regarded as 'charismatic' – which is misleading, because Paul's point is that all these gifts, including 'helping' and 'administration', are 'charismatic', are gifts of the spirit. Already we begin to see his point about one category not looking down on another.

Since we know from 9.1 what Paul thinks makes someone an 'apostle' (seeing the risen Lord), it should be clear that the gift he describes as 'first', and which also appears in that position in Ephesians 4.11, is not just a 'charismatic experience', but a fact about the way certain people were called to the service of the **Messiah**. These are, in other words, gifts *through which God establishes and builds up his church.* From Paul's point of view, there were no second-generation apostles; the next generation would have to build on the foundation he had laid, not lay it afresh. But that the church remains 'apostolic' in the sense of 'founded on the preaching and teaching of the apostles' is a thoroughly Pauline insight.

If this is what these gifts were, they were not given for people to enjoy the experience of receiving or exercising them. Of course, there is an exhilaration, a delight, in being fully what God has called and equipped you to be. But the point is that the 'gift' is God's gift *to* the whole church *through* the individual who has received it. God, naturally, gives gifts to different people in such a way that the church will be bonded together in ways that God sees as appropriate.

After 'apostles' we find, in all the lists, 'prophecy'. This is distinguished from 'teaching', and there is no agreement on what Paul meant by it or whether it is still important today. Some have seen it in terms of the teaching of scripture, opening the Bible with special insight for a new generation. Others have suggested that it has to do with speaking 'words of the risen Jesus' to the church, enabling Jesus to communicate with his people in the power of the spirit. This shades off into a special 'spiritual gift' which has nothing to do with learning or biblical study, but which comes instead, like tongues and healing, into the category of 'non-natural' or 'supernatural' workings. Perhaps, then, 'prophecy' is the activity through which particular words are given to particular individuals or groups by people speaking in church and claiming that the spirit is leading them to say such things, or that Jesus himself is speaking these words?

That kind of ministry undoubtedly happens, and Paul is comfortable with it. (According to Acts, he sometimes exercised it himself, for instance in 27.31–34.) But in the list in verse 8 it seems to be covered by 'words of wisdom' or 'words of knowledge', in which the speaker is suddenly able to say something, without previous ordinary-level knowledge of a person or situation, which nevertheless rings true and produces a sense of conviction. 'Prophecy' could then be a larger category of which these are subsets. Or it could, after all, be the special, God-given ability to understand what the Bible is saying and apply it to fresh hearers.

Paul will deal particularly with the relationship of prophecy and tongues in chapter 14. But we should note already that, though he has warned against an elitist approach to the whole question of 'gifts' and 'spiritual things', he can still urge them to 'be eager for the better gifts'. This too will be explained in chapter 14. And we should note, against those who from time to time make claims about this, that Paul assumes that none of these gifts are given to everybody. 'Do all speak in tongues?', like the other questions, expects the answer 'No'. And, though Paul is always eager for God to do new things in the lives of people and communities, he sees no need to suggest that the 'not all' categories of verses 29 and 30 should be challenged, that everyone should, after all, be prophets, or teachers, or tongue-speakers, or whatever.

It is all summed up in verse 27. These words should be engraved on the mind and heart of all church members. They should be especially taken to heart by those who are called to more high-profile office, or who have been given some special gift that, by thrusting them into the public eye, brings upon them the temptation to arrogance that was afflicting some in Corinth. 'You are the Messiah's body; individually, you're members of it.' That is the basis of all true understandings of the church, and of all humble service within it.

1 CORINTHIANS 12.31b—13.7

The Need for Love and the Character of Love

12.31b Now I'm going to show you a better way, a much better way.

13.1 If I speak in human languages, or even
in those of angels, but do not have love,
then I've become a clanging gong or else
a clashing cymbal. 2 And if I should have
prophetic gifts, and know all mysteries,
all knowledge, too; have faith, to move the mountains,
but have no love – I'm nothing. 3 If I give
all my possessions to the poor, and, for pride's sake,
my very body, but do not have love,
it's useless to me.

4 Love's great-hearted; love is kind,
knows no jealousy, makes no fuss,
is not puffed up, 5 no shameless ways,
doesn't force its rightful claim,
doesn't rage or bear a grudge,
6 doesn't cheer at others' harm,
rejoices, rather, in the truth.
7 Love bears all things, believes all things,
love hopes all things, endures all things.

When people say, as they sometimes do, that Paul must have been a very difficult person to have around – that he seems to have been awkward, cantankerous, argumentative and generally an unpleasant character – this passage is one I often quote in reply.

It seems to me impossible to imagine that this passage could have been written in a very personal letter by the founder of a community, to that community, *unless he knew, and he knew that they knew, that this is the kind of person he himself was*. Of course, that doesn't mean that Paul lived up to this stunning picture of love every minute of every day. But that he had (unlike some of the teachers in Corinth) spent his life and energy being what he was and doing what he was for the sake of other people, copying and embodying the love that Jesus himself had shown in dying on the cross, I think we can be sure.

Chapter 13, as we noted at the beginning of chapter 12, doesn't stand by itself – despite the fact that, for many people, it is known mainly through being read at weddings, as though it was simply a detached poem. In the illustration I used earlier, it is like the slow movement of a symphony, whose first movement is chapter 12 and whose final movement is chapter 14 – the 'symphony' of Paul's teaching about the corporate worship of the church, and especially about the use of different gifts by different members of the worshipping congregation. They need to understand that they all belong together in the body of the **Messiah**, and Paul has now set that out at length in chapter 12. But that won't be any good if they simply try to put the lesson into practice in a grudging or shoulder-shrugging fashion. They need to pause, to move into a different key and rhythm, and deepen their understanding of the highest virtue, the greatest quality, the most Jesus-like characteristic you can imagine: love.

The very word 'love' causes us all sorts of problems in the English language. Our vocabulary has become impoverished. Where Greek has four words, we have at most two – 'love' and 'affection'. All right, there are related ones like 'fondness' and 'compassion', but they none of them come near what Paul is talking about. The older word 'charity' has come to be associated so closely with the splendid work of organizing and administering relief for those in need that it has ceased to be useful as a translation here.

The description Paul gives in verses 4–7 is not an account of what Hollywood means by 'love'. Romantic or erotic love, at its best, is like a signpost to the thing Paul is talking about: when two people are 'in love', they often make promises which sound like verses 4–7, but the emotional and physical energy which gets them that far won't get them all the way to fulfilling the promises. It takes a commitment of mind and will – which often then, to its own surprise, brings erotic love along with it.

Nor is what Paul is talking about the same thing as we mean when we say 'I love tennis', or 'I love the colour orange'. But if we love tennis, or a colour, as much as that, we may again take the first steps of mind and will to do things which will enable us to play, or watch, more tennis, or to paint, or observe, our favourite colour.

No: what Paul has in mind is something which, though like our other loves in some ways, goes as far beyond them as sunlight goes beyond candles or electric light. Look closely for a moment at the type of person he describes in verses 4–7. This passage describes someone doing and being things which in the eyes of the world would be rubbish. The newspapers are full of the opposite every day; and most people, in ordering their own lives, assume a set of values in which what Paul is urging is at best a noble but far-off ideal.

And yet Paul insists that this 'love' is essential for Christian living, especially for communal Christian living and its shared worship. This chapter, itself (as we have seen) the short but vital middle section of a longer whole, likewise divides into three, with the middle part being the heart of it all. The first part (verses 1–3) insists on just how vital love is; without it, nothing else matters. The middle part (verses 4–7) describes love itself, in memorable though challenging language. The final part (verses 8–13, which is our next passage) explains that love is one of the things which will last into God's new world, and which therefore matters far, far more than the things which will pass away – which include most of the things the Corinthians were most bothered about.

In our present passage, then, Paul begins by insisting that it is love that gives meaning and appropriate flavour to all other Christian living. He stacks up all the impressive things that the Corinthians might do (he says 'though *I* do these things', but the assumption is that he's talking about them), and asserts firmly that none of them are of any advantage unless there is love as well. Just as the section (chapters 12—14) and the present chapter divide into three, so also does this passage, providing a crescendo of warnings. Verse 1 declares that, without love, speaking in tongues and languages of any and every kind is simply a way of making a loud but incomprehensible noise. Verse 2 lists several of the other 'gifts' that Paul mentioned in chapter 12 and will return to in chapter 14; this time he says that without love someone who does all these things will be 'nothing' – not even a noisy gong. Verse 3 imagines someone taking one of Jesus' commands to its literal extreme, giving away all one's possessions (Mark 10.21), perhaps in order to feed the poor (the same verb can mean something like that). Paul then imagines himself handing over his body, perhaps to be tortured or to death, in order to be able, like the martyrs of old, to feel that he really had something to boast of. (Some manuscripts say 'to be burnt', which in

Paul's language is a very similar word to 'boast'.) But even accomplishments like these, in the absence of love, 'won't do me any good at all'. As we have often seen, Paul clearly imagines that on the last day those who have been **justified** by **faith** in the present will be judged according to the life they have lived (see, for instance, 3.10–15); and the one thing that will count above all else on that day is love.

But what then does he mean by 'love'? Verses 4–7, the heart of the poem at the heart of the section, describe it. Line by line of the description is clear in itself. Perhaps the best thing to do with a passage like this is to take it slowly, a line at a time, and to reflect on at least three things: first, ways in which we see this quality in Jesus himself; second, ways in which we see it (or more likely, alas, don't see it) in ourselves; and third, ways in which, if we were like that, it would work out in practice.

Such an exercise should never be undertaken simply in order to feel either good about oneself or frustrated at one's lack of moral growth. It should always be done in prayer; and at the third stage, as we ask for grace to envisage situations where we could behave differently, we should try to imagine what doing that would feel like, what steps we would have to take to make it happen, to avoid lapsing back into our normal behaviour. Then, when we're faced with the relevant situation, we will at least have a choice which we have already thought about, instead of behaving as creatures of habit. And of course the ultimate aim is for *this* way of life, peculiar though it seems and almost unbelievable at points, to become the engrained way we habitually behave. Some people have taken steps along that road ahead of us. When we meet them it's like hearing gentle music, or seeing a beautiful sunrise. But this **life** is within reach of each one of us; because it is the life of Jesus, the life inspired by the **spirit**, the life which is our birthright within the Messiah's body.

What's more, as Paul insists – and this is the point of him saying all this here in the letter – this is the life which will bring the right sort of order to the chaos of faction-fighting and spiritual jealousy within the church. This poem serves a purpose, and in enjoying it and trying to make it our own we should have an eye on the equivalent purpose in our lives, and our churches, as well.

1 CORINTHIANS 13.8–13

Love: The Bridge to God's Future

[8]Love never fails. But prophecies will be
abolished; tongues will stop; and knowledge, too,
be done away. [9]We know, you see, in part;

we prophesy in part; [10]but, with perfection,
the partial is abolished. [11]As a child
I spoke, and thought, and reasoned like a child;
when I grew up, I threw off childish ways.

[12]For at the moment all that we can see
are puzzling reflections in a mirror;
then, face to face. I know in part, for now;
but then I'll know completely, through and through,
even as I'm completely known. So, now,
faith, hope, and love remain, these three; and, of them,
love is the greatest.

When Wolfgang Amadeus Mozart was a young man, living with his father Leopold (himself a fine musician) in Vienna, he is said to have played a trick on him from time to time. Young Wolfgang would come home from spending a riotous evening with his friends; his father would already be asleep in bed. Wolfgang would go to the piano, and would play, loudly, a rising scale of notes, getting slower and louder as they reached the resolution at the top of the scale . . . and then he would stop, one note short, and go to bed himself.

Old Leopold, so the story goes, would toss and turn in bed as the unfinished scale came into his dreams and imagination. The frustration of having one's musical senses aroused in that way without resolution would become too hard to bear. Eventually he would have to drag himself from his slumbers, stagger downstairs, and play the last note.

No doubt he had ways of getting his own back, but that is another story. What we are concerned with here is the way in which Paul describes the call of love, and of life itself, as an unfinished scale, going ahead of us into God's future. The music of love, which will one day be completed, is therefore not just our duty. It is our destiny.

Consider that distinction for a moment before we proceed. So often the moral demands of the Christian life are presented within a framework which speaks of duty: a cold, hard slog to attain a distant and seemingly impossible standard. But Paul sees all of life within the framework of God's future – God's future which has burst into the present in the person of Jesus of Nazareth, and especially in his **resurrection**, which has marked him out as God's **Messiah**, the world's true Lord. In that future, Paul sees a world of joy, delight and above all of love. So in the present there are three things which point into the future (verse 13): **faith**, which looks at the God made known in Jesus and trusts him for everything; hope, which looks ahead to God and what he will do in the future, which is already assured by Jesus' resurrection;

and love, which will finally know as it is known, and embrace as it is already embraced (see 8.3, and e.g. Galatians 2.19–20 and 4.9).

Why is love the greatest of these? Because, as the hymn says,

Faith will vanish into sight,
Hope be emptied in delight;
Love in **heaven** will shine more bright

– or, Paul would say along with Jesus, in the **kingdom of God** which will come on earth as in heaven. But the point should be clear. Love is the way of life in the new world to which, by grace, we are bound. We need to learn it here and now. It is the grammar of the language we shall speak there. The more progress we make in it here, the better we shall be equipped.

Paul places these abiding certainties over against the things which the Corinthians were priding themselves on. Prophecy? Who will need it in the world to come? Tongues? Why would we need to speak them in the world where everyone understands everyone else at once? Special knowledge? We shall all know everything we can know and need to know. These are things which belong to the country we live in at the moment. Love is God's river, flowing on into the future, across the border into the country where there is no pride, no jostling for position, no contention among God's people. We are invited to step into that river here and now, and let it take us where it's going.

Paul wants the Corinthians, above all, to learn to think in terms of God's future and its relation to the present. This, in part, is a matter of getting them to think *Jewishly*, instead of in the pagan thought-forms they tend so easily to lapse into. It is also a matter of getting them to place Jesus' resurrection at the centre of their view of the world, time, history and themselves. That is why chapter 15, which is already in view from this point, will form the great climax to the letter. And here, as he draws this poetic little chapter to its close, he uses three images that speak of the transition from the present to the future, the transition which makes it all the more important to make love the centre of their lives here and now.

The first image is of the child growing to maturity. 'When I grew up, I stopped behaving like a child.' Tongues, prophecy, clever-sounding words of knowledge: child's play, says Paul. Give me the grown-up stuff, the real spiritual, emotional and personal maturity. Give me the humanness that will last, enhanced and unimpeded, through to God's new world. Give me, in other words, love: the love described here, the love which is the highest form of knowing and being humans can attain in this world or the world to come.

The second image is of the mirror. Mirrors were made in Corinth, but the point Paul is making is familiar to many writers in the ancient world. When you look in the mirror everything is back to front, inside out. You can't always make out what it is you're looking at. That's what the present time is like, Paul is saying. You can see something of God's plan, something of what's going on, something of what God wants for his human creatures. But in the world to come all will be plain. 'Face to face' could be simply a way of saying 'so we won't be looking in mirrors any longer', but it is probably also a way of reminding his readers, as John puts it in his first letter, that when Jesus appears we shall be like him, 'because we shall see him as he is' (1 John 3.2).

This leads to the third way of saying the same thing, which picks up the contrast in verses 9 and 10 between things that are partial and things that are complete. 'Now I know in part'; there is such a thing as genuine Christian knowledge in the present, even though 'knowledge' can 'puff you up' (8.1). But then – in God's new world, the world waiting to be born, the world already glimpsed in Jesus' resurrection – 'then I shall know in the same way that I too have been known'. What matters at the moment, as in 8.2–3, is not your knowledge of God, but God's knowledge of you; but your knowledge, too, will be complete in the **age to come**.

Think within God's time-plan, Paul is urging them. If you do that, you will not only see how important love is, and will be able to resist the temptation to factional fighting, to perpetuating social divisions at the Lord's supper, and to boasting over spiritual gifts. You will also see the spiritual gifts themselves in their proper light. They are temporary helps for building up the church in the **present age**, and as such it's important to learn to use them aright. That's what the next chapter will be about. But love, at present an unfinished scale, is what will last into God's new world. One day the Son himself will come down and complete the music.

1 CORINTHIANS 14.1–5

Priorities in Worship

[1]Pursue love; and long for the spiritual gifts, especially that you may prophesy. [2]Someone who speaks in a tongue, you see, isn't speaking to human beings but to God. Nobody can understand such speakers, because they speak mysteries in the spirit. [3]But the one who prophesies speaks to other people, to build them up, to strengthen them, and to console them. [4]The one who speaks in a tongue builds up himself or herself; but the one who prophesies builds up the church.

[5]I would be delighted for all of you to speak in tongues, but I would be even more delighted to have you all prophesying. The one who prophesies is greater than the one who speaks in a tongue, unless they also give an interpretation so that the church may be built up.

One morning many centuries ago, two builders went off to work. The first walked through the twisting streets of the old town until he came to the little plot of land where he was labouring steadily day by day. He was building a small but beautiful house, just big enough for himself and his family to live in. The outside wasn't anything special to look at. In that part of the world, people didn't bother with decorating the bits that the general public would see. But inside, everything was magnificent. Around a tiny courtyard, the walls glistened with marble. The windows and their shutters were friendly and inviting. And the rooms and their fittings were glorious. Only he and his family would ever see it, but for them it would be a palace. The rest of the world could ignore them, for all he cared.

The second man walked down to the public square, where he took his place with dozens of others working together on a new building that would fill one whole side of the square, transforming it with a sense of space and grandeur. The foreman spoke eagerly to them as he allotted them their tasks for the day – this one to hauling pillars into position, that one to dressing stones for the upper storey, another to sorting tiny coloured stones for the mosaics, yet another to supervise the making of the great carved doors. Who cared what sort of a home they lived in? They were building a cathedral: a house of beauty, awe and above all prayer and worship to last a thousand years, a sign of God's love and power, an invitation to everyone to come gladly and humbly into his presence.

The contrast between the two builders indicates the contrast Paul makes throughout chapter 14. He has prepared his hearers for this in various ways. Now he focuses on a specific issue which, though at one level it simply relates to the ordering of public worship, at another level goes near the heart of what he wants to say to the Corinthians.

The contrast is between the person who builds up their private spirituality and the person who, in public worship, builds up the whole community. Paul has nothing against private spirituality. It is a fine thing (in the picture we have used) to adorn the inside of one's own house and make it a place of beauty, light and joy. Indeed, one often fears in many church circles today that Paul might need to remind some Christians that making time and effort to look after and beautify one's own house – to develop and enrich one's private, deeply personal awareness of God, his presence and his love – is actually a good thing, not at all necessarily a sign of self-centred individualism. There is no virtue in living in a spiritual slum. But Paul was aware – and, again, this warning is no doubt needed in various parts of today's church – that there are dangers in the opposite direction as well.

The problem centres on two 'gifts' from among those he listed in chapter 12. And the key question, which he highlights in the first verse, is: are you behaving according to the principle of chapter 13? Are you exercising the gifts God gives you in the spirit of love? The underlying contrast here is the same as we saw in chapter 8, verses 1–2: there are some things which can 'puff you up', making you proud and self-important, but what *builds* people up is love. And this chapter is all about making sure that public worship 'builds everybody up' rather than simply everybody developing their own spiritual giftedness and displaying it like so many strutting peacocks. When people come together to worship the God revealed in Jesus, they are not building their own private houses. They are building a great cathedral for all to share and enjoy.

The particular 'gifts' on which he concentrates in this passage are 'tongues' and 'prophecy', and we need to say a word about each of them here, before seeing how Paul develops his point. 'Tongues' refers to the gift of speech which, though making sounds, and using apparent or even actual languages, somehow bypasses the speaker's conscious mind. Such speech is experienced as a stream of praise in which, though the speaker may not be able to articulate what precisely is being said (a point to which Paul will draw attention later on), a sense of love for God, of adoration and gratitude, wells up and overflows. It is like a private language of love.

That is its delight, as Paul himself knew (see verse 18), but also its problem. It is essentially private. And when private wealth is displayed but not shared, it becomes a matter of showing off – which may have been exactly what some in Corinth had been doing, insisting on praying long and loud in public in words, or at least syllables, which made them feel ecstatic but which neither they nor anyone else could understand.

Part of the problem with tongues, then and now, is that in the world of Corinth there were many religions and cults offering different spiritual experiences, some of which involved the worshippers being carried away into ecstatic states and trances, and sometimes into various kinds of speech. Was the young Christian church just going to be another cult like that? Maybe that was what some were hoping for: an up-market version of a well-known product.

In many parts of today's world, we have the opposite problem. The 'secular' world has starved us of spirituality, and many are now eager for any kind of 'supernatural' or 'spiritual' manifestation, any sense of a power or life-source beyond the material world. Some would even argue (against what Paul says later) that such 'supernatural' signs are necessary today to convince sceptics of the existence of a 'spiritual' world in the first place. Such an approach is full of problems, particularly because it accepts the basis on which the 'secular' world has taught it to think: that God and the world are separate, detached beings, rather than (as in biblical thought) seeing the world as belonging to God, and seeing God as constantly, though strangely, present and active within it. Tongues, then and now, remain a gift of great value which God gives to some people (not all: see 12.30). But the purpose and use of this gift, especially in public, needs to be thought through carefully. Paul says in verse 5 that the only way tongues are able to be of real value in public worship is if the tongue-speaker is able to explain in coherent speech what is being said – a point to which we will return in verse 13.

In contrast to tongues, Paul highlights 'prophecy' as the gift which will build up the church, and hence as the gift people should seek and pray for if they want God to use them in constructing, beautifying and strengthening the whole community rather than their private spirituality. We shall say more about prophecy as the chapter develops. But what Paul means by this word must be made clear from the start.

When Paul says 'prophecy', he doesn't just mean 'foretelling the future', though that may sometimes happen. (Even the great Old Testament prophets were just as concerned with commenting on the present as with warnings and promises about the future.) Nor is he simply referring to sudden flashes of inspiration in which someone comes to know something, or understand something, they couldn't otherwise have imagined, and is moved at once to speak it out so that others – perhaps particularly the person about whom something is thus known – may learn and profit from it. That, too, happens, and Paul would be the last to disparage it. But his central emphasis is on the God-given wisdom, understanding, insight and teaching that the church badly needs if it is to go forward instead of round and round in circles, if it is to be built up as a community instead of as an accidental collection of private individuals. As the chapter develops, we shall see Paul insisting over and over again that prophecy, like all 'spiritual' phenomena, does not need to be 'spontaneous' to be genuine.

The climate of our own age has tended to see spontaneous utterance as inspired, while something that needs working at is thought of as less inspired. This owes more to the Romantic movement, in which poets such as Wordsworth and Keats would pour out verses as though from a hidden source–in contrast with most poets before and since, who have laboured carefully to polish and shape their original ideas – than to anything specifically Christian. As with tongues, some have felt that an 'inspired' word about a person or situation must be given priority over the careful and prayerful thinking through of a situation, in the light of scripture in particular, out of which wise and rich teaching and instruction can be given. As so often in 1 Corinthians, Paul needs to give the church wisdom about wisdom itself, spiritual teaching about spiritual teaching itself. Today's church urgently needs to listen in and see what lessons are still to be learned.

1 CORINTHIANS 14.6–12

Speaking Clearly in Church

> 6Well then, my brothers and sisters, if I come to you speaking in
> tongues, how am I going to bring you any benefit unless I speak to
> you either in a revelation or in a word of knowledge or in a prophecy
> or in teaching? 7It's the same with lifeless objects that make a sound,
> like a flute or a lyre. If they don't give a distinct note, how will anyone
> know what tune is being blown or plucked? 8Think about it: if the
> trumpet doesn't make a clear sound, who will get ready to fight?
> 9It's the same with you. Unless your tongue gives a distinct message,
> how will anyone be able to tell what you're talking about? You will be
> like someone speaking into thin air. 10To be sure, there are all kinds
> and types of languages in the world, and none of them is meaningless.
> 11But if I don't know the force of the words, I will remain a foreigner
> to the speaker, and the speaker will be a foreigner to me. 12It's the same
> with you. Since you are so eager for spiritual matters, try to specialize
> in doing things that will build up the church.

Two days ago I went to a meeting where seven or eight different languages were used in quick succession. There was a large crowd being addressed, including people from many parts of the world. One by one the speakers got up and spoke, repeating the same message so everyone could hear it.

I watched people's faces as this went on. With each new speaker, suddenly a whole section of the crowd would sit up, look eager and concentrate; at last, this was something they could understand. Then, with the next speaker, that section would settle down again and another group would come alive. And so on. Slowly the message got across to more and more until eventually the whole crowd had been included.

Paul's point here is that if the only thing people did in church was to speak in tongues, that moment would never come. Nobody would ever understand what was being said. He puts the point, tactfully, as though he himself were going to come to them and speak only in tongues (verse 6). This is both a way of saying that he can and does speak in tongues himself – in other words, this isn't a gift he scorns – and also a way of avoiding making a direct accusation against a particular group in the church.

His point is simple enough, but the way he says it deserves exploration. What is needed in church is not unintelligible speech but intelligible; a fresh vision of God; new knowledge that one person has acquired, whether through study or special God-given insight; 'prophecy' itself in the wide sense we mentioned earlier (including many different kinds of speaking, to exhort, rebuke, encourage, give insight, open the scriptures, and so on); or simply 'teaching', an ordered exposition either of a passage of scripture or of a topic of Christian instruction. All of these, if done in the right spirit, will be of profit for the church in a way that any amount of tongue-speaking simply won't.

Paul uses three different illustrations to make his point. To begin with, think of musical instruments. The flute was one of the most common wind instruments of the time, and the small 'lyre', maybe a type of harp, was one of the most common of stringed instruments. But if the person playing them doesn't make a clear noise, if it comes out as a strangled squawk on the flute or a discordant twang on the strings, nobody will know what tune is supposed to be being played. That's what it's like with tongues. As far as the listeners are concerned, the result is meaningless noise. Notice how this ties in with what Paul said at the beginning of chapter 13: however many tongues I speak in, if I don't have love – in this context, if I don't try to bring benefit to other people – I'm like a noisy gong or a clanging cymbal, which are precisely instruments that don't have a definite pitch.

The second illustration is a military one. Paul may not be thinking explicitly of the Christian life as a battle (as in 1 Thessalonians 5.8, Ephesians 6.10–20 and 1 Timothy 6.12), but his point is now that the listeners should not only be able to *understand* what is being said but that if something is worth saying in church it's because it will result in people *doing* something. Blowing the trumpet is supposed to make people get ready for their various military tasks; speaking in church is supposed to make people get ready to serve God in the world, whatever their calling may be.

The third illustration (verses 10–11) is like the picture I began with. Supposing at that great assembly every language had been spoken except my own, and that I couldn't understand any of the others. I would have been excluded, kept on the outside of what was going on. That, in fact, seems to be part of Paul's point, which he will develop presently. The danger with those who are eager to use their new gifts in public is that they will forget the real point of coming together, which is that the church family as a whole should be 'built up'. If the Corinthians are as keen as they seem to be on having the **spirit** work in and through them, the thing they ought to be longing for, praying for, and working towards is that they would all be able to do and say things which make the body of Christ work together in harmony and be built up in love.

What Paul says here is relevant to much wider issues than simply speaking in tongues – and hence to many churches which don't have the same problem that the Corinthians had. What is the point, for instance, of choosing hymn-tunes which may be musically very fine and sophisticated but which the average congregation can't sing? What is the point of reading scripture in such a mannered or 'elevated' tone of voice that, instead of it being heard as the exciting, life-changing **word** it really is, it comes across as a lofty oracle, very grand perhaps but totally unrelated to the ordinary life of the listeners? 'You might as well be speaking into thin air', says Paul in verse 9, and most readers of this book will be able to think of occasions when that has been the effect of something done or said in church.

There are other examples of the same danger, in churches which wouldn't dream of using over-clever hymn-tunes or over-elevated tones of voice. The personality of those who lead in worship – especially where 'leading' means standing as though one were a rock star facing an audience – can easily intrude, so that, as with the Corinthian tongue-speakers, the spiritual experience of one person is put on display for others to see, instead of the others being built up in their own **faith** and understanding.

That is what Paul is most concerned for. He longs for a genuinely human, grown-up worship in the church. He sees that an overemphasis on some of the spiritual gifts can make people and communities unbalanced and keep them immature. These are the two issues he is now going to address.

1 CORINTHIANS 14.13–19

Praying with Mind as Well as Spirit

> 13So the one who speaks in a tongue should pray to be able to say the
> same thing in clear speech. 14If I pray in a tongue, you see, my spirit
> prays, but my mind remains fruitless. 15Why is that important? I will
> pray with the spirit, and I will pray with the mind as well. I will sing
> with the spirit, and I will sing with the mind as well. 16You see, if you
> say a blessing in the spirit, how can someone who isn't one of the
> inner circle say the 'Amen' to your prayer? They won't know what
> you're talking about! 17You may well be giving thanks in fine style, but

the other person isn't being built up. [18]I thank God that I speak in tongues more than all of you. [19]But in the assembly I would rather speak five words with my mind, to teach other people, than a thousand words in a tongue.

When you look at another person, what do you see? I don't mean what shape, what colour, what size of person are you looking at; I mean, how do you think about who they are? How do you observe them as a whole, an entire person and personality?

Some modern traditions, like some ancient ones, have hugely emphasized the importance of the body itself. From fashion models to movie stars, from exercise regimes to slimming programmes, the Western world in particular has given people the message that the most important thing about you is the shape and appearance of your body.

Some other traditions, both ancient and modern, have focused on the mind. Education has sometimes been seen as developing and training the mind, filling it with useful and important information and teaching it how to process it to maximum effect. Those who have not found their education a happy experience have sometimes rebelled against this approach, but focusing on the mind as an almost detachable part of the person is clearly possible.

Other traditions have insisted on the importance of the feelings, the emotions, as the clue to everything. Such an idea often downplays the importance of the mind in favour of things which entrance and delight, which excite and stimulate, which bring a joy or a thrill that doesn't need to be thought about or analysed. Sometimes when people want to talk about this approach they refer to it as the 'heart', knowing quite well that the physical heart itself, the central organ in the body's circulation system, isn't actually where such emotions are located, even though sometimes the physical heart itself does literally beat faster, or experience a sense of warmth or intensity, under strong emotion.

Where in all this do you put the '**spirit**'? It's one of the oldest puzzles in Paul that sometimes when he says 'spirit' he is referring to the deepest awareness that a human being is capable of, and sometimes he is referring to God's spirit, the **holy spirit**. We saw this back in chapter 2, where the reason for the possible confusion became obvious. When God pours out the holy spirit on someone, their awareness of God through the spirit's presence is experienced precisely in what they would call their own 'spirit'.

The problem with all of these ways of looking at or talking about human beings is that we all too easily imagine that humans really are constructed in segments or compartments, which can be addressed or related to one by one in distinct ways. In particular, whenever people in the modern West hear someone talk about 'spirit' or 'spiritual', our culture makes us assume that the person means '*not* material, '*not* bodily'. And that is to misunderstand Paul. Part of the whole problem he faced in Corinth was precisely that some of the Christians had allowed themselves to compartmentalize, to split up their full, God-given humanness into different bits and pieces, and to develop one without reference to the other. In particular, there was a danger that those with the gift of tongues would neglect the vital dimension of the mind.

Of course (as some would quickly remind us today) there is an equal and opposite danger. There are always some who, perhaps not least because they are afraid of their own and other people's emotions, prefer to keep their religious experience and expression a cerebral thing, analysing theological concepts and praising God in the cool, detached way that you might praise a fine painting or a first-rate wine. That, too, is a problem and needs to be addressed. But the problem Paul sees here is that of those whose high-powered languages of praise encourage them to leave their minds behind at the church door. And that isn't just an impoverishment; it is a failure to realize what it means to be a truly human being.

Paul, rooted as he was in Jewish thinking, saw a human being as a rich, many-sided, complicated but integrated whole. 'Body', 'mind', 'heart', '**soul**' and 'spirit' were not, for him, words to describe different *parts* that you could in principle separate out. They were words to describe *the whole person seen from one angle.* In particular, 'spirit' describes the whole person at his or her deepest level of consciousness – which is in fact linked in a thousand ways to mind, heart and body. And 'mind' describes the whole person as a thinking, reasoning being, which is again linked to everything else we are and do.

Paul often has occasion to instruct Christians to let their mind be renewed by God's spirit, as part of their most basic discipleship, living in God's new world. He wants them to think through, and come to know for themselves, what God wants them to do and be (see, for example, Romans 12.1–2). And here he applies this point to worship.

It isn't just that he wants them to engage the mind in order to apply a kind of brake to the unthinking, and hence unchecked, use of spiritual gifts. Nor is it simply – though this is important – that mindless babbling in tongues nobody else can understand is a way of excluding those who don't have a gift like that, or who perhaps are at a very early stage of Christian experience and haven't a clue what's going on (that may be the point he is making in verse 16). These things matter, but there is a bigger issue still.

The underlying point is that Paul wants them to grow to maturity as whole human beings, using and celebrating to the full the various aspects of their created selves, made in God's image. One of the most basic laws of the spiritual life is that you become like what you worship; and if you are worshipping the true God, the creator of all things, the one in whose image you are made, you should be developing as a wise, many-sided human being, not letting one aspect get out of proportion as though God were only interested in the 'spiritual' side, meaning by that not only the non-bodily but also the non-rational. Of course, those who live in a world that has overemphasized the body, or the reasoning mind, may find that they need to redress the balance in other ways than the one Paul stresses here. But the point is this: especially in public worship, what matters is to bring mind, spirit and body together. When you look at a worshipping Christian, what you should see is a whole human being, with every aspect united in giving praise to God.

1 CORINTHIANS 14.20–25

Signs for Believers and Unbelievers

[20]Brothers and sisters, don't be children in your thinking. Be babies
when it comes to evil, but in your thinking be grown-ups. [21]This is
what it says in the law: 'I will speak to this people in foreign languages
and with the lips of strangers, and even so they won't listen to me, says
the Lord.' [22]So tongues are not meant for believers, but are a warning
for unbelievers; while prophecy is not designed for unbelievers, but
for those who come to faith. [23]What I mean is this: if the whole assem-
bly comes together and everybody speaks in tongues, and outsiders
or unbelievers come in, they'll say you're crazy, won't they? [24]But if
everyone prophesies, and outsiders or unbelievers come in, they will
be called to account by everyone, judged by everyone, [25]the secrets of
their hearts will be laid bare, and so they will fall down on their faces
and worship God, declaring that 'God is truly among you.'

'We need to take an adult attitude to this . . .'

'Of course, if we are to approach the problem as adults . . .'

'Since we're all adults here, perhaps I could say . . .'

What do you think these people are talking about? It would be nice to think that such sentences really did introduce serious and informed discussion of important and difficult issues. But in much modern speech the language of 'adult' has been used in a different sense. As with shops and bookstores that offer 'Adult' products, and with movies that proclaim themselves as 'Adult Entertainment', we have to conclude that the word has ceased, almost entirely, to mean 'grown-up' in the sense of 'mature, wise, responsible', and has come to mean 'people who have forgotten the moral constraints of their younger days'. The three speakers are most likely saying, 'Now that we've grown out of the silly restrictions that less mature people still regard as important . . .' And of course from the same stock of words we get 'adultery' – adults behaving selfishly without thought for long-term consequences, especially for children.

When Paul appeals for 'adult' or 'grown-up' thinking in verse 20, the last thing he means is that one should have 'grown out of' careful moral thinking. On the contrary: when it comes to evil, he says, you should still be babies. There is no shame, no immaturity, in simply not knowing about the depths of evil and perversity in the world. Nobody is diminished in their humanness by being ignorant, innocent or even naive when it comes to knowing all the things that the twisted human mind can devise. (Of course, those called to pastoral work, and to various kinds of work in the community, need to know what they're dealing with; but this no more connives at evil than a doctor connives at sickness by learning how to treat it.)

Instead, Paul wants them to grow to maturity in their thinking. This is a problem we still face, even in the church. There are people who pride themselves on knowing about evil, but can't be bothered to think through serious issues from a biblical or theological point of view. There are many Christians who can tell you which film star is getting divorced but can't tell you where in the Bible you might find teaching on the subject.

This general introduction in verse 20 applies, as I have suggested, to all kinds of situations. But Paul gives the general principle about maturity in order to home in on yet another aspect of the problem he has been addressing throughout the chapter. Not only does he want them to worship God with mind as well as innermost **spirit**; he wants them to reflect intelligently about the whole problem of what should happen in the church's public meetings. And when they do there are surprises in store.

He begins by quoting what to us seems a strange passage from Isaiah 28, where God says that, as a mark of his displeasure with unbelieving, rebellious Israel, he will address them by the lips of foreigners, babbling in a tongue they can't understand. This won't persuade them to turn back to him, but the very fact of being addressed in this way will be a sign to them of just how far they have gone astray.

So, he says, tongues are not a sign for believers; those who believe don't need to be addressed in this way as a mark of God's displeasure. But if those outside, the 'unbelievers', come into the house where Christians are worshipping, and discover people speaking in tongues, they will be repelled. Paul may be thinking that such outsiders would conclude that Christianity was just another of various cults in which people went into trance-like ecstasies and uttered strange things; or he may just be thinking, as he says in verse 23, that they will think the Christians are simply mad; but either way the effect will be negative. Tongues, then, are not likely to be useful in a public worship service, unless the tongue-speaker can also express in plain speech the meaning of what has been uttered.

With prophecy, however, it's different. The way Paul has said this in the second half of verse 22 seems a bit puzzling, and different translations have struggled to remain faithful to his original words while making sense of the passage. He seems to be saying that prophecy – speaking God's **word** intelligibly, both under spontaneous prompting by the spirit and after mature and careful thought – is designed to further the work of bringing people to **faith**. He envisages a situation where 'outsiders' hear powerful words, preaching, exhortation, specially given wisdom, and so on, and find themselves captivated by it. The prophetic words shine a spotlight that goes right into their innermost selves, bringing a sense of unworthiness, conviction and judgment. No other power has been able to do that to them, and (Paul paints a dramatic picture here, but we must assume this sort of thing did happen in the communities he knew) they will fall down in worship to the one true God whom they have recognized as present in and with the congregation.

This is clearly another argument against the use of untranslated or uninterpreted tongues in public worship, and in favour of words which are intelligible and powerful in their appeal to the mind as well as the heart and the spirit. His appeal for maturity (which reflects the child/adult contrast of 13.11) may also hint at another criticism of tongues; they belong to a childish stage of Christian experience. Of course, no wise adult ever loses touch with the child he or she once was and in a sense still is; but Paul insists that maturity is what matters. One must learn to progress beyond childish babblings into articulate and wise speech. We should not overstress this, because Paul himself still clearly uses the gift of tongues in his personal and private prayers, and he doesn't see this as a sign of immaturity (verse 18). Maturity comes in knowing what behaviour is appropriate in which context.

Paul rounds the argument off with another quotation from Isaiah, this time from chapter 45, something of a favourite of his. There, the prophet speaks of the pagan nations coming to recognize that the one true God is present in Israel and nowhere else, and so coming to worship. As with many parts of Isaiah, Paul sees this fulfilled in his own day; this may be a hint to us of one aspect at least of what he means by 'prophecy'. He is, after all, quoting two prophetic texts in his own discussion *about* prophecy; could it be that this passage is itself an example of what he has in mind?

If so, we can glimpse how it might come about. Through prayer, careful reflection and creative thought about the way in which God's long purposes have been fulfilled in Jesus **Christ**, Paul and other early Christian prophets would gain the courage to say new things, to offer fresh interpretations of scripture, to apply previously unimagined insights to the life of the church. This ministry of fresh, prayerful reading of scripture, coupled with a desire to think through the practical, social and cultural issues facing the church – as well as the great theological questions, of course – is still urgently needed in the church. Paul urges the Corinthians to seek such gifts for the building up of the whole church, and there is every reason for Christians today, too, to pray for such gifts and to seek to bring them to maturity.

1 CORINTHIANS 14.26–40

Final Instructions for Worship

26So where does this leave us, my brothers and sisters? When you come
together, one person has a psalm, another some teaching, another a
revelation, another a tongue, and another some interpretation. Let
everything be done for the general upbuilding. 27If anyone speaks in a
tongue, there should be two or at most three, each taking their turn,
and one of them should put it into plain speech. 28But if none of them
can do that, let them be silent in the assembly, and speak to themselves
and to God.

29As for prophets, let two or three speak, and the others evaluate
what is said. 30If fresh revelation comes to someone sitting there, the
first person should be silent. 31You can all prophesy one by one, so
that everyone can learn, and everyone can be encouraged. 32The spirits of prophets are under the control of prophets, 33since God is the
God, not of chaos, but of peace.

As in all the assemblies of God's people, 34the women should keep
silence in the assemblies. They are not permitted to speak; they should
remain in submission, just as the law declares. 35If they want to understand something more, they should ask their own husbands when
they get home. It's shameful, you see, for a woman to speak in the
assembly. 36Do you suppose God's word began with you? Are you the
only ones it has reached?

37If anyone thinks they are a prophet, or spiritual, they should
acknowledge that what I write to you is the Lord's command. 38If anyone disregards this, they can be disregarded.

39So, my brothers and sisters, be eager to prophesy, and don't forbid
speaking in tongues. 40But everything should be done in a seemly
fashion, and in proper order.

Last night I stood in awe at a mosaic dating from the sixth century. It is a picture of Jesus himself, 'coming on the clouds', and it's in the domed apse above the altar in a church in Rome. Peter and Paul are standing on either side of Jesus, presenting to the risen Lord two saints of the period, the brothers Cosmas and Damian. As often in ancient mosaics, there are animals and birds, and the whole thing looks incredibly bright and vivid. It's hard to believe it is a millennium and a half old.

Or at least, that most of it is. There was an earthquake in Rome in the Middle Ages, and the great bell-tower that used to stand there collapsed onto the roof of the apse, crashing through and damaging part of the picture. It was restored; but in restoring it the new artists added a few touches of their own, making allusions to their own time. This doesn't spoil the picture, and indeed it adds a sense of continuity as different generations made their contribution.

Similar things happened from time to time to ancient books (and indeed some modern ones). It didn't always take an earthquake; sometimes it was simply a careless **scribe**, or in other cases an overzealous one. We know this because the manuscripts of the New Testament that we possess – there are hundreds of them – all differ slightly in (mostly) very small details. In one or two well-known cases, with the ending of Mark being a good example, it seems that some early Christian scribes were determined to make good what they saw as gaps or deficiencies.

(We should note, in saying this, that the New Testament is by far the best preserved book from the ancient world. Most of the great classical texts such as Homer and Virgil, Sophocles and Cicero, are preserved in only a few copies, all much later than most of the New Testament manuscripts we've got, some of which date from very early on, some even from within one or two hundred years of the time of Jesus.)

This problem about variations between different manuscripts doesn't greatly affect the letters of Paul, except for one or two examples; and this present passage includes one of the most famous. Verses 34 and 35 – the command to women to 'keep silence in the assemblies' – don't occur here in some of the manuscripts. Instead, they are added on at the end of chapter 14, seemingly as a kind of appendix. Since the verses are in any case very odd – Paul clearly assumes in 11.2–16 that women are going to speak during worship – many serious scholars have concluded that the verses were not by Paul, and were added by a scribe who was anxious to keep public worship a matter of male leadership only.

This could be the case, although equally wise and learned people have concluded that Paul really did write the passage. But if he did, as on balance I am inclined to believe, what can he have meant by it?

He clearly doesn't mean that no women must speak during worship. As we saw, chapter 11 assumes that women will take leadership roles in praying and 'prophesying' just as much as men will. And I simply don't think Paul has any agenda about keeping women in a downtrodden condition, as has often been suggested. What we have to reckon with is a possible scenario, or a set of possible scenarios, that might explain the sudden need for a commandment of this type.

The whole passage, and indeed most of this long chapter, is about speaking and being silent in public worship, and about making sure that everything is done out of a concern to build up God's people, and out of a belief that the God we worship is the God of peace, not of confusion or chaos. This suggests that, if Paul did indeed write these words, one or both of the following problems may have occurred.

It is likely that the men and women were segregated during worship, as in synagogues, and as in some churches to this day in the Middle East and elsewhere. But if public worship was conducted in the main formal language of the day – in Corinth, obviously, mainstream Greek – many of the women, who might only understand their local dialects, would not always be able to grasp what was being said. (Like some other things in this letter, this isn't to say that Paul approves of a situation where women would be less educated than men, but he has to deal with the real problems he faces, not with an ideal situation.) As still sometimes happens today in such cases, the women might become bored and begin to talk among themselves. Or they might start calling across the central division to their husbands to explain what had been said. Either way, Paul says, this can be disruptive and should not be allowed.

That is one possibility. Another is that with Paul's instructions in verse 29, according to which the congregation should reflect on what a prophet said and 'evaluate' it, some of the women in the congregation might have taken it upon themselves to 'evaluate' what their own husbands had said, and do so rather too personally and sharply. In that case, it would be far better, Paul believes, to have them take the matter up at home, rather than airing what could be, at least by extension, a domestic disagreement within the context of public worship.

Either of these may describe the situation Paul faced; or there may have been another possibility. We don't know. What is clear is that this is a particular problem posed from within the cultural setting of the time, and that Paul's overriding concern (if the passage is indeed written by him) is for order, peace and mutual upbuilding when the congregation comes together for worship, rather than for chaos, interruption and dissension.

Of course, there are many churches today where there is so much order and peace that Paul might have wondered if everyone had gone to sleep. That poses different problems, which a fresh and lively engagement with the **gospel** itself, and the personal challenges it poses, should begin to address. But in Corinth at least the problem was one of worship meetings bordering on the chaotic – and chaos, as always, provides an opportunity for those with the loudest voices or the slickest operating skills to come out on top, while those with gentler voices and more humility can get crushed in their path. The issue, in other words, may well not be simply about how to order public worship, but how to prevent bossy and overbearing Christians exploiting an extemporaneous worship service in order to show off their gifts and strengths. That problem is not unique to 'free' services such as those in Corinth.

In particular, Paul issues specific instructions as to the exercise of the gifts he has been talking about. The main principle remains that everything should be done with an eye to building up the church. Beyond that, at most three people should speak in tongues, and then only if one of them can 'interpret', in other words, put into plain speech what it is that has been said. Paul would have no time for people who wanted to go on and on in a free-floating way with different gifts being exercised. Spontaneity is no guarantee of spirituality, and to think otherwise is to entertain wrong ideas about God himself (verse 33).

When it comes to prophecy, again two or three is to be the rule; the rest must be silent, but certainly not passive; they must consider carefully what has been said. Nobody must try to shout down another; if God gives a second person something to say, the first should give place. Again, spontaneity is not enough. Prophets must take charge of what's going on in their own 'spirits', and should be self-disciplined in their speaking (verses 29–33).

The final commands, after the puzzling passage about the women keeping silent, comment ironically on what's just been said (verses 37–38): anyone who thinks they have prophetic or spiritual gifts should see, by such means, that what Paul has said really is a command of the Lord! He doesn't want to squash the work of the **spirit** (see 1 Thessalonians 5.19–20); he wants to encourage it. But the important thing is that everything be done in a fitting and appropriate manner, and with proper order. It's better to drink wine from a wine glass than to lick it off the tablecloth.

1 CORINTHIANS 15.1–11

The Gospel of the Messiah, Crucified, Buried and Risen

[1]Let me remind you, brothers and sisters, about the good news which
I announced to you. You received this good news, and you're standing
firm on it, [2]and you are saved through it, if you hold fast the message
I announced to you – unless it was for nothing that you believed!

[3]What I handed on to you at the beginning, you see, was what I
received, namely this: 'The Messiah died for our sins in accordance
with the Bible; [4]he was buried; he was raised on the third day in
accordance with the Bible; [5]he was seen by Cephas, then by the
Twelve; [6]then he was seen by over five hundred brothers and sisters at
once, most of whom are still with us, though some fell asleep; [7]then he
was seen by James, then by all the apostles; [8]and, last of all, as to one
ripped from the womb, he appeared even to me.'

[9]I'm the least of the apostles, you see. In fact, I don't really deserve
to be called 'apostle' at all, because I persecuted God's church! [10]But I
am what I am because of God's grace, and his grace to me wasn't
wasted. On the contrary. I worked harder than all of them – though it
wasn't me, but God's grace which was with me. [11]So whether it was me
or them, that was the way we announced it, and that was the way you
believed.

The old man made me a cup of tea, and took me through to his sitting room. 'Now you must see this,' he said, passing me a much-handled photograph album. 'This tells you how we came here.'

The pictures told their own story. The happy family at home in Armenia. The sudden journey with what they could carry and nothing else. The key figures – father, grandfather, an uncle. On board the ship. And then the arrival: staying with distant relatives, finding their own home, settling down, making a new life.

'And this is where I come in,' he smiled, turning the last page. 'I'm not really an Armenian, you see.' There he was, a little baby, born just after the family arrived in their new world.

I wanted to know more of the history of this strange, proud people who had retained their sense of identity despite being hunted almost to extinction. He gave me a book, also showing signs of being read many times. 'This gives you the whole picture', he said. 'When we read this we realize why it's important that we came here and have carried on our way of life.'

Two stories, one old and long, the other sudden and short. Weave them together and you create a new community. And that's what Paul is doing in this passage. He tells how the Christian movement had begun: it's a kind of family album, explaining what had happened to bring this little family to birth in its new existence. He adds himself at the end of the list, though there is something odd about his being there at all. And he gives the tell-tale hints that reveal this story as simply the most recent, and decisive, moment in a much longer story, for which you need the Book, the Book that gives the whole picture and explains why these new events are so important.

The chapter which is now beginning is one of the greatest sustained discussions of a topic which Paul ever wrote. The theme is the **resurrection** – the resurrection of Jesus, and the future resurrection of those who believe in Jesus.

Some in Corinth have a problem with this, as we'll find out at verse 12. But there is a much wider reason why Paul gives this topic such a lengthy treatment and places it here as the final major theme of the letter. We have seen over and over again that he is trying to get the Corinthians to understand where they are, and who they are, in God's long story. They are in danger of forgetting their roots – the roots which they have because they belong to the **Messiah**, who has brought Israel's long story to its climax. They have to learn to live 'according to the scriptures' (verses 3 and 4): not in the sense that they must take little bits and pieces of the Bible as their guide to life (though they could do a lot worse) but in the much larger sense that the whole Bible tells a story which has now exploded into new life with the Messiah, particularly with his death and resurrection.

If they understand where they belong in this story, so many other things that have troubled them will be seen in the correct light. Think, for instance, how the Messiah's death and resurrection were crucial in the discussion of sexual morality in chapter 6. God 'bought' you for himself through Jesus' death, and God will raise your body to new **life** as he raised Jesus; so who you are and what you do in and with your present body matters vitally. Think how the discussion of the **eucharist** in chapter 11 encouraged the Corinthians to see this meal in the light of the longer story, looking back now to Jesus' death and on to when he comes again. Think of the lyrical passage about love in chapter 13, and how the deepest point there is that love is the thing which will last into the new world that God will make. The fact that there is a new world, that it's already been launched in Jesus' resurrection, and that all God's people will be given new bodies in order to share in it, is basic to everything he has said. This is where the photograph-album illustration can't help; what we would need is some photographs of the future.

Paul wants to be clear that the resurrection is rock-bottom reality for the Christian. It isn't a strange idea that he's dreamed up himself. He and all the others tell the same story; it's already become a carefully guarded tradition (verses 1, 3, 11). The story, in fact, forms the **gospel**, the announcement of the good news of Jesus the Messiah. This was the message that Paul announced wherever he went, and it was this message that carried God's power and brought people, by the **spirit**, into a living knowledge and love of him, into the rule of the Messiah, into the **kingdom of God**. The only point in being a Christian at all is if this message continues to be the solid ground on which you stand.

The message is like the photograph album: this is the story which makes sense of who we are. Here are the snapshots. The Messiah. His shameful death. His burial. His resurrection on the third day. The people who saw him – Cephas, the **Twelve**, five hundred at once, James (Jesus' own brother). Then, at the end of the story, the man born a bit late, torn from the womb just in time to be part of the sequence: the last person to see the risen Jesus before the appearances stopped. Paul himself.

And it all happened 'according to', or 'in accordance with', the Bible. This doesn't refer to the biblical accounts of the New Testament, the gospel stories of Jesus' death and resurrection. They hadn't been written at this stage. Nor does it mean that Paul could quote half a dozen 'proof-texts' of passages from the Old Testament which predicted that the Messiah would die and rise again, though he could certainly have done that. No. The Bible which Paul had known and loved as a young man was like a story in search of an ending; and when Jesus rose from the dead the ending was now revealed. This was where it was all going. You need the Bible not least to remind you what, if this was the ending, the story itself was about; but you need the gospel to remind you that this was the ending that God himself had provided, giving meaning to the whole thing.

We need to be clear about what the word 'resurrection' itself meant for Paul and his hearers. It didn't mean 'life after death'. It was never a general term for any and every belief about what might happen to people after they die. It meant, very specifically, that people already dead would be given new bodies, would return to an embodied life not completely unlike the one they had had before.

This belief had begun to be popular in Judaism in the two or three centuries before Paul's day; but it had always been denied not only throughout the pagan world (with the possible exception of the Zoroastrians) but also by many Jewish groups, including the powerful aristocrats (the **Sadducees**). The point is this: when Paul spoke of Jesus having been raised from the dead, and pointed on to resurrection as God's promise for all Jesus' people, nobody in Corinth would have thought he meant simply that Jesus had gone after his death into some kind of glorious but non-bodily existence. (Think about it; if that was what Paul and the others had meant, why did they suggest it happened 'on the third day', rather than straight away?) People sometimes talk vaguely about Jesus being 'raised to **heaven**', but that simply isn't what the word meant.

What *sort* of body Jesus had, and what sort his people will have, is an important question. Paul will get to it later in the chapter. But the fact of there being a body is all-important.

Paul's personal conclusion to this introduction (verses 9–11) serves as a reminder: what we're talking about here is God's grace, God's powerful grace, at work in and through the most unlikely people. But Paul is also careful to underline what the Corinthians already knew, namely that this message was the same, whichever **apostle** was announcing it. The Corinthians had heard Cephas and others. They knew this wasn't a strange idea that only Paul had spoken of. This was and is the central thing about Christianity.

Christianity, you see, isn't a set of ideas. It isn't a path of spirituality. It isn't a rule of life. It isn't a political agenda. It *includes*, and indeed gives energy to, all those things; but at its very heart it is something different. It is good news about an event which has happened in the world, an event because of which the world can never be the same again. And those who believe it, and live by it, will (thank God!) never be the same again either. That's what 1 Corinthians 15 is all about.

1 CORINTHIANS 15.12–19

What If the Messiah Wasn't Raised?

> 12Well, then: if the royal proclamation of the Messiah is made on the
> basis that he's been raised from the dead, how can some of you say
> that there is no such thing as resurrection of the dead? 13If there is no
> such thing as resurrection of the dead, the Messiah hasn't been raised,
> either; 14and if the Messiah hasn't been raised, our royal proclamation
> is empty, and so is your faith. 15We even turn out to have been misrep-
> resenting God, because we gave it as our evidence about God that he
> raised the Messiah, and – if the dead really are not raised – he didn't!
> 16For if the dead aren't raised, the Messiah wasn't raised either; 17and if
> the Messiah wasn't raised, your faith is pointless, and you are still in
> your sins. 18What's more, people who have fallen asleep in the Mes-
> siah have perished for good. 19If it's only for this present life that we
> have put our hope in the Messiah, we are the most pitiable members
> of the human race.

Robert had longed to play in the school football team. He had watched every game since he had come to the school. He had idolized the players and thought about the different styles of play, the different skills that were needed, and (of course) the excitement of running out on to the pitch himself to do his best for the school.

He worked hard at his game, made sure he was fit, and played in one of the junior teams. Then one day a friend came running up to him.

'You've made it!' he said. 'You're in the team! I've seen it on the notice-board! Congratulations!'

Robert was on his way to a lesson at the time and couldn't check the notice-board for himself, but instead spent the following hour in a haze of excitement. It had happened. His dream had come true. Life was going to be different from now on.

As he came out of class, he whispered to another friend,

'I'm on the team! Sam saw it on the notice-board!'

The friend looked puzzled.

'But they never put up the team list this early in the week,' he said. 'Sam must have made a mistake. They wouldn't do that. It doesn't happen that way!'

Robert's state of mind at that moment is exactly the state of mind Christians ought to be in if someone says '**Resurrection**? Things just don't happen that way!' People have often tried to reinvent Christianity as something quite different. Some have supposed that to say 'The **Messiah** was raised from the dead' was simply a fancy first-century way of saying 'God's cause continues!' or 'I still regard Jesus as my leader and teacher'. That's all very well if Christianity was simply a set of ethical commands, or if Jesus was simply one guru among others, teaching a way to God which one could follow or not as one chose. There are some today who want Christianity to be that kind of thing. It is, after all, much less demanding on several levels. Sometimes the desire that Christianity should be this sort of thing has even been made a reason for denying that Jesus was raised from the dead. 'We can't say the resurrection happened,' someone once said to me, 'because that would make Christianity different from all the other faiths.'

But the **gospel** which Paul and the others announced was that Jesus was the Messiah – Israel's Messiah, God's Messiah, and hence the world's true Lord. This meant that there was 'another king' (Acts 17.7): a king who would trump Caesar himself, a king at whose name every knee would bow (Philippians 2.10–11). That kingship over the world is precisely what Paul is going on to talk about in verses 20–28. And as far as Paul is concerned the evidence, the demonstration, that Jesus is the true King is that God has raised him from the dead (Romans 1.3–4). This is what he means in verse 12: it isn't just (a) that Jesus is Messiah and (b) that he's been raised from the dead, but that we know Jesus is Messiah, and we announce him as such, *because* he's been raised from the dead. It's only the resurrection that makes the crucifixion appear anything other than a horrible end for another failed Messiah.

Paul's careful argument in this section is designed to show the Corinthians, starkly, what would follow if you were to declare that there is no resurrection. Since this is what virtually all ancient pagans believed, the best explanation for why some in Corinth were denying the resurrection is that it made no sense within their surrounding world-view. There was no room for it in the culture they had grown up in. But Paul wants them to see that the Christian world-view is different, and that it has the power at the personal level and the rigour at the intellectual level to take on the old pagan world-views and win. The resurrection is the foundation of the Christian counterculture. And the immediate results go beyond culture into the world of royal claims: Jesus is Lord, so Caesar isn't.

This takes us, too, into the deeper world of moral and spiritual reality, and by that route into the very structure of the cosmos itself. Paul's strongest argument in this passage is to point up the link between sin and death (verse 17). If Jesus has been raised, the power of death has been broken, and final victory over it is assured (verse 26). Death, as always in biblical thought, is the result of sin, as humans turn away from the life-giving God and vainly attempt to find life elsewhere (see Romans 5.12–14). So if death has been defeated it must mean that sin has been defeated as well.

We could spell it out like this:

1. If Jesus has been raised, that proves he really was the Messiah, since God has clearly reversed the verdict of the court, which found him guilty of being a messianic pretender, and wrote that as the charge above his head. But if he really was the Messiah, and has now been raised from the dead, his death itself turns out not to have been simply a tragic and ghastly end but God's strange means of dealing with the sin of the world.

2. However, if he wasn't raised from the dead, he wasn't and isn't the Messiah, and his cross had no such effect. Sin has not been dealt with; the world is still as it was.

But Paul doesn't believe that for a moment. With Jesus' resurrection, he insists, a new world has opened up, in which the all-embracing power of sin and death no longer holds sway. The world we know – the world whose loveliness, majesty, fragrance and teeming life are mocked by death, decay, corruption and sheer entropy – has heard the news that there is after all a way forward, a way into a **life** yet greater, more beautiful, more powerful, than this one. Take away Jesus' resurrection and all that is put into doubt.

With that, you lose any sense that the individual follower of Jesus really does live in a new world in which the power of sin has been defeated. 'If the Messiah isn't raised, your **faith** is worthless, and you are still in your sins.' What's more (verse 18), Christians who have died in the meantime are dead and gone; when some in Corinth denied the resurrection they were declaring, in effect, that the ancient pagan view of life after death (a shadowy half-existence in the world of Hades) was the best they could hope for.

And, as Paul says, without the hope of resurrection, what is the point of being one of the Messiah's people in the first place? Hated, reviled, persecuted, struggling – if this is all there is, surely it would be better to throw in the towel, to admit that many other philosophies gave you an easier life, and to stop wasting your time with this Jesus nonsense? He will develop this later in the chapter, but already the point is coming through loud and clear.

Those who deny the resurrection, then, are not simply tinkering with one negotiable element of Christian belief. (Not long ago there was a survey among bishops in my part of the church; most of them said they did believe in Jesus' resurrection, but some said that whether or not this was a *bodily* event didn't really matter – you could believe it or not as you chose. That is a total misunderstanding of what Paul is talking about – and Paul is our earliest witness for the gospel itself.) They are cutting off the branch on which the gospel, and those who embrace it, are sitting. They are even accusing the **apostles** of 'bearing false witness' about God himself (verse 15). But, most importantly, they are declaring that no great event has yet happened through which the world has been changed. They are reducing Christianity to a form of spirituality, a new 'religion' to take its place alongside the others in the marketplace of ancient pluralism. This danger is as present today as it was in the first century.

1 CORINTHIANS 15.20–28

The Reign of the Messiah

[20]But in fact the Messiah has been raised from the dead, as the first
fruits of those who have fallen asleep. [21]For since it was through a
human that death arrived, it's through a human that the resurrection
from the dead has arrived. [22]All die in Adam, you see, and all will be
made alive in the Messiah.

[23]Each, however, in proper order. The Messiah rises as the first
fruits; then those who belong to the Messiah will rise at the time of his
royal arrival. [24]Then comes the end, the goal, when he hands over the
kingly rule to God the father, when he has destroyed all rule and all
authority and power. [25]He has to go on ruling, you see, until 'he has
put all his enemies under his feet'. [26]Death is the last enemy to be
destroyed, [27]because 'he has put all things in order under his feet'. But
when it says that everything is put in order under him, it's obvious
that this doesn't include the one who put everything in order under
him. [28]No: when everything is put in order under him, then the son
himself will be placed in proper order under the one who placed
everything in order under him, so that God may be all in all.

'The whole place is a mess. I want you to go in there and tidy it up.'

The chairman of the college council was appointing a new principal, and giving him his marching orders. The college had been in bad shape for a while, and the time had come to sort it out, to put everything in proper order. There are times when institutions can be allowed to develop unchecked, to float free and see what happens; but there comes a time when someone has to take things firmly by the scruff of the neck and bring them back into shape.

The **resurrection** of Jesus was the moment when the one true God appointed the man through whom the whole cosmos would be brought back into its proper order. A human being had got it into this mess; a human being would get it out again. The story of Genesis 1—3 – the strange, haunting tale of a wonderful world spoiled by the rebellion of God's image-bearing creatures – is in Paul's mind throughout this long chapter. But his more pressing concern is with the job that the **Messiah** has been given to do. This passage is near the heart of Paul's understanding of Jesus, God, history and the world. It's near the heart of what Jesus himself spent his short public career talking about, too. It's about the coming of God's **kingdom**.

God's kingdom was what many Jews of Paul's day longed for, and we are right to assume that he grew up longing for it too. They imagined that God would become king over the whole world, restoring Israel to glory, defeating the nations that had oppressed God's people for so long, and raising all the righteous dead to share in the new world. Quite *how* this would all happen was seldom clear; *that* it would have to happen, if God really was God, there could be no doubt. And the resurrection of Jesus of Nazareth had revealed to Paul that it had happened at last, though not at all in the way he had imagined.

Instead of all God's people being raised at the end of history, one person had been raised in the middle of history. That was the shocking, totally unexpected thing. But this meant that the coming of God's kingdom was happening in two phases. When Paul talks about things happening 'in their proper order' in verse 23, he has two things in mind: the 'order' of events, and the eventual 'order', the putting-into-shape, that God intends to bring to the world.

The order of *events* is explained first. Jesus, following his resurrection, is already the Lord of the world, already ruling as king (verse 25 is as clear a statement as anywhere in Paul of what he means when calling Jesus 'Messiah': he is God's anointed king, already installed as the world's true Lord). Paul understands the present time as the time when Jesus is already reigning. But the purpose of his reign – to defeat all the enemies that have defaced, oppressed and spoiled God's magnificent world, and his human creatures in particular – has not yet been accomplished. One day this task will be complete: the final enemy, death itself, will be defeated (verse 26), and God will be 'all in all' (verse 28). The world will have been put back to rights.

That brings us to the 'ordering' of God's final *putting-into-shape* of the world. In that final 'ordering', the son (this is the first time Paul has called Jesus the son in this passage, but it fits with the clear implication of what he has been saying all along) will be 'placed in order' under the father. Paul never used the word 'Trinity', but at several points in his writing he says things which point towards what later theologians would say. Jesus remains the son, intimately related to the father but subordinated to him. The father shares his unique glory with him (Philippians 2.9–11). If the father is the one *from* whom everything comes, the son is the one *through* whom it comes (1 Corinthians 8.6). And so on. Paul envisages the entire cosmos sorted out at last, put into the shape the creator intended; and part of that shaping is the status of Jesus himself, revealed as the father's true and only son.

Into this picture, of a world put back to rights, Paul has woven several strands taken from the Old Testament. He quotes two psalms which were often used in the early church to speak of Jesus' messianic rule. Psalm 110, quoted in verse 25, is about the king whom God will place at his right hand until all his enemies are brought into subjection. This, Paul declares, is now being fulfilled in Jesus. Psalm 8, quoted in verse 27, belongs closely with this, speaking of God 'putting all things into order under his feet'. But instead of talking about the Messiah, as Psalm 110 does, Psalm 8 talks about the human being. This role, of being under God and over the world, is not just the task of the Messiah; it's what God had in mind from the very start when he created humans in his own image. This is how Paul ties the passage tightly together: the achievement of the Messiah, and his present reign in which he is bringing the world back to order, is the fulfilment of what God intended humans to do (see verse 21). The story told in Genesis is completed by the story told in the Psalms.

At the centre of this story is a point which remains central to all Jewish and Christian thinking, spirituality and hope. Death is the *enemy*.

This is blindingly obvious to anyone who has recently been bereaved – though some, thinking to be kind, have often tried to soften the blow by pretending death doesn't really matter that much, which is a piece of blasphemous nonsense. To say that death is anything other than an enemy is to deny the goodness, beauty and power of God's good creation. And the point of resurrection is that it is the *defeat* of death. It isn't a way of saying that death isn't so bad after all. It certainly isn't a way of saying that after death we go into some other realm, perhaps called '**heaven**' (notice how Paul never mentions heaven throughout this passage). The only thing Paul says here about where people are after they die is that they 'belong to the Messiah' (verse 23), as in verse 18 he had spoken of people who had 'fallen asleep in the Messiah'.

No: 'resurrection' isn't the *immediate* future for those who die; it's what happens at the *subsequent* moment, the moment when Jesus reappears as king (that's what 'his royal arrival' refers to, picking up the language of the emperor coming back to Rome after being away). At that final moment death itself will be conquered. And, since death is the unmaking of God's creation, resurrection will be its remaking. That, and nothing less, is the Christian hope.

1 CORINTHIANS 15.29–34

Resurrection Gives Meaning to Present Christian Living

[29]Otherwise, what are people doing when they get baptized on behalf
of the dead? If the dead simply aren't raised, why should people get
baptized on their behalf?
[30]And why should we face danger every hour? [31]I die every day –
yes, that's something for you to boast about, my dear family, and that's
the boast I have in the Messiah, Jesus our Lord! [32]If, in human terms,
I fought with wild animals at Ephesus, what use is that to me? If the
dead are not raised, 'let's eat and drink, for tomorrow we die'!
[33]Don't be deceived: 'bad company kills off good habits'! [34]Sober up;
straighten up; stop sinning. Yes, some of you simply don't know God!
I'm saying this to bring shame on you.

We stood in the great Colosseum in Rome, and stared at the chambers and passages underneath where the floor would have been.

'This is where they kept the wild animals', our guide said. 'They used ropes and pulleys to winch up the cages, and then the animals would come out of a trapdoor straight into the arena.' We looked around and imagined the crowd, half the city packed into the vast stadium for a holiday spectacle full of excitement, blood and death. We imagined the gladiators, trained up for this moment, sharing their last meal together the previous night, knowing that by the following day many if not all of them would be dead.

And I thought of Paul, speaking here (verse 32) of fighting with wild beasts in Ephesus. This is strange, because Paul almost certainly didn't actually fight animals in an arena like a gladiator would have done. It seems most likely that he means it metaphorically. Something had happened at Ephesus (that's where he is while writing this letter) which had been, for him, just like fighting wild beasts.

Some people think this is a reference to a huge moral struggle he's had to go through, with the wild animals of temptation coming up from the floor to devour him. Others think it's a battle with spiritual forces, using the weapons of prayer and fasting. I am inclined to think it's to do with the enormous opposition that the **gospel** aroused, not least from those who saw it as a political threat (Ephesus was a great centre of the new imperial cult), an economic threat (if Paul was right, man-made idols were a nonsense, but lots of people made a living by making and selling them), and a religious threat (if Jesus was the world's true Lord, the other gods and goddesses at Ephesus, whose worship was woven into the fabric of local culture, were downgraded). In chapter 19, Acts describes a riot in the huge theatre in Ephesus because of this explosive combination. As far as Paul was concerned, it was like being in the arena, facing a horde of wild beasts, with nothing but the weapons of the gospel for help.

Paul was good at breaking up a heavy discussion with a change of pace and style, and that's what he's doing in this little passage. The point he's making is that if he went through all that in order simply to die, with no hope of **resurrection**, he would be just like those gladiators, eating, drinking and making merry the night before the big show, knowing that this was the end. Paul does not even contemplate the idea, popular though it was in some philosophical circles, that there might be a wonderful, glorious *non*-bodily life after death. For him, as for most ordinary pagans at the time, if there was no resurrection, then death was basically the end, with nothing much to look forward to.

The other little comments which come thick and fast in this short passage all make the same point from different angles. The question of '**baptism** for the dead' (verse 29) has long been a puzzle. It may be that some Christians had died without being baptized, and that the practice had grown up (if so, it didn't last long) of other people undergoing baptism on their behalf as a sign and symbol that they really did belong to the **Messiah**. Or it may be that 'being baptized on behalf of the dead' refers to non-Christians who, after the death of close relatives or friends who were Christians, decided to become Christians themselves, undergoing baptism so that they would continue to be with their loved ones in the final resurrection. But, whichever conclusion we come to (and every student of Paul knows that this verse is a difficult one), the overall point is clear. Something the Corinthians knew about as a regular practice makes no sense unless there is in fact a resurrection to look forward to.

His own sufferings, and the dangers he faces, are a further argument (verses 30–31), leading to the passage about the metaphorical 'wild beasts'. This then brings him, suddenly, to a quotation from the Greek poet Menander: 'bad company kills off good habits'. What Paul is saying – and quoting a pagan poet is a heavily ironic way of making the point – is that the Corinthian Christians, who ought by now to be able to show and tell the truth of the one living God to their pagan neighbours, are instead continuing to allow the pagan thought-forms of those neighbours to distort and even deny the central beliefs they should be gladly holding. There is a danger, as present today as it was in Paul's day, of being deceived: it is possible to allow the influence of the surrounding culture and the ideas it promotes to seep into a Christian world-view until the truth has been turned into a lie. Part of the point of the gospel is that, through it, people come to know the true God (see 8.1–6); but some of these Christians have simply forgotten who God is (verse 34). They need the sharp rebuke Paul already issued in 6.5: I'm saying this to make you ashamed.

Nothing in this little section is actually an *argument* that the resurrection (of Jesus, or of Christians) is *in fact* true; it is all designed to say 'just think what it would mean if it isn't'. Someone might conclude, from these verses alone, that since it still isn't true all these consequences really do follow: baptism (especially on behalf of the dead) is a waste of time; Paul has been suffering and struggling unnecessarily; and one might just as well eat and drink and wait for death. But pointing things out in this fashion is useful alongside the formal, step-by-step exposition of the Christian world-view in verses 20–28 and the detailed discussion of the resurrection body which will now follow (verses 35–49). When faced with a new idea, especially the questioning of some central aspect of the faith, the wise Christian will ask: does this fit with what we regularly do as Christians? Does it make sense of the suffering which many have undergone for the faith? Does it show the tell-tale signs of being imported from pagan ideas? And, above all, does it show a true understanding and knowledge of the one true God, the creator, the **life**-giver?

1 CORINTHIANS 15.35–49

The Transformed Resurrection Body

[35]But someone is now going to say: 'How are the dead raised? What
sort of body will they come back with?' [36]Stupid! What you sow
doesn't come to life unless it dies. [37]The thing you sow isn't the body
that is going to come later; it's just a naked seed of, let's say, wheat, or
some other plant. [38]God then gives it a body of the sort he wants, with
each of the seeds having its own particular body.

[39]Not all physical objects have the same kind of physicality. There is
one kind of physicality for humans, another kind for animals, another
for birds, and another for fish. [40]Some bodies belong in the heavens,

and some on the earth; and the kind of glory appropriate for the ones
in the heavens is different from the kind of glory appropriate for the
ones on the earth. [41]There is one kind of glory for the sun, another for
the moon, and another for the stars, since the stars themselves vary,
with different degrees of glory.

[42]That's what it's like with the resurrection of the dead. The body is
sown decaying, and raised undecaying. [43]It is sown in shame, and
raised in glory. It is sown in weakness, and raised in power. [44]It is
sown as the embodiment of ordinary nature, and raised as the embod-
iment of the spirit. If ordinary nature has its embodiment, then the
spirit too has its embodiment. [45]That's what it means when the Bible
says, 'The first man, Adam, became a living natural being'; the last
Adam became a life-giving spirit.

[46]But you don't get the spirit-animated body first; you get the nature-
animated one, and you get the spirit-animated one later. [47]The first
man is from the ground, and is made of earth; the second man is from
heaven. [48]Earthly people are like the man of earth; heavenly people are
like the man from heaven. [49]We have borne the image of the man made
of earth; we shall also bear the image of the man from heaven.

Imagine standing outside a car showroom, a hundred or more years from now. An advertisement has brought you and lots of others to see a new type of car. Different from all that went before, the slogan had said.

'Looks pretty much the same to me,' says one person.

'Well, it's similar,' replies another, 'but the engine seems different somehow.'

The inventor makes a short speech.

'I know it may look like an ordinary car,' he says, 'but what makes this one totally different is what it runs on. We've developed a new fuel, nothing to do with oil or petrol. It's clean, it's safe, and there are limitless supplies. And because of the type of fuel, the engine will never wear out. This car is going to last for ever.'

A fantasy, of course – or perhaps not, since you never know what inventions are going to come next (who in 1880 would have predicted the jet engine or the microchip?). But it gets us to the point of this long, dense and hugely important discussion. What sort of a body will the **resurrection** produce? And what will it 'run' on?

We may as well go to the heart of the passage, to the verse that has puzzled people many times in the past, and still does. In verse 44 Paul contrasts the two types of bodies, the present one and the resurrection one. The words he uses are technical and tricky. Many versions translate these words as 'physical body' and 'spiritual body', but this is highly misleading. That is as though the difference between the old car and the new one was that, whereas the old one was *made of* steel, the new one is *made of* something quite different – plastic, say, or wood, or some as-yet-uninvented metal alloy. If you go that route, you may well end up saying, as many have done, that Paul is making a contrast simply between what we call a 'body', that is a physical object, and what we might call a ghost, a 'spiritual' object in the sense of 'non-physical'. But that is exactly what he is *not* saying.

The contrast he's making is between a body *animated by* one type of **life** and a body animated by another type. The difference between them is found, if you like, in what the two bodies run on. The present body is animated by the normal life which all humans share. The word Paul uses for this often means '**soul**'; he means it in the sense of the ordinary life-force on which we all depend in this present body, the ordinary energy that keeps us breathing and our blood circulating. But the body that we shall be given in the resurrection is to be animated by God's own **spirit**. This is what Paul says in a simpler passage, Romans 8.10–11: the spirit of Jesus the **Messiah** dwells within you at the moment, and God will give life to your mortal bodies through this spirit who lives inside you.

But when the spirit creates a new body, it won't wear out. Here, in order to make the illustration of the new car really work, we would have to say that the new fuel will not only preserve the engine for ever, but the bodywork too. That would be straining even fantasy-imagination a bit far. But we need to say something like that to do justice to what Paul has written here.

Paul does in fact think that the resurrection body will be a different kind of thing to the present one, because in verses 51 and 52, and again in Philippians 3.20–21, he declares that Christians who have not died at the moment when Jesus returns as Lord will need to be *changed*. But the contrast he then makes between the present body in itself, and the future body in itself, is not the contrast between 'natural' and 'spiritual'. That, as we've seen, has to do with what energizes these two bodies, what they run on. The contrast between the two bodies in themselves is stated in verses 42 and 43. It is the contrast between corruption (our present bodies fall sick, bits wear out, we decay, die, and return to dust) and incorruption (the new body won't do any of those things). It is the contrast between shame (we know we were made for more than this decaying, corrupting life, and we are ashamed of frailty and death) and honour (the new body will be splendid, with nothing to be ashamed of). It is the contrast between weakness and power.

We can now stand back from the detail in the middle of the passage and see how the whole argument works.

The first paragraph (verses 35–38) introduces the idea of the seed which is sown looking like one thing and which comes up looking quite different. Paul doesn't of course mean that when you bury a body in the ground, a new one 'grows' like a plant from its seed. The point he is making is simply that we understand the principle of transformation, of a new body in continuity with the old yet somehow different. And he emphasizes particularly that this happens through the action of God: 'God gives it a body.' That's the first thing to grasp: the resurrection is the work of God the creator, and it will involve transformation – not merely resuscitation, as though the seed, after a while underground, were to emerge as a seed once again.

The second paragraph (verses 39–41) establishes a different point: that we are all used to different types of physicality, all the way from the fish in the sea to the stars in the sky. When Paul speaks of some of these physical objects having 'glory', he means of course 'brightness'; but this doesn't mean he's preparing us for the idea that people raised from the dead will shine like electric light bulbs. When he describes the new body as having 'glory', it's in contrast to 'shame' or 'humiliation' (verse 43, and Philippians 3.21), not to 'darkness'. His point is simply to note that there are different types of created physicality, each with its own properties.

Throughout the passage so far, he's been echoing Genesis 1, where God creates the sun, the moon and the stars, and particularly trees and plants that have their seed within them. (As I typed that sentence, a gust of wind blew a little shower of seeds in through the window from the tree outside.) The underlying theme of the whole chapter, remember, is new creation, new Genesis: God will complete the project he began at the beginning, and in the process he will reverse and undo the effects of human rebellion, especially death itself, the great enemy that drags God's beautiful world down into decay and dissolution. Paul will now move to the climax of Genesis 1, the creation of human beings in God's own image (Genesis 1.26–28). As with Jesus' resurrection, so with ours: this will not be a strange distortion of our original humanity, but will be the very thing we were made for in the first place.

The final paragraph (verses 42–49) brings him to the crunch. The ultimate contrast between the present body and the future one is between two basic types of humanness. God already has the new model in store, he says, waiting to bring it out on show at the proper time – though, of course, the prototype, the resurrection body of Jesus himself, has already been launched.

Paul's word for the place where God keeps things safe before unveiling them at the proper time is of course '**heaven**'. When he speaks of the 'earthly' humanity and the 'heavenly' humanity, he doesn't mean that we will 'go to heaven' to become the new type. Rather, God will bring this new humanity, our new bodies, *from* heaven to earth, transforming the present bodies of Christians who are still alive, and raising the dead to the same kind of renewed, deathless, glorious body.

That is the hope set before us in the resurrection; and it is all based, of course, on the fact that Jesus himself, the Messiah, already possesses the new type of body. He is 'the man from heaven'; and, as we have borne the image of the old, corruptible humanity (see Genesis 5.3), so we shall bear the image of Jesus himself (see Romans 8.29). The overall point of the chapter is that in the resurrection of Jesus himself the power of the creator God was at work to bring about the renewal of the world, and that through the work of the spirit this same creator God will give new, glorious, deathless bodily life to all his people.

1 CORINTHIANS 15.50–58

The Mystery and the Victory

> 50This is what I'm saying, my dear family. Flesh and blood can't inherit
> God's kingdom; decay can't inherit undecaying life. 51Look! I'm telling
> you a mystery. We won't all sleep; we're all going to be changed – 52in
> a flash, at the blink of an eye, at the last trumpet. This is how it will be,
> you see: the trumpet's going to sound, the dead will be raised undecaying, and we're going to be changed. 53This decaying body must put
> on the undecaying one; this dying body must put on immortality.
> 54When the decaying puts on the undecaying, and the dying puts on
> the undying, then the saying that has been written will come true:
>
> Death is swallowed up in victory!
> 55Death, where's your victory gone?
> Death, where's your sting gone?
>
> 56The 'sting' of death is sin, and the power of sin is the law. 57But
> thank God! He gives us the victory, through our Lord Jesus the Messiah.
>
> 58So, my dear family, be firmly fixed, unshakeable, always full to overflowing with the Lord's work. In the Lord, as you know, the work you're doing will not be worthless.

He stood there in baggy jeans, trainers and an old sweater. 'You can't come in like that,' I said. 'This is a smart lunch, and we're the guests. We've got to get it right.'

'No problem,' he replied, and within three minutes had changed, as though miraculously, into a dark suit, a smart tie, and polished black shoes. The transformation seemed almost instantaneous.

Of course, social convention doesn't have much to do with the **kingdom of God**. Indeed, Paul had hard words to say in chapter 11 about the social divisions in the Corinthian community. But that's not the point. This passage is all about the instant transformation which will change, not just the outward appearance, but the inner reality of who and what we are.

Paul is here talking about the people – he assumes he will be one of them – who are still alive at the great moment when **heaven** is unveiled, the royal Lord reappears, the dead are raised to their new bodies, and (as he says in Romans 8) the whole creation is liberated from decay to share the freedom of the glory of God's children. There is one apparent problem remaining: what happens to those who are still alive?

In 1 Thessalonians 4.17 Paul uses picture-language of one sort, borrowed from Daniel 7: we will be caught up on the clouds to meet the Lord as he comes, so that we can then escort him royally into his kingdom, here in God's new world. But in the present passage and Philippians 3.20–21 he speaks of the same event in terms of what happens to the bodies of those concerned. The answer is simple: they will be transformed.

They need to be transformed, because the way they are at the moment is inappropriate for God's new world. It's not just like someone wearing scruffy jeans at a smart lunch; it's like somebody who is, so to speak, *made of the wrong stuff*. At the moment we are people made of corruptible, decaying material; we need to be transformed into non-corruptible, undecaying material, so that we become people over whom death has no more control.

People get puzzled when Paul says 'flesh and blood can't inherit God's kingdom'. Hasn't he just insisted on the bodily **resurrection**? And isn't 'flesh and blood' a way of saying 'body'? Does he, they wonder, mean after all that the new existence will be 'non-bodily', 'spiritual' in the sense that we insisted he did *not* mean in verse 44?

No. When Paul uses the word 'flesh', he regularly means that there's something wrong with the material in question. Either it's in rebellion against God; or it is perishable, decaying; or both. What he here means by 'flesh and blood' is explained immediately afterwards. The present 'flesh and blood' will decay and die, but God intends to create a world – and, in Jesus, he has decisively inaugurated the project – in which decay and death are not accommodated but defeated. That is the whole point of the present passage, summing up and celebrating the entire long chapter.

The point then is that 'we shall not all sleep' – in other words, not all Christians will die before the great day – but 'we shall all be changed'. We shall be transformed. It will happen in a flash, in a great act of new creation, echoing round the cosmos like the blast of a great trumpet. When this happens, the ancient story which the Bible told in a thousand different ways will come true: the story of creation reaching its intended goal; the story of the enemies being defeated (Egypt, Assyria, Babylon, Syria and many others – and now the ultimate ones, sin and death); the story of God's victory, the creator's victory, over all the forces of chaos and destruction.

Paul here quotes from two biblical passages, Isaiah 25 and Hosea 13, which pointed in this direction. But this truth, like that of Jesus' own death and resurrection, is not simply established through one or two proof-texts. It is in line with the entire narrative. Death has claimed a victory, and the pagan world shrugs its shoulders and acknowledges it. The Jewish world at its best declares that God remains the creator and will do a new thing. The Christian message is that he *has already done the new thing* in the **Messiah**, Jesus, and that he *will* do it for all Jesus' people through the power of the **spirit**. And in that new thing death and decay will be gone, swallowed up for ever.

Paul pauses to glance sideways at the ways in which death has worked. It gets its peculiar character, its unpleasant 'sting', through sin, the dark power that entices humans to rebellion, to turn away from God the **life**-giver. And sin gets its particular power, in Paul's world, from the **law**. Paul doesn't explain what he means here, and we need Romans 7.1—8.11 to get inside this cryptic throwaway line. But his main point is clear: through our Lord Jesus, the Messiah, God *has* given us the victory over all the powers that drag us down, he *will* give it to us in the future, and he *is* giving it to us here and now.

The 'here and now' is where Paul ends up. You might think, after a spectacular chapter like this one, that he would conclude by saying something like, 'So let's rejoice at the wonderful hope we can look forward to!' But he doesn't. And this isn't just because he is a solid and sober practical theologian, true though that is. It's because the truth he has been expounding, the truth of the resurrection of the dead and the transformation of the living, is not just a truth about the future hope. It's a truth about the present significance of what we are and do. *If it is true that God is going to transform this present world, and renew our whole selves, bodies included, then what we do in the present time with our bodies, and with our world, matters.* For far too long many Christians have been content to separate out future hope from present responsibility, but that is precisely what Paul refuses to do. His full-bodied doctrine and promise of resurrection sends us back to our present world, and our present life of bodily obedience to our Lord, in the glorious but sobering knowledge (as we saw in 6.14, 13.8–13 and elsewhere) that, if there is continuity between who and what we are in the present and who and what we will be in the future, we cannot discount the present life, the present body and the present world as irrelevant.

On the contrary. It is a matter of the greatest encouragement to Christian workers, most of whom are away from the public eye, unsung heroes and heroines, getting on faithfully and quietly with their God-given tasks, that what they do 'in the Lord' during the present time will last, will matter, will stand for all time. *How* God will take our prayer, our art, our love, our writing, our political action, our music, our honesty, our daily work, our pastoral care, our teaching, our whole selves – how God will take this and weave its varied strands into the glorious tapestry of his new creation, we can at present have no idea. *That* he will do so is part of the truth of the resurrection, and perhaps one of the most comforting parts of all.

1 CORINTHIANS 16.1–9

The Collection and Paul's Plans

1Now when it comes to the collection for God's people, you should do
the same as I laid down for the churches in Galatia. 2On the first day
of each week, every one of you should set aside and store up whatever
surplus you have gained, so that when I come I won't have to take an
actual collection. 3Then, when I get to you, I will write formal letters
to commission the people you approve, whoever they are, to go to
Jerusalem with your gift. 4If it's appropriate for me to go as well, we
can travel together.
5I shall come to you when I've been through Macedonia. I intend to
pass through Macedonia, you see, 6and I may well end up staying with
you, perhaps even through the winter. Then you will be able to send
me on to wherever I shall be going to next. 7I don't want just to see you
for a short time; I'm hoping to remain with you for a while, if the Lord
allows me to. 8I shall be staying on in Ephesus until Pentecost. 9A huge
and important door has opened for me here, and there is plenty of
opposition.

Advertisements in many cosmopolitan cities offer easy and efficient ways of transferring money from one part of the world to another. Many families are now divided by oceans; sometimes those who find work are able to support relatives back home who are not so fortunate. All you have to do is to walk into a local branch of whichever bank or travel agent is offering the required service, and within minutes your family the other side of the world will be able to collect the money.

Now imagine what it would be like without telephones, telexes, e-mail, and 'wire transfers' of various kinds. What would you do? Well, of course, you could send the money by post. And if you didn't want to send actual banknotes, you would send a cheque or something equivalent. But what would you do if there was no paper money, and no central banking service? You would have to send somebody in person to carry the cash.

The nature of Paul's project now becomes apparent. The little church in Jerusalem had suffered grievously by persecution, the scattering of its members, and perhaps also from the enthusiastic pooling of resources in its early days (as described in Acts). Paul had promised the Jerusalem leaders that he would 'continue to remember the poor' (Galatians 2.10). It's not clear whether they had expected Paul to keep his promise in quite this way, but he has worked out this plan and is determined to bring it to a successful conclusion. He isn't just interested in raising money to help those who don't have very much. He wants this to be a sign of something more, something bigger, something so momentous that later on, when it's all been collected and he's ready to go, he becomes anxious about the reaction he's going to get (Romans 15.31).

The problem arises from the very purpose that Paul is using the collection for: to signal to the **Gentile** Christians that they are part of the same family as the Jewish Christians in Jerusalem; and, more importantly still, to signal to the Jewish Christians that those Gentiles out there, who have come to **faith** in Jesus as the **Messiah** and the true Lord of the world, are part of the same family as they are, even though they haven't become Jews in the process.

That was the issue Paul faced in Galatians. Now he has developed this plan for the collection as a long-term strategy for making both 'sides' of the great ethnic divide in the early church understand the truth of the matter. So this letter, which has addressed the problem of divisions within the church, and of the urgent need for love at the heart of everything, brings it all into focus with a practical, hard-headed scheme. And now he's concerned about the detailed arrangements for making it all work.

Paul has, it seems, already made arrangements for the churches in central Turkey to contribute in this way. He now plans to travel round northern Greece (Macedonia in his day included the area where Philippi and Thessalonica are) and then come south to Corinth. And when he arrives he doesn't want to have to start a fund-raising campaign from scratch.

He wants them – all of them, not just the wealthy – to put something aside on the first day of every week. (This is the first mention in the New Testament of a special significance being given to Sunday. Some will give a wry smile at the thought that the first time anyone refers to Sunday the point at issue is taking a collection. We should be glad, though, that the church from the very beginning was called to share its resources.) Then there will be the business of how the money is to be taken. Much better that the churches themselves should commission other people to take it than that Paul and his travelling companions should do it by themselves. However much people trust Paul, there is no point leaving a loophole for potential accusations of fraud.

Much better, too, that actual Gentile Christians should come with Paul, so that they can meet the Jewish part of the family face to face (though this good idea became the flashpoint for trouble, according to Acts 21.29). But the real problem was going to be how to carry the money. We can only assume that the eventual sum collected would be turned into a small number of high-value coins, and that a party of several members would have these concealed about their persons for the journey. They had a long way to go, by land and sea, and would be in danger from robbers almost every mile of the way.

When we hear of this project again, it is in the very different context of Paul's second letter (2 Corinthians 8 and 9), where we learn that all sorts of things have happened which make the collection at one level more difficult and at another level even more necessary. This has to do, as well, with Paul's travel plans. Here he is cheerfully planning a midsummer trip round northern Greece, after completing his present stay in Ephesus; but this, too, was postponed, for reasons that will also become clear in the second letter. Paul is very much aware that all his plans are subject to the will of the Lord (verse 7), which is not usually clear until the last minute! But even he can hardly have expected the difficulties and painful experiences he was going to have to face any day now. Overhearing this part of the letter, but knowing what is to come, we are now in the position of someone watching a movie for the second time, knowing that the car driving so merrily along the road is about to go over a cliff . . .

Even if Paul had known of all this, however, we can be sure that he wouldn't have backed away. As he knew already from his time in Ephesus, where you get an open door for the **gospel** you also usually get opposition. The church today is just as liable as Paul was to all this, and hence just as much in need of humble planning, strategic thinking, and putting all things under the sign of 'if the Lord wills'.

1 CORINTHIANS 16.10–14

Timothy and Apollos

[10]If Timothy comes, take care that he isn't fearful when he's with you.
He's doing the Lord's work, after all, just as I am. [11]Nobody should

look down on him. Send him on in peace, so that he can come to me.
I'm expecting him, and so is the family here.
12As for our brother Apollos, I did my best to persuade him to go to
you with the other family members, but it simply wasn't for the best
that he should come just now. He will come when the right moment
appears.
13Keep alert, stand firm in the faith, be brave, be strong! 14Whatever
you do, do it with love.

I have a vivid memory of the first time I stood up in front of a group of people to make an announcement. It was at school, and I had been given responsibility for organizing something; and suddenly the room went quiet, everybody was looking at me, and I heard my voice, as though coming from someone else and somewhere else entirely, speaking more or less what I'd planned to say. Nobody had warned me that it is a quite different experience, almost a different *physical* experience, to ordinary speaking in ordinary personal contact. It's not just about being nervous. It's about a different feeling altogether.

Now imagine that, instead of a room full of schoolfriends, I'm standing in front of people I haven't seen for some time, many of whom in fact I don't know at all. Some of them are much older than me. Many are better speakers, and know more about the issues than I do – or at least they think they do. Some of them are likely to be cross that I'm making the announcement instead of the senior man whose place I'm taking. Now I really do have reason to be nervous. And now I am more or less in the situation Timothy would be in when he arrived in Corinth.

Timothy was considerably younger than Paul, and Paul refers to him as working with him like a son with his father – this in a world, of course, where sons were regularly apprenticed to fathers (4.17; see also Philippians 2.22). But Timothy was not, it seems, the bold, who-cares type who could stroll into a place like Corinth and charm everyone with fluent, impressive oratory.

He didn't lack courage, that's quite clear. No coward would have stuck it out alongside Paul for very long. But he seems not to have been what we would call a forceful personality. And there was a danger that the sophisticated Corinthians might look down on him, might make him feel afraid, might prevent him doing the work he'd been sent to do, not least in teaching and giving instruction. Paul's warning to the church that they shouldn't make him feel afraid is therefore a ground-level, nuts-and-bolts application of what he's been saying in much of the letter. When the Corinthian Christians welcome Timothy and give him the encouragement to teach and instruct as he is able, they will be backing off from the 'puffed-up' arrogance that has bedevilled so much of their life, and taking a more appropriately Christian stance.

Ministry is a delicate matter. Many whom God wants to use powerfully in church work are not what the world regards as 'natural leaders'. Indeed, sometimes the 'natural leader' can allow his or her personality to get in the way of the **gospel**. That is, in fact, one of the problems Paul identified in Corinth. Sending Timothy begins to look like another of Paul's strategic moves.

Whatever we say about that, his mention of Apollos (who is obviously with Paul in Ephesus) is certainly calculated to defuse any lingering suspicions the party-spirited Corinthians might have about the relationship between these two leaders. The Corinthians may have played them off against one another, but Paul and Apollos themselves are not at loggerheads with each other. Paul, so far from being anxious about Apollos going to Corinth in case the church there should join his 'party' instead of Paul's, had actually encouraged Apollos to make a visit. This hadn't been possible; the way Paul expresses that leaves it open as to whether this was Apollos's own decision, or whether circumstances, in which Paul and Apollos would both see the hand of the Lord, had ruled it out. What is also ruled out, though, is any suggestion that there is rivalry between them. This once more cuts the ground from under the factional fighting Paul criticizes in the early chapters.

The final sentences are generalized, but none the less bracing. The four commands correspond to what an army commander might say to someone on guard, and they form an ascending scale: keep awake, stand firm, be brave, be strong! The guard must stay awake and alert in case of any danger. Not only so; he must know his ground and not give way. When actual danger threatens, bravery is required to face up to it. When he has to deal with it, he needs to act with all his strength.

Paul sees the church in Corinth in danger from many things. You can't just drift along in the Christian life, hoping things will work out somehow. Precisely because of the nature of the gospel itself, those who are embraced and called by it have to take responsibility for what's going on. He wants them now to assume that responsibility for their own spiritual health, and for the ongoing work of the gospel. At every stage they will need each one of these commands. But, in the process, they must never imagine that the gospel can be helped forwards by brute force, bullying or arrogance. 'Everything you do must be done in love'; that has been the keynote of the whole letter, and Paul wants to remind them of it as he moves towards the close.

1 CORINTHIANS 16.15–24

The Love That Stitches It All Together

> 15One more word of exhortation for you, my dear family. You know the household of Stephanas: they were the first fruits of Achaea, and they have set themselves to serve God's people. 16You should submit to people like that, and to everyone who is working with them and labouring hard. 17I have thoroughly enjoyed the visit of Stephanas, Fortunatus and Achaicus; they have made up for the fact that I haven't been able to see you. 18They have refreshed my spirit and yours. Give proper recognition to such people.
>
> 19The churches in Asia send you greetings. Aquila and Prisca send you many greetings in the Lord, together with the church in their house. 20All the family send you greetings. Greet one another with the holy kiss.
>
> 21I, Paul, add my greetings in my own hand.
>
> 22If anyone doesn't love the Lord, let them be accursed! Come, Lord, come! 23The grace of the Lord Jesus be with you. 24My love be with you all in Messiah Jesus.

A young woman I met the other day was complaining about a new outfit she had bought at considerable expense in a fashionable store. She had worn it precisely once; and at the end of the evening she discovered that the seams were coming unstitched. The visual effect of trying it on, and wearing it for one occasion, had been terrific; but the workmanship had been very poor. Whoever had been in charge of the detailed, painstaking task of making sure the stitching was in good shape had not been concentrating. What was worse, the outfit had been bought abroad, and the event was back home, so no complaint could be registered without making an expensive journey.

Paul, writing to Corinth from the other side of the Aegean Sea, takes every care in this final passage that the stitching which holds together his relationship with the church in Corinth isn't going to come undone. What started with excitement, as the church in southern Greece was born, mustn't end in frustration as it tears itself loose from its founder after such a short time. As he himself says in another letter (Colossians 3.14), what ties the whole Christian family together, and stitches it up tight, is of course love.

But it isn't enough simply to *talk* about love. It's important to point to the places where it wears skin and flesh. Stephanas, Fortunatus and Achaicus have brought Paul the letter from the Corinthian church, and they have stayed with him while he has pondered it and dictated his reply. This visit has been, for Paul, a breath of friendly and supportive

Corinthian air. As long as there are people like this in Corinth, Paul knows that all is not lost.

Presumably Stephanas wasn't among those who were proclaiming 'I am of Paul', because otherwise verse 16 would look as though Paul was simply backing 'his own party'. The point is that they have proved themselves trustworthy and faithful, and the church should be proud of them and give them the respect they deserve. Stephanas, in particular, had with his family been the 'first fruits' of southern Greece. Paul uses this well-known harvest picture quite often, most recently in 15.20, 23. It means that Stephanas and his family were the first people in the area to believe the **gospel**, and Paul regarded them with joy, like the first sheaf of corn at harvest-time, a sign that there was much more to come.

The fine things Paul says about these three from Corinth is the first major bit of 'stitching' that he does. He is bound to these three in special affection and gratitude; they are central to the life of the Corinthian church; together they will help to maintain the bond and keep it strong.

The second piece of 'stitching' comes with the mention of Aquila and Prisca. They were Jewish Christians who had had to leave Rome when Claudius expelled the Jews (see Acts 18.2); they had gone to Corinth, where they had met Paul, and now, it seems, they had gone on to Ephesus. By the time Paul writes Romans they are back in Rome again (Romans 16.3–5); they seem almost as well travelled as Paul himself. In any case, they had been members of the Corinthian church from its earliest days, and their greetings, and the reminder of their close friendship with Paul himself, was another bond between the **apostle** and his people.

Looking wider, all the Christian communities in the area sent greetings. Paul wants to remind the Corinthians, as he has done at various points in the letter, that they are not the only people the gospel has reached. They are part of a much larger family, sewn into a much larger fabric. Every reminder of the mutual love and respect that this implied is another stitch holding it all together.

So, too, is the 'kiss of peace', which from the very earliest times in the church was the greeting during worship which demonstrated reconciliation, affection, mutual care and support between all members. It was, of course, the *holy* kiss; some later writers had to point out the dangers of over-familiarity, of allowing Christian greetings to acquire romantic or erotic overtones. It is a measure, though, of how far some Western Christianity had diverged from Paul's ideal that when 'the Peace', even in the form of a handshake, was reintroduced in many churches in the twentieth century, it met with huge resistance from those who preferred to worship in as it were hermetically sealed compartments, sitting close to other people but maintaining a strict line between them.

Paul takes the pen, as we do today after dictating or typing a letter, both to write a signature and to add a few closing remarks – which of course gain all the more significance both by coming at the end and by being in his own hand. Now the stitching is not so much between apostle and congregation, but between the whole church and its Lord. As in 8.1–6, and by implication in so much of the argument, what really matters is the love that Christians have for the Lord himself. This grows, in Paul's mind, out of the ancient prayer and command to Israel, to 'Love the Lord your God with all your heart . . .' (Deuteronomy 6.5). That command formed the heart and centre of the **covenant**, the bond of love, of God's promise and Israel's faithfulness, the stitching together of the one God and the chosen people.

But when the Bible speaks of covenant, it regularly speaks of the results of covenant obedience and disobedience: obedience brings more blessing, disobedience or infidelity brings curse. So it is here. Anyone who does not love the Lord, Paul says, must be 'cursed': the word is *Anathema*, which refers to the solemn 'ban' placed on those in the Old Testament who rejected the true God and spurned his ways. Paul doesn't want to end the letter simply with the sense that all will be well and there's nothing to worry about; there *are* things to worry about in Corinth, and central to them is the danger that some Christians will be so in love with their own spiritual and philosophical attainments that they forget the love (which includes loyalty, devotion and obedience, not just warm feelings), that they owe to the Lord who bought them with his own life and death.

The warning of the curse for those who turn away from the Lord and his love is reinforced by the strange phrase *Maran Atha*, which is actually Aramaic (the native language of Palestine in Jesus' and Paul's day). This means that it is probably a very ancient Christian prayer used by the church from the time before the gospel spread out into the **Gentile** world. It means, 'Our Lord, Come', and is almost certainly a prayer, in line with the Lord's own prayer, that the **kingdom** would come, that Jesus would return as king and Lord (see 15.20–28), and that through his defeat of every enemy, including death itself, God would be Lord of all. To pray for the coming of the Lord is the most natural prayer of those who love him; the fact that the church must and should pray this prayer regularly ought to serve as a warning to those whose love is growing cold.

But cold love, and warnings of judgment, cannot be Paul's final word in this letter in which grace and love have been central strands. Grace and love are the two final stitches which Paul puts into the fabric of his relationship with the turbulent, energetic, often muddled but greatly beloved people of Corinth: the grace of the Lord, more than adequate to meet every need, and the love which he himself has for them, a love that no rebellion or accusation can change. As we see when we turn to the second letter to Corinth, this love was going to be tested far more severely than had yet happened, and Paul himself was going to need fresh resources of grace to deal with the next stage of the relationship.

GLOSSARY

age to come, ***see*** **present age**

apostle, disciple, the Twelve

'Apostle' means 'one who is sent'. It could be used of an ambassador or official delegate. In the New Testament it is sometimes used specifically of Jesus' inner circle of twelve; but Paul sees not only himself but several others outside the Twelve as 'apostles', the criterion being whether the person had personally seen the risen Jesus. Jesus' own choice of twelve close associates symbolized his plan to renew God's people, Israel; after the death of Judas Iscariot (Matthew 27.5; Acts 1.18), Matthias was chosen by lot to take his place, preserving the symbolic meaning. During Jesus' lifetime they, and many other followers, were seen as his 'disciples', which means 'pupils' or 'apprentices'.

baptism

Literally, 'plunging' people into water. From within a wider Jewish tradition of ritual washings and bathings, **John the Baptist** undertook a vocation of baptizing people in the Jordan, not as one ritual among others but as a unique moment of **repentance**, preparing them for the coming of the **kingdom of God**. Jesus himself was baptized by John, identifying himself with this renewal movement and developing it in his own way. His followers in turn baptized others. After his **resurrection**, and the sending of the **holy spirit**, baptism became the normal sign and means of entry into the community of Jesus' people. As early as Paul it was aligned both with the **Exodus** from Egypt (1 Corinthians 10.2) and with Jesus' death and resurrection (Romans 6.2–11).

Christ, ***see*** **Messiah**

circumcision, circumcised

The cutting off of the foreskin. Male circumcision was a major mark of identity for Jews, following its initial commandment to Abraham (Genesis 17), reinforced by Joshua (Joshua 5.2–9). Other peoples, e.g. the Egyptians, also circumcised male children. A line of thought from Deuteronomy (e.g. 30.6), through Jeremiah (e.g. 31.33), to the **Dead Sea Scrolls** and the New Testament (e.g. Romans 2.29) speaks of 'circumcision of the heart' as God's real desire, by which one may become inwardly what the male Jew is outwardly, that is, marked out as part of God's people. At periods of Jewish assimilation into the surrounding culture, some Jews tried to remove the marks of circumcision (e.g. 1 Maccabees 1.11–15).

covenant

At the heart of Jewish belief is the conviction that the one God, **YHWH**, who had made the whole world, had called Abraham and his family to belong to him in a special way. The promises God made to Abraham and his family, and the requirements that were laid on them as a result, came to be seen in terms either of the agreement that a king would make with a subject people, or sometimes of the marriage bond between husband and wife. One regular way of describing this relationship was 'covenant', which can thus include both promise and **law**. The covenant was renewed at Mount Sinai with the giving of the **Torah**; in Deuteronomy before the entry to the promised land; and, in a more focused way, with David (e.g. Psalm 89). Jeremiah 31 promised that after the punishment of **exile** God would make a 'new covenant' with his people, forgiving them and binding them to him more intimately. Jesus believed that this was coming true through his **kingdom** proclamation and his death and **resurrection**. The early Christians developed these ideas in various ways, believing that in Jesus the promises had at last been fulfilled.

Dead Sea Scrolls

A collection of texts, some in remarkably good repair, some extremely fragmentary, found in the late 1940s around Qumran (near the north-east corner of the Dead Sea), and virtually all now edited, translated and in the public domain. They formed all or part of the library of a strict monastic group, most likely Essenes, founded in the mid-second century BC and lasting until the Jewish–Roman war of 66–70. The scrolls include the earliest existing manuscripts of the Hebrew and Aramaic scriptures, and several other important documents of community regulations, scriptural exegesis, hymns, wisdom writings and other literature. They shed a flood of light on one small segment within the Judaism of Jesus' day, helping us to understand how some Jews at least were thinking, praying and reading scripture. Despite attempts to prove the contrary, they make no reference to **John the Baptist**, Jesus, Paul, James or early Christianity in general.

demons, *see* **the satan**

devil, *see* **the satan**

disciple, *see* **apostle**

Essenes, *see* **Dead Sea Scrolls**

eucharist

The meal in which the earliest Christians, and Christians ever since, obeyed Jesus' command to 'do this in remembrance of him' at the Last Supper (Luke 22.19; 1 Corinthians 11.23–26). The word 'eucharist' itself comes from the Greek for 'thanksgiving'; it means, basically, 'the thank-you meal', and looks back to the many times when Jesus took bread, gave thanks for it, broke it and gave it to people (e.g. Luke 24.30; John 6.11). Other early phrases for the same meal are 'the Lord's Supper' (1 Corinthians 11.20) and 'the breaking of bread' (Acts 2.42). Later it came to be called 'the mass' (from the Latin word at the end of the service, meaning 'sent out') and 'holy communion' (Paul speaks of 'sharing' or 'communion' in the body and blood of Christ). Later theological controversies about the precise meaning of the various actions and elements of the meal should not obscure its centrality in earliest Christian living and its continuing vital importance today.

exile

Deuteronomy (29—30) warned that if Israel disobeyed **YHWH**, he would send his people into exile, but that if they then repented he would bring them back. When the Babylonians sacked Jerusalem and took the people into exile, prophets such as Jeremiah interpreted this as the fulfilment of this prophecy, and made further promises about how long exile would last (70 years, according to Jeremiah 25.12; 29.10). Sure enough, exiles began to return in the late sixth century (Ezra 1.1). However, the post-exilic period was largely a disappointment, since the people were still enslaved to foreigners (Nehemiah 9.36); and at the height of persecution by the Syrians, Daniel 9.2, 24 spoke of the 'real' exile lasting not for 70 years but for 70 *weeks* of years, i.e. 490 years. Longing for the real 'return from exile', when the prophecies of Isaiah, Jeremiah, etc. would be fulfilled, and redemption from pagan oppression accomplished, continued to characterize many Jewish movements, and was a major theme in Jesus' proclamation and his summons to **repentance**.

Exodus

The Exodus from Egypt took place, according to the book of that name, under the leadership of Moses, after long years in which the Israelites had been enslaved there. (According to Genesis 15.13f., this was itself part of God's covenanted promise to Abraham.) It demonstrated, to them and to Pharaoh, King of Egypt, that Israel was God's special child (Exodus 4.22). They then wandered through the Sinai wilderness for 40 years, led by God in a pillar of cloud and fire; early on in this time they were given the **Torah** on Mount Sinai itself. Finally, after the death of Moses and under the leadership of Joshua, they crossed the Jordan and entered, and eventually conquered, the promised land of Canaan. This event, commemorated annually in Passover and other Jewish festivals, gave the Israelites not only a powerful memory of what had made them a people, but also a particular shape and content to their faith in **YHWH** as not only creator but also redeemer; and in subsequent enslavements, particularly the **exile**, they looked for a further redemption which would be, in effect, a new Exodus. Probably no other past event so dominated the imagination of first-century Jews; among them the early Christians, following the lead of Jesus himself, continually referred back to the Exodus to give meaning and shape to their own critical events, most particularly Jesus' death and **resurrection**.

faith

Faith in the New Testament covers a wide area of human trust and trustworthiness, merging into love at one end of the scale and loyalty at the other. Within Jewish and Christian thinking faith in God also includes *belief*, accepting certain things as true about God, and what he has done in the world (e.g. bringing Israel out of Egypt; raising Jesus from the dead). For Jesus, 'faith' often seems to mean 'recognizing that God is decisively at work to bring the **kingdom** through Jesus'. For Paul, 'faith' is both the specific belief that Jesus is Lord and that God raised him from the dead (Romans 10.9) and the response of grateful human love to sovereign divine love (Galatians 2.20). This faith is, for Paul, the solitary badge of membership in God's people in **Christ**, marking them out in a way that **Torah**, and the works it prescribes, can never do.

Gehenna, hell

Gehenna is, literally, the valley of Hinnom, on the south-west slopes of Jerusalem. From ancient times it was used as a garbage dump, smouldering with a continual fire. Already by the time of Jesus some Jews used it as an image for the place of punishment after death. Jesus' own usage blends the two meanings in his warnings both to Jerusalem itself (unless it repents, the whole city will become a smouldering heap of garbage) and to people in general (to beware of God's final judgment).

Gentiles

The Jews divided the world into Jews and non-Jews. The Hebrew word for non-Jews, *goyim*, carries overtones both of family identity (i.e., not of Jewish ancestry) and of worship (i.e., of idols, not of the one true God **YHWH**). Though many Jews established good relations with Gentiles, not least in the Jewish Diaspora (the dispersion of Jews away from Palestine), officially there were taboos against contact such as intermarriage. In the New Testament the Greek word *ethne*, 'nations', carries the same meanings as *goyim*. Part of Paul's overmastering agenda was to insist that Gentiles who believed in Jesus had full rights in the Christian community alongside believing Jews, without having to become **circumcised**.

good news, gospel, message, word

The idea of 'good news', for which an older English word is 'gospel', had two principal meanings for first-century Jews. First, with roots in Isaiah, it meant the news of **YHWH**'s long-awaited victory over evil and rescue of his people. Second, it was used in the Roman world of the accession, or birthday, of the emperor. Since for Jesus and Paul the announcement of God's inbreaking **kingdom** was both the fulfilment of prophecy and a challenge to the world's present rulers, 'gospel' became an important shorthand for both the message of Jesus himself, and the apostolic message about him. Paul saw this message as itself the vehicle of God's saving power (Romans 1.16; 1 Thessalonians 2.13).

The four canonical 'gospels' tell the story of Jesus in such a way as to bring out both these aspects (unlike some other so-called 'gospels' circulated in the second and subsequent centuries, which tended both to cut off the scriptural and Jewish roots of Jesus' achievement and to inculcate a private spirituality rather than confrontation with the world's rulers). Since in Isaiah this creative, life-giving good news was seen as God's own powerful word (40.8; 55.11), the early Christians could use 'word' or 'message' as another shorthand for the basic Christian proclamation.

gospel, *see* **good news**

heaven

Heaven is God's dimension of the created order (Genesis 1.1; Psalm 115.16; Matthew 6.9), whereas 'earth' is the world of space, time and matter that we know. 'Heaven' thus sometimes stands, reverentially, for 'God' (as in Matthew's regular '**kingdom of heaven**'). Normally hidden from human sight, heaven is occasionally revealed or unveiled so that people can see God's dimension of ordinary life (e.g. 2 Kings 6.17; Revelation 1, 4—5). Heaven in the New Testament is thus not usually seen as the place where God's people go after death; at the end the New Jerusalem descends *from* heaven *to* earth, joining the two dimensions for ever. 'Entering the kingdom of heaven' does not mean 'going to heaven after death', but belonging in the present to the people who steer their earthly course by the standards and purposes of heaven (cf. the Lord's Prayer: 'on earth as in heaven', Matthew 6. 10) and who are assured of membership in the **age to come**.

hell, *see* **Gehenna**

holy spirit

In Genesis 1.2, the spirit is God's presence and power *within* creation, without God being identified with creation. The same spirit entered people, notably the prophets, enabling them to speak and act for God. At his **baptism** by **John the Baptist**, Jesus was specially equipped with the spirit, resulting in his remarkable public career (Acts 10.38). After his **resurrection**, his followers were themselves filled (Acts 2) by the same spirit, now identified as Jesus' own spirit: the creator God was acting afresh, remaking the world and them too. The spirit enabled them to live out a holiness which the **Torah** could not, producing 'fruit' in their lives, giving them 'gifts' with which to serve God, the world and the church, and assuring them of future resurrection (Romans 8; Galatians 4—5; 1 Corinthians 12—14). From very early in Christianity (e.g. Galatians 4.1–7), the spirit became part of the new revolutionary definition of God himself: 'the one who sends the son and the spirit of the son'.

John (the Baptist)

Jesus' cousin on his mother's side, born a few months before Jesus; his father was a **priest**. He acted as a prophet, baptizing in the Jordan – dramatically re-enacting the **Exodus** from Egypt – to prepare people, by **repentance**, for God's coming judgment. He may have had some contact with the **Essenes**, though his eventual public message was different from theirs. Jesus' own vocation was decisively confirmed at his **baptism** by John. As part of John's message of the **kingdom**, he outspokenly criticized Herod Antipas for marrying his brother's wife. Herod had him imprisoned, and then beheaded him at his wife's request (Mark 6.14–29). Groups of John's disciples continued a separate existence, without merging into Christianity, for some time afterwards (e.g. Acts 19.1–7).

justified, justification

God's declaration, from his position as judge of all the world, that someone is in the right, despite universal sin. This declaration will be made on the last day on the basis of an entire life (Romans 2.1–16), but is brought forward into the present on the basis of Jesus' achievement, because sin has been dealt with through his cross (Romans 3.21—4.25); the means of this present justification is simply **faith**. This means, particularly, that Jews and **Gentiles** alike are full members of the family promised by God to Abraham (Galatians 3; Romans 4).

kingdom of God, kingdom of heaven

Best understood as the king*ship*, or sovereign and saving rule, of Israel's God **YHWH**, as celebrated in several psalms (e.g. 99.1) and prophecies (e.g. Daniel 6.26f.). Because YHWH was the creator God, when he finally became king in the way he intended this would involve setting the world to rights, and particularly rescuing Israel from its enemies. 'Kingdom of God' and various equivalents (e.g. 'No king but God!') became a revolutionary slogan around the time of Jesus. Jesus' own announcement of God's kingdom redefined these expectations around his own very different plan and vocation. His invitation to people to 'enter' the kingdom was a way of summoning them to allegiance to himself and his programme, seen as the start of God's long-awaited saving reign. For Jesus, the kingdom was coming not in a single move, but in stages, of which his own public career was one, his death and **resurrection** another, and a still future consummation another. Note that 'kingdom of **heaven**' is Matthew's preferred form for the same phrase, following a regular Jewish practice of saying 'heaven' rather than 'God'. It does not refer to a place ('heaven'), but to the fact of God's becoming king in and through Jesus and his achievement. Paul speaks of Jesus, as **Messiah**, already in possession of his kingdom, waiting to hand it over finally to the father (1 Corinthians 15.23–28; cf. Ephesians 5.5).

law, *see* **Torah**

leper, leprosy

In a world without modern medicine, tight medical controls were needed to prevent the spread of contagious diseases. Several such conditions, mostly severe skin problems, were referred to as 'leprosy', and two long biblical chapters (Leviticus 13—14) are devoted to diagnosis and prevention of it. Sufferers had to live away from towns and shout 'unclean' to warn others not to approach them (13.45). If they were healed, this had to be certified by a **priest** (14.2–32).

life, soul, spirit

Ancient people held many different views about what made human beings the special creatures they are. Some, including many Jews, believed that to be complete, humans needed bodies as well as inner selves. Others, including many influenced by the philosophy of Plato (fourth century BC), believed that the important part of a human was the 'soul' (Gk: *psyche*), which at death would be happily freed from its bodily prison. Confusingly for us, the same word *psyche* is often used in the New Testament within a Jewish framework where it clearly means 'life' or 'true self', without implying a body/soul dualism that devalues the body. Human inwardness of experience and understanding can also be referred to as 'spirit'. *See also* **holy spirit, resurrection.**

message, *see* **good news**

Messiah, messianic, Christ

The Hebrew word means literally 'anointed one', hence in theory either a prophet, **priest** or king. In Greek this translates as *Christos*; 'Christ' in early Christianity was a title, and only gradually became an alternative proper name for Jesus. In practice 'Messiah' is mostly restricted to the notion, which took various forms in ancient Judaism, of the coming king who would be David's true heir, through whom **YHWH** would bring judgment to the world, and in particular would rescue Israel from pagan enemies. There was no single template of expectations. Scriptural stories and promises contributed to different ideals and movements, often focused on (a) decisive military defeat of Israel's enemies and (b) rebuilding or cleansing the **Temple**. The **Dead Sea Scrolls** speak of two 'Messiahs', one a priest and the other a king. The universal early Christian belief that Jesus was Messiah is only explicable, granted his crucifixion by the Romans (which would have been seen as a clear sign that he was not the Messiah), by their belief that God had raised him from the dead, so vindicating the implicit messianic claims of his earlier ministry.

miracles

Like some of the old prophets, notably Elijah and Elisha, Jesus performed many deeds of remarkable power, particularly healings. The **gospels** refer to these as 'deeds of power', 'signs', 'marvels' or 'paradoxes'. Our word 'miracle' tends to imply that God, normally 'outside' the closed system of the world, sometimes 'intervenes'; miracles have then frequently been denied as a matter of principle. However, in the Bible God is always present, however strangely, and 'deeds of power' are seen as *special* acts of a *present* God rather than as *intrusive* acts of an *absent* one. Jesus' own 'mighty works' are seen particularly, following prophecy, as evidence of his messiahship (e.g. Matthew 11.2–6).

Mishnah

The main codification of Jewish law (**Torah**) by the **rabbis**, produced in about AD 200, reducing to writing the 'oral Torah' which in Jesus' day ran parallel to the 'written Torah'. The Mishnah is itself the basis of the much larger collections of traditions in the two Talmuds (roughly AD 400).

parousia

Literally, it means 'presence', as opposed to 'absence', and is sometimes used by Paul with this sense (e.g. Philippians 2.12). It was already used in the Roman world for the ceremonial arrival of, for example, the emperor at a subject city or colony. Although the ascended Lord is not 'absent' from the church, when he 'appears' (Colossians 3.4; 1 John 3.2) in his 'second coming' this will be, in effect, an 'arrival' like that of the emperor, and Paul uses it thus in 1 Corinthians 15.23; 1 Thessalonians 2.19; etc. In the **gospels** it is found only in Matthew 24 (verses 3, 27, 39).

Pharisees, lawyers, legal experts, rabbis

The Pharisees were an unofficial but powerful Jewish pressure group through most of the first centuries BC and AD. Largely lay-led, though including some **priests**, their aim was to purify Israel through intensified observance of the Jewish law (**Torah**), developing their own traditions about the precise meaning and application of scripture, their own patterns of prayer and other devotion, and their own calculations of the national hope. Though not all legal experts were Pharisees, most Pharisees were thus legal experts.

They effected a democratization of Israel's life, since for them the study and practice of Torah was equivalent to worshipping in the **Temple** – though they were adamant in pressing their own rules for the Temple liturgy on an unwilling (and often **Sadducean**) priesthood. This enabled them to survive AD 70 and, merging into the early rabbinic movement, to develop new ways forward. Politically they stood up for ancestral traditions, and were at the forefront of various movements of revolt against both pagan overlordship and compromised Jewish leaders. By Jesus' day there were two distinct schools, the stricter one of Shammai, more inclined towards armed revolt, and the more lenient one of Hillel, ready to live and let live.

Jesus' debates with the Pharisees are at least as much a matter of agenda and policy (Jesus strongly opposed their separatist nationalism) as about details of theology and piety. Saul of Tarsus was a fervent right-wing Pharisee, presumably a Shammaite, until his conversion.

After the disastrous war of AD 66–70, these schools of Hillel and Shammai continued bitter debate on appropriate policy. Following the further disaster of AD 135 (the failed Bar-Kochba revolt against Rome) their traditions were carried on by the rabbis who, though looking to the earlier Pharisees for inspiration, developed a Torah-piety in which personal holiness and purity took the place of political agendas.

present age, age to come, the life of God's coming age

By the time of Jesus many Jewish thinkers divided history into two periods: 'the present age' and 'the age to come' – the latter being the time when **YHWH** would at last act decisively to judge evil, to rescue Israel and to create a new world of justice and peace. The early Christians believed that, though the full blessings of the coming age lay still in the future, it had already begun with Jesus, particularly with his death and **resurrection**, and that by **faith** and **baptism** they were able to enter it already. For this reason, the customary translation 'eternal life' is rendered here as 'the life of God's coming age'.

priests, high priest

Aaron, the older brother of Moses, was appointed Israel's first high priest (Exodus 28—29), and in theory his descendants were Israel's priests thereafter. Other members of his tribe (Levi) were 'Levites', performing other liturgical duties but not sacrificing. Priests lived among the people all around the country, having a local teaching role (Leviticus 10.11; Malachi 2.7), and going to Jerusalem by rotation to perform the **Temple** liturgy (e.g. Luke 2.8).

David appointed Zadok (whose Aaronic ancestry is sometimes questioned) as high priest, and his family remained thereafter the senior priests in Jerusalem, probably the ancestors of the **Sadducees**. One explanation of the origins of the **Qumran** Essenes is that they were a dissident group who believed themselves to be the rightful chief priests.

Qumran, *see* Dead Sea Scrolls

rabbis, *see* Pharisees

repentance

Literally, this means 'turning back'. It is widely used in the Old Testament and subsequent Jewish literature to indicate both a personal turning away from sin and Israel's corporate turning away from idolatry and back to **YHWH**.

Through both meanings, it is linked to the idea of 'return from **exile**'; if Israel is to 'return' in all senses, it must 'return' to YHWH. This is at the heart of the summons of both **John the Baptist** and Jesus. In Paul's writings it is mostly used for **Gentiles** turning away from idols to serve the true God; also for sinning Christians who need to return to Jesus.

resurrection

In most biblical thought, human bodies matter and are not merely disposable prisons for the **soul**. When ancient Israelites wrestled with the goodness and justice of **YHWH**, the creator, they ultimately came to insist that he must raise the dead (Isaiah 26.19; Daniel 12.2–3) – a suggestion firmly resisted by classical pagan thought. The longed-for return from **exile** was also spoken of in terms of YHWH raising dry bones to new **life** (Ezekiel 37.1–14). These ideas were developed in the second-**Temple** period, not least at times of martyrdom (e.g. 2 Maccabees 7). Resurrection was not just 'life after death', but a newly embodied life *after* 'life after death'; those at present dead were either 'asleep', or seen as 'souls', 'angels' or 'spirits', awaiting new embodiment. The early Christian belief that Jesus had been raised from the dead was not that he had 'gone to **heaven**', or that he had been 'exalted', or was 'divine'; they believed all those as well, but each could have been expressed without mention of resurrection. Only the bodily resurrection of Jesus explains the rise of the early church, particularly its belief in Jesus' messiahship (which his crucifixion would have called into question). The early Christians believed that they themselves would be raised to a new, transformed bodily life at the time of the Lord's return or **parousia** (e.g. Philippians 3.20f.).

sabbath

The Jewish sabbath, the seventh day of the week, was a regular reminder both of creation (Genesis 2.3; Exodus 20.8–11) and of the **Exodus** (Deuteronomy 5.15). Along with **circumcision** and the food laws, it was one of the badges of Jewish identity within the pagan world of late antiquity, and a considerable body of Jewish **law** and custom grew up around its observance.

sacrifice

Like all ancient people, the Israelites offered animal and vegetable sacrifices to their God. Unlike others, they possessed a highly detailed written code (mostly in Leviticus) for what to offer and how to offer it; this in turn was developed in the **Mishnah** (*c.* AD 200). The Old Testament specifies that sacrifices can only be offered in the Jerusalem **Temple**; after this was destroyed in AD 70, sacrifices ceased, and Judaism developed further the idea, already present in some teachings, of prayer, fasting and almsgiving as alternative forms of sacrifice. The early Christians used the language of sacrifice in connection with such things as holiness, evangelism and the **eucharist**.

Sadducees

By Jesus' day, the Sadducees were the aristocracy of Judaism, possibly tracing their origins to the family of Zadok, David's **high priest**. Based in Jerusalem, and including most of the leading priestly families, they had their own traditions and attempted to resist the pressure of the **Pharisees** to conform to theirs. They claimed to rely only on the Pentateuch (the first five books of the Old Testament), and denied any doctrine of a future life, particularly of the **resurrection** and other ideas associated with it, presumably because of the encouragement such beliefs gave to revolutionary movements. No writings from the Sadducees have survived, unless the apocryphal book of Ben Sirach ('Ecclesiasticus') comes from them. The Sadducees themselves did not survive the destruction of Jerusalem and the **Temple** in AD 70.

the satan, 'the accuser', demons

The Bible is never very precise about the identity of the figure known as 'the satan'. The Hebrew word means 'the accuser', and at times the satan seems to be a member of **YHWH**'s heavenly council, with special responsibility as director of prosecutions (1 Chronicles 21.1; Job 1—2; Zechariah 3.1f.). However, it becomes identified variously with the serpent of the garden of Eden (Genesis 3.1–15) and with the rebellious daystar cast out of **heaven** (Isaiah 14.12–15), and was seen by many Jews as the quasi-personal source of evil standing behind both human wickedness and large-scale injustice, sometimes operating through semi-independent 'demons'. By Jesus' time various words were used to denote this figure, including Beelzebul/b (lit. 'Lord of the flies') and simply 'the evil one'; Jesus warned his followers against the deceits this figure could perpetrate. His opponents accused him of being in league with the satan, but the early Christians believed that Jesus in fact defeated it both in his own struggles with temptation (Matthew 4; Luke 4), his exorcisms of demons, and his death (1 Corinthians 2.8; Colossians 2.15). Final victory over this ultimate enemy is thus assured (Revelation 20), though the struggle can still be fierce for Christians (Ephesians 6.10–20).

scribes

In a world where many could not write, or not very well, a trained class of writers ('scribes') performed the important function of drawing up contracts for business, marriage, etc. Many would thus be legal experts, and quite possibly **Pharisees**, though being a scribe was compatible with various political and religious standpoints. The work of Christian scribes was of vital importance in copying early Christian writings, particularly the stories about Jesus.

son of God

Originally a title for Israel (Exodus 4.22) and the Davidic king (Psalm 2.7); also used of ancient angelic figures (Genesis 6.2). By the New Testament period it was already used as a **messianic** title, for example in the **Dead Sea Scrolls**. There, and when used of Jesus in the **gospels** (e.g. Matthew 16.16), it means, or reinforces, 'Messiah', without the later significance of 'divine'. However, already in Paul the transition to the fuller meaning (one who was already equal with God and was sent by him to become human and to become Messiah) is apparent, without loss of the meaning 'Messiah' itself (e.g. Galatians 4.4).

soul, *see* **life**

spirit, *see* **life, holy spirit**

Temple

The Temple in Jerusalem was planned by David (*c.* 1000 BC) and built by his son Solomon as the central sanctuary for all Israel. After reforms under Hezekiah and Josiah in the seventh century BC, it was destroyed by Babylon in 587 BC. Rebuilding by the returned **exiles** began in 538 BC, and was completed in 516, initiating the 'second Temple period'. Judas Maccabaeus cleansed it in 164 BC after its desecration by Antiochus Epiphanes (167). Herod the Great began to rebuild and beautify it in 19 BC; the work was completed in AD 63. The Temple was destroyed by the Romans in AD 70. Many Jews believed it should and would be rebuilt; some still do. The Temple was not only the place of **sacrifice**; it was believed to be the unique dwelling of **YHWH** on earth, the place where **heaven** and earth met.

Torah, Jewish law

'Torah', narrowly conceived, consists of the first five books of the Old Testament, the 'five books of Moses' or 'Pentateuch'. (These contain much law, but also much narrative.) It can also be used for the whole Old Testament scriptures, though strictly these are the 'law, prophets and writings'. In a broader sense, it refers to the whole developing corpus of Jewish legal tradition, written and oral; the oral Torah was initially codified in the **Mishnah** around AD 200, with wider developments found in the two Talmuds, of Babylon and Jerusalem, codified around AD 400. Many Jews in the time of Jesus and Paul regarded the Torah as being so strongly God-given as to be almost itself, in some sense, divine; some (e.g. Ben Sirach 24) identified it with the figure of 'Wisdom'. Doing what Torah said was not seen as a means of earning God's favour, but rather of expressing gratitude, and as a key badge of Jewish identity.

the Twelve, *see* **apostle**

word, *see* **good news**

YHWH

The ancient Israelite name for God, from at least the time of the **Exodus** (Exodus 6.2f.). It may originally have been pronounced 'Yahweh', but by the time of Jesus it was considered too holy to speak out loud, except for the **high priest** once a year in the Holy of Holies in the **Temple**. Instead, when reading scripture, pious Jews would say *Adonai*, 'Lord', marking this usage by adding the vowels of *Adonai* to the consonants of YHWH, eventually producing the hybrid 'Jehovah'. The word YHWH is formed from the verb 'to be', combining 'I am who I am', 'I will be who I will be', and perhaps 'I am because I am', emphasizing YHWH's sovereign creative power.

STUDY/REFLECTION GUIDE

This study/reflection guide is designed to help you engage the major themes in *1 Corinthians for Everyone*, either as part of a small group (for a four-week study) or in a time of personal reflection.

If using the guide with a group, each group member will need a copy of the book and should read the pages indicated prior to the group session. Because every group is unique, this guide is designed to give you flexibility and choice in customizing your group experience. You may use the format outlined below or adapt it however you wish to meet the needs, interests and schedule of your group. (The times indicated within parentheses are merely estimates. You may move at a faster or slower pace, making adjustments as desired.)

Suggested Format: 60 minutes

Opening Prayer (3 minutes)
Icebreaker (5–7 minutes)
Biblical Content and Commentary Highlights (5 minutes)
Group Discussion/Personal Reflection (30 minutes)
Application Exercise (10 minutes)
Closing Prayer (5 minutes)

Preceding each session outline is a brief section for the group facilitator, which includes a list of the scripture texts, the main idea and suggestions for preparation/materials needed. The opening and closing prayers are intended to cover the group in prayer. Feel free to use these prayers as printed, expand them or create your own. You also may want to include prayer requests of the group in the closing prayer. The icebreaker is provided to involve every group member from the beginning of the session, connecting with the overarching idea that the content of 1 Corinthians is meant for *everyone*. The biblical content and commentary highlights recap the major themes, setting the stage for group discussion. Read this material aloud or summarize it for the group. The application exercise, which is intended to be done in groups of two to three people, will help you begin thinking about how God may be inviting you to apply or respond to what you've read.

If using the guide in a time of personal reflection, modify the icebreaker as appropriate for a fun way to begin engaging the content. You may find it helpful to journal in response to some or all the reflection questions and then choose one or more to discuss with a friend. After reflecting on the questions in the application exercise, identify one invitation you sense God is extending to you personally. Write it down, journal about it or talk with God about it throughout the coming week.

SESSION 1: 1 CORINTHIANS, CHAPTERS 1—4 (PAGES 1-37)

For the Group Facilitator

Scripture Texts

1 Corinthians 1.1–9	Thankful for God's Grace
1 Corinthians 1.10–17	Beware of Divisions!
1 Corinthians 1.18–25	God's Folly
1 Corinthians 1.26–31	Boasting in the Lord
1 Corinthians 2.1–5	The Powerful Message of the Cross
1 Corinthians 2.6–13	God's Strange Wisdom
1 Corinthians 2.14—3.4	Spiritual or Merely Human?
1 Corinthians 3.5–11	God's Farm, God's Building
1 Corinthians 3.12–17	The Coming Day, the Coming Fire
1 Corinthians 3.18–23	Everything Belongs to You
1 Corinthians 4.1–5	Judgment Then Rather Than Now
1 Corinthians 4.6–13	Apostles on Display
1 Corinthians 4.14–21	Puffed Up or Powerful?

The Main Idea

As followers of Christ, we are called to live by God's wisdom rather than the world's wisdom. There is no place for jealousy, quarrelling or boasting, because everything we have received is a gift from God. Christianity is a matter of grace from start to finish.

Suggestions for Preparation/Materials Needed

- Prepare the meeting space by arranging seats in a circle, if possible, so that everyone can see one another.
- If group members do not already know one another, have name tags and pens or markers available.

- Have on hand a whiteboard or large sheet of paper with markers for writing.
- Remind group members to read 1 Corinthians 1—4 before the session and to bring their copies of this book and, if desired, a Bible (optional, since the text is included in the book). You might consider having some additional Bibles in various translations on hand.

Session Outline

Opening Prayer (3 minutes)

Jesus, we know there are to be no divisions among us, yet so often we get caught up in comparison, competition and conflict. We find ourselves living according to the wisdom of the world instead of your wisdom. Open our eyes as we study Paul's letter so that we may understand what it means to live in you – to have you at the center of every thought and action. Amen.

Icebreaker (5–7 minutes)

In advance, write the following scripture on a whiteboard or chart: '*Don't let anyone deceive themselves. If anyone among you supposes they are wise in the present age, let them become foolish, so that they can become wise*' *(1 Corinthians 3.18)*. Read the scripture aloud and then say: *The world pressures us to either deny we know anything or adopt a know-it-all position. But genuine Christianity is learning to be foolish in the world's eyes in order to become wise; it is embracing the wisdom of God, which is open access to the mind of Christ through the spirit.* Now draw two columns on the board or chart, labeling them 'Wisdom of the World' and 'Wisdom of God'. Invite group members to suggest descriptions and examples of each kind of wisdom as you write them in the appropriate columns for discussion later.

Biblical Content and Commentary Highlights (5 minutes)

Paul's central concern in his first letter to the Christians in Corinth is helping them to place Jesus at the center of their lives, rather than dividing into different factions according to their preferred teacher – much in the same way that the citizens of Corinth would align themselves with visiting intellectual teachers, or 'sophists'. In chapter 1, Paul digs beneath the surface issue of their infighting and urges them to make a choice between the wisdom of the world and the wisdom of God. His basic claim is that although the message of the Messiah and the cross invites mockery, it carries a power far greater than any human rhetoric. He reminds them that although they once were 'nobodies', God has made them 'somebodies', giving them the same status as the Messiah himself – all as a gift of grace, so they have no reason to boast. Everything they need is found in Christ.

In chapter 2, Paul says that the secret to life, to everything, is found in Jesus. He reminds the Corinthian Christians that the power of the gospel message – Jesus' death and resurrection – is the wisdom of God, which comes through the spirit, not through persuasive speech. The spirit is poured out on believers, bringing them to faith and opening their hearts and minds to the wisdom of God. But the rulers of 'this present age' and those who are 'merely human' (lacking in spiritual maturity) do not understand this wisdom.

Paul goes on in chapter 3 to point out that the Corinthians' infighting is evidence of their spiritual immaturity. He says that he fed them with milk when they were babies in the Messiah, and even now they are not able to take solid food. In other words, they are still at the infancy stage and not yet ready for serious teaching. He then uses analogies of planting and building to say that all teachers are fellow workers or servants of the Lord. Jesus is the foundation of the church, and God is the one who brings the growth. So those who work to build up the church must use lasting materials, and when the Lord returns, it will be seen what each has accomplished. Builders who use wrong materials will suffer loss but be saved themselves. Paul's point is that the various tasks and responsibilities of Christians, especially teachers and leaders, is serious business, and so we must not deceive ourselves with human wisdom or boast in our own abilities but trust in the spirit of God, who lives within us.

In chapter 4, Paul uses another image of a servant of the Messiah, describing a household manager for God's mysteries – which are like treasures in a storehouse. The household manager is simply to be faithful with what has been entrusted to his or her care. Paul warns the Corinthian Christians not to pass judgment on anything before the final judgment, because then everything will be made right. He then instructs the warring factions not to get puffed up in favor of one person or another but to remember what the scriptures say. Using the image of a Roman 'triumph' – a victorious parade of soldiers with prisoners at the back of the procession – he shows them what the work of an apostle is like and urges them to remember the way he has conducted his own life and to follow his example.

Group Discussion/Personal Reflection (30 minutes)

1. Read 1.1–9. How many times does the name Jesus occur in these verses? In light of this and Paul's opening words in these verses, what would you say is Paul's primary concern in this letter?

2. What is the presenting issue or conflict that Paul is addressing in 1.10–17? What does baptism have to do with the quarrels of the Corinthian Christians?
3. How does Paul contrast the 'wisdom of the world' with the 'wisdom of God' in 1.18–25? How was the cross foolishness to the people of Paul's day, and how is it foolishness to people today? How have you experienced and witnessed the power of the cross?
4. What is the important point Paul is making in 1.26–31? According to these verses, why are we not to boast in ourselves? What does Paul say in verse 30 that we receive from Jesus? Read Jeremiah 9.23–24, which Paul quotes in verse 31. Based on all these verses, how would you explain what it means to boast in the Lord?
5. According to 2.1–5, what and how did Paul preach to the Corinthians? Though this does not mean that Paul spoke only of the cross and never mentioned the resurrection, why does the author suggest that Paul emphasized Jesus' crucifixion? (See page 15.) What is the wisdom of God described in 2.6–16, and how is it revealed? Who receives this wisdom, and who does not? What does it mean to have 'the mind of the Lord' (verse 16)?
7. According to 3.1–4, what is the difference between those who are 'spiritual' and those who are 'merely human'? What analogy does Paul use to describe the Corinthians, and what does he give as evidence for this assessment? What words might Paul use for today's church? For your own church?
8. What two images does Paul use in 3.5–11 to describe the work of a teacher? In each analogy, what is the teacher's role, and what is God's role? The author suggests that every church worker should ask, 'Is what I'm doing encouraging and enabling people to worship the true and living God, in holiness and truth?' How would you answer this question? What do verses 12–17 tell us about 'building materials', and what is Paul's point here?
9. What warning does Paul give in 3.18? What explanation or support does he offer for this warning in verses 19–23?
10. In Paul's comparison of teachers and apostles to household managers, found in 4.1–5, what is the main requirement of a manager? Why does the author suggest that believing in God's final judgment is believing in God's wisdom and goodness? (See the comments on page 31.) How can we know when to judge and when not to judge; when to listen to whispers of criticism and when to dismiss them as irrelevant and a waste of time?
11. How does Paul address the problem of rivalry and enmity within the Corinthian church in 4.6–21? What analogies does he use, and for what purpose? How does the message of the cross come

through in verses 12–13 and Paul's heart come through in verses 14–21?

Application Exercise (10 minutes)

Break into groups of two or three and discuss the following:

- Of all the content we've covered today, what is something that strongly resonates or stands out to you?
- How does it connect with your current life experience?
- How do you sense God inviting you to respond or make application in your daily life?

Closing Prayer (5 minutes)

Lord, we're no different than the Corinthians. We divide into factions and elevate concerns that are mere folly while ignoring important matters. We need your wisdom to be a healthy church. Help us to discern when judgment is needed and when criticism is irrelevant. Give us wisdom, holy spirit, so that we will boast only in you, not in ourselves. Remind us that all is grace. Amen.

SESSION 2: 1 CORINTHIANS 5—9 (PAGES 37–82)

For the Group Facilitator

Scripture Texts

1 Corinthians 5.1–5	Scandal and Judgment
1 Corinthians 5.6–13	Get Rid of the 'Leaven'!
1 Corinthians 6.1–8	Lawsuits in the Church?
1 Corinthians 6.9–11	Inheriting God's Kingdom – Or Not
1 Corinthians 6.12–20	What Is the Body For?
1 Corinthians 7.1–7	Life within Marriage
1 Corinthians 7.8–16	Marriage and Divorce
1 Corinthians 7.17–24	Stay the Way You Were Called
1 Corinthians 7.25–31	On Remaining Unmarried
1 Corinthians 7.32–40	Divided Loyalties
1 Corinthians 8.1–6	Meat Offered to Idols
1 Corinthians 8.7–13	Respecting Weak Consciences
1 Corinthians 9.1–12a	The 'Rights' of an Apostle
1 Corinthians 9.12b–18	Giving Up Rights for the Gospel

1 Corinthians 9.19–23	The Apostle's Freedom – to Be Enslaved to Everyone
1 Corinthians 9.24–27	The Christian Athlete

The Main Idea

It is up to us as believers to recognize the ways in which the deceitfulness of sin is distorting our thinking and behavior so that we may live as the people we truly are in Christ. We must be able to think through issues for ourselves, which means exploring who the true God is and what it means to love and serve God.

Suggestions for Preparation/Materials Needed

- Prepare the meeting space by arranging seats in a circle, if possible, so that everyone can see one another.
- If group members do not already know one another, have name tags and pens or markers available.
- Have on hand a whiteboard or large sheet of paper with markers for writing.
- Remind group members to read 1 Corinthians 5—9 before the session and to bring their copies of this book and, if desired, a Bible (optional, since the text is included in the book). You might consider having some additional Bibles in various translations on hand.

Session Outline

Opening Prayer (3 minutes)

Jesus, we admit that, at times, it can be confusing and difficult to navigate morality and freedom in our culture. As Christians and as the church, we find ourselves holding different views on some issues, and we're often seen as either judgmental and unloving or too loving and permissive. We desperately need your wisdom and guidance to discern between Christian freedom and immoral behavior. Open our eyes as we study and discuss your word so that we may avoid both moral indifference and legalism. Amen.

Icebreaker (5–7 minutes)

In advance, write these words of Paul from Philippians on a whiteboard or chart: *'Live clean, innocent lives as children of God, shining like bright lights in a world full of crooked and perverse people' (Philippians 2.15 NLT)*. Read the verse aloud and then say: *Paul says we should be like bright lights shining into a dark world. Where and how in today's church are we behaving in such a way? Where and how are we shaming the gospel in the eyes of the world?* Invite participants to share their thoughts as you write their responses in two columns on the board or chart for discussion later.

Biblical Content and Commentary Highlights (5 minutes)

Chapter 5 opens with a sex scandal that sounds as of it could be a reality TV show – a man is living with his own stepmother, presumably his father's second wife. Paul does not waste time arguing that the behavior is wrong but focuses on how the Corinthians' tolerance of the behavior is threatening the life and witness of the church. Drawing on images of Passover, Paul suggests that the leaven of the 'old life' must be exchanged for the 'unleavened bread' of genuine Christian living, which requires sincerity and truth. In other words, it matters how we live, and moral indifference is like a cancer that spreads. Paul suggests it is the church's right and responsibility to distinguish between those who are living in the way of Christ and those who are not and to enforce appropriate discipline.

In chapter 6, Paul begins by chastising the Corinthian Christians for taking one another to court. Rather than addressing their disputes themselves, they are showing the world that they are no different than everyone else. Paul goes on to say there are certain behaviors that no longer are fitting for a follower of Jesus. Becoming a Christian, he explains, means receiving a new identity and living a new lifestyle, which involves recognizing the deceitfulness of sin that distorts our thinking. He makes it clear that sexual immorality is one of their most serious issues, and he implores them to learn to use the human body in the right way, for the right purpose. His point is that a Christian belongs to Jesus and is part of his body, resulting in a union of spirit that can be damaged or threatened by inappropriate unions of the flesh. In fact, every Christian is a Temple of God, a dwelling place of the holy spirit, and therefore should glorify God in his or her body.

In chapter 7, Paul addresses various issues pertaining to those who are married, divorced or unmarried – with a section on circumcision and enslavement sandwiched in the middle. In addition to advising married couples to have sexual relations so that they avoid being tempted toward immoral pursuits and encouraging those who are widowed and unmarried not to feel pressured to marry, he advocates against divorce, especially for those Christians who are married to unbelievers. After all, the unbelieving partner might be won over by the believing spouse – though the Christian should not oppose an unbelieving spouse's desire to separate. Paul then discusses circumcision and slavery, emphasizing that what counts is not one's social status but one's status in the Messiah. Though his comments on enslavement are debated, the author suggests Paul is in favor of enslaved people pursuing freedom when an opportunity presents itself without spending every waking moment thinking about how to become free. His point is that our primary focus as Christians should be our calling in Christ.

Chapters 8 and 9 explore our rights and freedom in Christ, which do not permit us to do whatever we like but, paradoxically, enable us to be 'slaves of all'. In other words, we willingly choose to forfeit our rights for the sake of others and the service of God and the gospel. This kind of obedient self-denial is like athletic training, shaping us into the persons God intends us to be. Paul admonishes the Corinthians, for example, to forfeit their freedom to eat food sacrificed to idols if it causes someone to stumble – if it leads those with weaker consciences astray. And he himself forfeits his right to receive compensation for his ministry. Our freedom always must be freedom *for* – for Christ, for God's people, and for those who need the gospel.

Group Discussion/Personal Reflection (30 minutes)

1. According to 5.1–5, what is the scandal going on in the Corinthian church, and what is Paul's position on the matter? What does he want them to do about it? In the author's view, what does pride have to do with the church's response? (See the comments on pages 38–39.)
2. What does Paul mean when he talks of cleansing out the leaven in 5.6–13? What is the significance of the reference to Passover here?
3. Paul was adamant that anything that would spread within the body of Christ like cancer, destroying the Christian community, must be cut out. Such a suggestion in today's church likely would elicit a strong reaction. What do you think is the appropriate role of the church today in matters of morality? Do you think there is a place for discipline in the church? Why or why not? If so, what kind of discipline is appropriate in cases of severe misconduct?
4. Read aloud 6.1–8. What is Paul concerned about in these verses, and why? What was the Corinthians' behavior communicating to the watching world? Where and how in today's church are we shaming the gospel in the eyes of the world? Where and how are we behaving in such a way that we are shining like bright lights into a dark world? Refer to and discuss the responses recorded during the icebreaker.
5. Paul's words in 6.9–11 are often seen as a list of moral rules. What difference does it make when we view these verses as a warning

about behaviors that become liabilities for ourselves and others, preventing us from reflecting the full image of Christ?

6. How can we recognize the ways in which the deceitfulness of sin is distorting our own thinking and behavior? What role should the community of faith play in this discernment? How can the church help us to live into our new identity as image bearers of Christ?
7. According to Paul, what is the body meant for (6.13)? Why does what we do with our bodies matter? What does it mean to 'glorify God in your body' (verse 20)?
8. According to the author, why does Paul offer 'wise Christian advice' for sexual relations for those who are married, those who are widowed or unmarried, and Christians considering divorce – including those married to unbelieving spouses? Discuss the advice he shares in chapter 7 and your thoughts about it. (See the author's comments on pages 52–54 and 55–57.)
9. Why does Paul seem to change topics and address circumcision and enslavement in 7.17–24? What point is he making for the Corinthian Christians, and how does it apply in our lives today? (See pages 58–61.)
10. Why does Paul warn the Corinthians about eating meat offered to idols in 8.1–6? What might be a contemporary example for us today? What does he mean by a 'weak conscience' in 8.7? If the conscience is like a compass that can easily malfunction, what is our responsibility in helping others keep a clear conscience before God?
11. What does Paul say about a Christian's rights and freedom in chapter 9? What rights did Paul forfeit for the sake of the gospel? What rights or freedoms have you given up for the sake of the gospel? How does Christian obedience benefit both us and others?
12. What does Paul mean when he says I 'enslaved myself to everyone' (9.19)? Some say that becoming 'all things to all people' (verse 22) requires inconsistency and hypocrisy. How would you respond to that?

Application Exercise (10 minutes)

Break into groups of two or three and discuss the following:

- Of all the content we've covered today, what is something that strongly resonates or stands out to you?
- How does it connect with your current life experience?
- How do you sense God inviting you to respond or make application in your daily life?

Closing Prayer (5 minutes)

Lord, thank you for reminding us that Christian freedom is not freedom to do whatever we want but freedom from all the things that stop us from being the people you want us to be. Our freedom is always *for* – for your kingdom work on behalf of others. Help us to be people who are willing to practice self-denial and discipline for the sake of the gospel. Our desire is to glorify you in all things. Amen.

SESSION 3: 1 CORINTHIANS 10—13 (PAGES 82–122)

For the Group Facilitator

Scripture Texts

1 Corinthians 10.1–5	The First Exodus
1 Corinthians 10.6–13	Don't Make the Same Mistake Again!
1 Corinthians 10.14–22	The Table of the Lord and the Table of Demons
1 Corinthians 10.23—11.1	Do Everything to God's Glory
1 Corinthians 11.2–16	Male and Female in the Worshipping Church
1 Corinthians 11.17–22	Rich and Poor at the Table of the Lord
1 Corinthians 11.23–34	Recognizing the Body
1 Corinthians 12.1–11	The Same Spirit at Work
1 Corinthians 12.12–20	Many Members, One Body
1 Corinthians 12.21–26	The Responsibilities of Each Member
1 Corinthians 12.27–31a	Gifts and Ministries
1 Corinthians 12.31b—13.7	The Need for Love and the Character of Love
1 Corinthians 13.8–13	Love: The Bridge to God's Future

The Main Idea

Love is the way of life in the world to come, so we must learn it here and now. As Christians, love is our duty and our destiny, and it is the only way to resist evil and temptation so that we may be one body reflecting Christ's light in the world.

Suggestions for Preparation/Materials Needed

- Prepare the meeting space by arranging seats in a circle, if possible, so that everyone can see one another.

- If group members do not already know one another, have name tags and pens or markers available.
- Have on hand a whiteboard or large sheet of paper with markers for writing.
- Remind group members to read 1 Corinthians 10—13 before the session and to bring their copies of this book and, if desired, a Bible (optional, since the text is included in the book). You might consider having some additional Bibles in various translations on hand.

Session Outline

Opening Prayer (3 minutes)

Jesus, when we join your family, we do not automatically reach perfection but must exert effort to resist those behaviors and attitudes that pull us toward unholy living. There are forces at work in this world that distort and damage your creation and your people. Open our eyes as we study your word today so that we may more fully embrace and embody the better way of love. Amen.

Icebreaker (5–7 minutes)

Say: *I invite you to close your eyes and listen as I read aloud 1 Corinthians 13 through two times. As I read it the first time, simply take in this beautiful description of the better way of love. Then as I read it a second time, listen for a particular phrase that stands out to you or touches your heart.* After reading the passage aloud twice, pausing briefly between the readings, go around the circle and invite each person to share the phrase that stood out to them, saving comments about the phrase for later discussion.

Biblical Content and Commentary Highlights (5 minutes)

In chapter 10, Paul develops the idea that the Corinthians – and all of Jesus' followers – are the true Exodus people, enacting the same drama as the children of Israel through baptism and the Lord's supper. Yet just as the Israelites did not act responsibly with the privileges they received in the wilderness, so the Corinthians are at risk of not living up to the blessings that are theirs because they belong to the Messiah. Paul warns them not to think their freedom in Christ exempts them from moral responsibility, urging them to be careful that they do not fall back into paganism, idolatry and immoral behaviours. He offers some encouragement by saying that God is faithful and will always provide a way to escape temptation. He also says they must take seriously the

Lord's table and not become a partner with evil forces by eating and drinking in the temple of an idol. Though the food sacrificed to idols is not off limits, the place where it is sacrificed is. In short, he urges them to do everything to the glory of God, not giving offense to anyone.

The author suggests that the material in chapter 11 on males and females in worship, which is debated, expresses more of a concern about honouring God by being true to who we were created to be than a concern for male authority (patriarchy). Paul's primary aim, he proposes, is to ensure that the physical marks of difference between the sexes are not blurred in worship so that God's creation, and its ultimate fulfillment in the new creation, is honoured. Another concern Paul raises is the division between rich and poor during the Lord's supper – which, at this time, is a full meal taking place in a private house. It seems that social customs, in which hosts give preferential treatment to the more affluent guests, are reinforcing this problem. Paul urges them to examine themselves, making sure their behaviouur at this meal is appropriate, or face the judgment of the Lord himself (11.27–31). His desire is for them to treat one another as equals, declaring that they are one body.

Paul continues to address the issue of unity in chapter 12, where he clarifies that no gift of the spirit is more spiritual than any other. Though he is acknowledging that every member of the church has an important gift to contribute, he is saying much more than that. Those in whom the holy spirit lives are the true family of God, who reflect the image of God in the world – all indispensable members of one body that cuts across every social division. He wants them to value and care for one another. In naming various gifts that the spirit gives to believers, Paul emphasizes that the gifts are given by the same spirit for the purpose of building up the church.

In chapter 13, the famous 'love chapter', Paul deepens the Corinthians' understanding of the highest virtue necessary for living in unity as one body: love. In verses 1–3, he shows how vital love is. In verses 4–7, he describes love itself. And in verses 8–13, he explains that love is one of the things that will last into God's new creation – and, therefore, matters more than the things that will pass away, which include most of the things the Corinthians are concerned about. A life of love is the only way to bring order to the chaos in the Corinthian church – as well as in our churches today.

Group Discussion/Personal Reflection (30 minutes)

1. In 10.1–13, how does Paul compare the Corinthian Christians to the Israelites in the wilderness, making the case that they – and all

Christians – are the true Exodus people? What do the cloud, the sea, the food and the drink represent? What warnings does he give, and what is his primary point?

2. Read aloud 10.12–13. Why is it dangerous to think we are immune to temptation? How would you explain the promise of verse 13 in your own words? How does it encourage you?
3. In 10.14–22, Paul is expressing the danger of having anything to do with idolatry. How do these verses apply to our lives and worship today?
4. What is your faith tradition's understanding of the elements of the Lord's supper or eucharist? How does this holy meal make us one body in Christ?
5. What basic principles and practical guidelines does Paul offer in 10.22–30? What is the application for us today? How can we live in a world where there are both moral absolutes and grey areas? What happens when we get confused about which is which – or try to eliminate one or the other? Share an example if one comes to mind.
6. Read aloud 10.31–33. Practically speaking, how can we live out verse 31? What does Paul mean in verse 33, and how is this different from our understanding of 'people pleasing'?
7. Review the author's comments regarding Paul's puzzling words in 11.2–16 (see pages 95–98). What insights do you find helpful? Do you agree with the author's suggested interpretation? Why or why not? What remaining questions do you have about this passage?
8. What concern does Paul address in 11.17–34? What additional insights does the author provide that help us understand the problem? (See pages 98–104.) What warnings and instructions does he give in verses 23–34? What did Paul mean by suggesting they should 'test' or 'judge' themselves before the meal?
9. Take a look at 12.1–31a. What does Paul want the Corinthian Christians to understand about the gifts of the spirit? What underlying issue within the church is he addressing? How does the analogy of the body help us to understand the value and purpose of every gift? What does it teach us about the importance of unity and equality among all members and the need to care for one another?
10. Do you know your own spiritual gifts, and if so, how are you currently using them to build up the church?
11. What is the 'better way' (12.31b) Paul describes in chapter 13, and what does this have to do with all that Paul has said about spiritual gifts? Recall the phrase that stood out to you from the chapter during the icebreaker and share why it resonates with you today.

12. What does each section of chapter 13 teach us about love?
    - Verses 1–3
    - Verses 4–7
    - Verses 8–13
13. How do we see the qualities described in 13.4–7 in Jesus? The author says this life of love is within reach of each of us because it is the life of Jesus inspired by the spirit. What, then, can we do to nurture this love in us? How do verses 8–13 encourage you and give you hope?

Application Exercise (10 minutes)

Break into groups of two or three and discuss the following:

- Of all the content we've covered today, what is something that strongly resonates or stands out to you?
- How does it connect with your current life experience?
- How do you sense God inviting you to respond or make application in your daily life?

Closing Prayer (5 minutes)

Jesus, we can get fixated on things that have no lasting meaning, but we know love is the only thing that truly matters and lasts. Help us to love as you love. May we remember that love is not a lofty ideal we aspire to but our very birthright as members of your family, because you are love. We desire to embody your love so that the world will see you in us and be drawn to your light. Amen.

SESSION 4: 1 CORINTHIANS 14—16 (PAGES 122–164)

For the Group Facilitator

Scripture Texts

1 Corinthians 14.1–5	Priorities in Worship
1 Corinthians 14.6–12	Speaking Clearly in Church
1 Corinthians 14.13–19	Praying with Mind as Well as Spirit
1 Corinthians 14.20–25	Signs for Believers and Unbelievers
1 Corinthians 15.1–11	The Gospel of the Messiah, Crucified, Buried and Risen
1 Corinthians 15.12–19	What If the Messiah Wasn't Raised?
1 Corinthians 15.20–28	The Reign of the Messiah

1 Corinthians 15.29–34	Resurrection Gives Meaning to Present Christian Living
1 Corinthians 15.35–49	The Transformed Resurrection Body
1 Corinthians 15.50–58	The Mystery and the Victory
1 Corinthians 16.1–9	The Collection and Paul's Plans
1 Corinthians 16.10–14	Timothy and Apollos
1 Corinthians 16.15–24	The Love that Stitches It All Together

The Main Idea

We all should pray and work toward being able to do and say things that make the body of Christ work together in harmony and be built up in love in an orderly way, especially in worship. Christianity isn't a personal path of spirituality but good news about the resurrection of Jesus, who one day will resurrect our bodies and restore the entire cosmos.

Suggestions for Preparation/Materials Needed

Prepare the meeting space by arranging seats in a circle, if possible, so that everyone can see one another.

- If group members do not already know one another, have name tags and pens or markers available.
- Have on hand a whiteboard or large sheet of paper with markers for writing.
- Remind group members to read 1 Corinthians 14—16 before the session and to bring their copies of this book and, if desired, a Bible (optional, since the text is included in the book). You might consider having some additional Bibles in various translations on hand.

Session Outline

Opening Prayer (3 minutes)

Jesus, your resurrection means everything to us. It is the good news that ushers in the kingdom of God, the solid ground on which we stand. Open our eyes as we study your word today so that we are transformed and motivated by this central reality of the gospel message. May we believe it, live by it and never be the same again because of it. And may all that we do and say – in our personal lives and in our corporate worship – help to bring others to faith in you. Amen.

Icebreaker (5–7 minutes)

Say: *The author says that the resurrection is what makes Christianity different from all other faiths.* Ask: *Why is the resurrection central to the good news of Christianity?* Invite group members to share brief responses as you write them on a whiteboard or chart for further discussion later.

Biblical Content and Commentary Highlights (5 minutes)

On one level, chapter 14 is about orderly public worship, but on a deeper level, it gets at the difference between displaying personal spiritual experience and building up the whole community in public worship. Paul is not against personal spirituality, but his message is that public worship is to be about building up everyone in faith and love – as opposed to showcasing personal giftedness like strutting peacocks. Specifically, he explains how the gifts of tongues and prophecy should and should not be used in corporate worship, emphasizing that the gift of prophecy – which includes God-given wisdom, understanding, insight and teaching – is more beneficial for building up the church than uninterpreted tongues. Essentially, he wants the Corinthians to grow to maturity as whole human beings, using and celebrating all their created selves – mind, spirit, soul and body – in worship.

The author points out that it is debated whether Paul wrote verses 34 and 35, which instruct women to 'keep silence in the assemblies', or whether they were added later. If Paul indeed wrote them, the author suggests they are more about orderly worship than prohibiting women from speaking in worship. In chapter 11, Paul clearly assumes that women will take leadership roles in praying and prophesying, just as much as men. Two problems might have prompted this instruction. If public worship was conducted in the mainstream Greek language, many women might not have understood what was being said and could have begun to talk among themselves or call across to their husbands sitting on the other side for interpretation. Either way it would have been disruptive. Another possibility is that some of the women took it upon themselves to critique what their husbands had spoken in worship, according to Paul's instruction in verse 29 to evaluate what a prophet says. This also would have caused interruption and perhaps dissension. Paul's overarching concern throughout the chapter seems to be restoring peace to worship services bordering on the chaotic.

Chapter 15 focuses on the resurrection of Jesus and the future resurrection of those who believe in him. Jesus' resurrection – and its implications for our lives in this world and the world to come – is central to all that Paul wrote in this letter, as well as what he preached wherever he went. It was this good news, empowered by the spirit, that brought people into the kingdom of God. One day we will be raised to new, eternal bodies just as Jesus was, and the final enemy, death itself, will be defeated once and for all. Then all creation will be liberated from decay and made new, sharing in the freedom of the glory of God's children. Somehow there will be continuity between who and what we are now and who and what we will be in the future, which means that what we do in this present time matters and will stand for all time. How God will take our work and weave it into the tapestry of the new creation is mysterious but comforting.

In this letter that has addressed divisions within the church and the need for love at the heart of everything, Paul brings it all into focus in the final chapter with a practical plan for collecting money for the Jerusalem church, which had suffered greatly. Paul isn't simply interested in raising money but wants to show the Jewish and Gentile Christians in Jerusalem that they are part of the same family. He also asks the Corinthians to welcome and encourage Timothy, followed by four commands: 'keep alert, stand firm in the faith, be brave, be strong'. Recognizing that the church in Corinth is in danger from many things, Paul urges them to assume responsibility for their own spiritual health and the ongoing work of the gospel. He concludes his letter by lifting up three people in the church who have exemplified love, extending final greetings, calling for Jesus – and his kingdom – to come, and offering the grace and love of the Messiah, Jesus.

Group Discussion/Personal Reflection (30 minutes)

1. What is Paul's overarching concern in chapter 14? What does he say about the gifts of tongues and prophecy, and what specific instructions does he give for public worship?
2. Read the author's comments about prophecy on page 125. What are some examples of this kind of prophecy in your church? What have been the benefits or results of this prophecy – in your life and the life of the church?
3. The author writes, 'If the Corinthians are as keen as they seem to be on having the spirit work in and through them, the thing they ought to be longing for, praying for and working towards is that they would all be able to do and say things which make the body of Christ work together in harmony and be built up in love'. How do these words speak to us as the body of Christ today? How can we know when we are showcasing personal spiritual experience in corporate worship rather than building up the body of believers?
4. Throughout the centuries, Christian communities have often compartmentalized their humanness in worship, emphasizing the mind or emotions more than the other. Does your congregation tend to

lean toward one or the other in worship? How can we bring mind, spirit and body together in worship so that we praise God with our whole beings?

5. Read aloud 14.34–35. What has been your perspective on these verses to date? How do the author's comments on pages 135–37 give you new insight or understanding into these verses? How might verse 40 give credence to the view that Paul's instruction in these verses has more to do with orderly worship than prohibiting women from speaking in worship?
6. What is the theme of chapter 15? According to the author, why does Paul give this topic such a lengthy treatment as the final major theme of the letter (see pages 139–41)?
7. After reading chapter 15 and the author's commentary, how would you summarize Paul's understanding of resurrection and our resurrection bodies? What questions does this chapter raise for you? What stands out or speaks to you, and why?
8. Some in Corinth denied the resurrection because it made no sense within the surrounding pagan worldview. What are some popular worldviews today, and what might they have to say about the resurrection? Why is it important for Christians to affirm the bodily resurrection of Jesus? In other words, what difference does Jesus' bodily resurrection make for us and for the world?
9. How do Paul's instructions regarding the collection for the church in Jerusalem bring together the letter's themes of divisions within the church and the need for love at the heart of everything? How are both spontaneity and planning important when it comes to demonstrating love? How might humble planning, strategic thinking and surrendering to God's direction be beneficial to your church in this season?
10. Read aloud 16.10–24. What do these final words of Paul's letter have to say to us today? How might we assume responsibility for our own spiritual health and the ongoing work of the gospel?

Application Exercise (10 minutes)

Break into groups of two or three and discuss the following:

- Of all the content we've covered today, what is something that strongly resonates or stands out to you?
- How does it connect with your current life experience?
- How do you sense God inviting you to respond or make application in your daily life?

Closing Prayer (5 minutes)

Jesus, thank you for reminding us, through your life and the writings of Paul, that what matters most is love – our love for you and our love for one another. Help us to keep love at the heart of all things, not only in our personal lives but also in the life of the church. May your kingdom come fully, and until then, may we be faithful in serving you and living the gospel message in all we say and do. Amen.